England and the 1966 W[

Manchester University Press

England and the 1966 World Cup

A cultural history

JOHN HUGHSON

Manchester University Press

Published by Manchester University Press
Altrincham Street, Manchester M1 7JA

www.manchesteruniversitypress.co.uk

British Library Cataloguing-in-Publication Data
A catalogue record for this book is available from the British Library

Library of Congress Cataloging-in-Publication Data applied for

ISBN   978 0 7190 9615 0 hardback
ISBN   978 0 7190 9616 7 paperback

First published 2016

Typeset by
Servis Filmsetting Ltd, Stockport, Cheshire
Printed in Great Britain by
Bell and Bain Ltd, Glasgow

Contents

Figures

Acknowledgements

I am grateful to many people for making various contributions related to this book over the last few years, including those who have shared personal memories of the 1966 World Cup Final. A number of colleagues have shared information and materials relevant to the book and in this regard I would like to thank Alan McDougall, Stacey Pope, Chris Stride and Jean Williams. Thank you also to Jean for giving me the opportunity to speak publicly on aspects of the research. A special thank you to Graham Deakin for the many conversations over the last couple of years relevant to the 1966 World Cup and for the insights from his designer's eye. For their assistance in the research archive at the National Football Museum, I am especially grateful to Peter Holme and Alex Jackson. For comments on the manuscript and constant support, I am gladly indebted to Kevin Moore. Thanks to Tom Dark and Tony Mason at Manchester University Press for supporting the project. I am grateful for the funding made available to the International Football Institute at the University of Central Lancashire to assist research activity for the book. Finally, my heartfelt thanks to Marina Hughson. Marina's personal and professional support has been unstinting and invaluable on the long and winding road back to 1966.

1

This is England '66: an introduction

Let homage be rendered to the various sports, and in particular to football. For, still more than the king of sports, football is the king of games. (Jean Giraudoux)

English people of a certain age may well remember where they were when England won the World Cup on 30 July 1966.[1] During the preparation and writing of this book I have informally heard a number of firsthand memories in this regard, both from people I know, and people I have met in passing.[2] In each case the memory of seeing the World Cup Final, mostly on television, was recalled with such apparent vividness to confirm my belief, held from the outset, that this is a topic well worthy of thoroughgoing academic attention. Fifty years on, this may not be the only book by an academic published in 2016 on England's World Cup victory, but it is likely to be the only one written by someone over the age of fifty-five who did not watch the match at the time. In July 1966 I was eight years old and, while the World Cup Final was being played at Wembley Stadium, I was asleep in my bed at home in the early hours of a western Sydney morning. Had I been able to watch the match, I may well have done so. Attending state schools with a significant number of fellow students from the diversity of European migrant communities residing in my neighbourhood, I developed an interest in the sport we referred to as soccer from a fairly young age. I have my own memories – perhaps more hazy than vivid, but certain enough to remark upon – of standing around in the school-yard discussing the replays of either *Match of the Day* or *The Big Match* on local television. As it was only these broadcasts of football from abroad that we got to see on a weekly basis, for an Australian child, becoming a soccer fan meant developing a keen interest in the English League.

I have no memory of first hearing about England winning the World Cup in 1966. It just seems to have lodged within my awareness, at a formative stage, as an accepted fact of football history. This taken for granted understanding was accompanied by an assumption that winning the World Cup would involve a fairly uncomplicated response of national pride for English people. Facile views of this kind came under challenge once I took up studying sport seriously,

yet the example of the 1966 World Cup did not return to my attention until I
started living and working in Britain as an academic in the 1990s. When it came
to my attention it did so as a matter of surprise. The surprise was not so much
to read academic criticism of England's victory being manipulated for ideological and commercial reasons, but journalistic criticism of the victory itself, based
on dissatisfaction with the way in which the England team had gone about playing football. Of related surprise was seeing depictions of the England manager,
Sir Alf Ramsey, as a figure of ridicule. I remembered seeing photographs in my
childhood and youth of Ramsey as a distinguished looking and understandably
proud man.[3] That his popular image in England did not necessarily match to
that which I had assumed for him became a matter of intrigue that festered away
for some time and has now taken shape as a point of inquiry in this book. I now
understand the reasons why some mock the persona of Ramsey, although, like
his biographer Leo McKinstry, I think the representations are based in snide
caricature.[4] However, rather than the primary interest here being in defending
Ramsey's image, it is in understanding how his caricaturing connects to criticism of the circumstances surrounding England's winning of the World Cup in
1966. If there is a key protagonist in this book, then it is Ramsey. Criticisms of
England's World Cup victory are so closely tied to him that he demands more
than the already considerable attention he would receive in a study of this topic.
A central argument in my book is that criticism of Ramsey, for the style of football he had England play in the 1966 World Cup, fails to recognise that he was
a modernist in a way not unrelated to art. His innovation to playing strategy has
not been denied, but references to him 'modernising' football tend to regard
him as a ruthless technocrat devoid of aesthetic sensibility. The case presented
here suggests otherwise and is intended to free Ramsey from an association
with sterile scientific management.

The one particular episode that supposedly highlights Ramsey's lack of
appreciation for the aesthetics of football is his exclusion of the virtuoso player
Jimmy Greaves from the World Cup Final team. Ramsey's treatment of Greaves
offers an indictment that no critic of the England manager can miss. From the
outset of the World Cup finals tournament Greaves looked an uncomfortable
fit within the playing 'system' Ramsey had developed. However, Greaves's
undeniable goal-scoring potential secured his selection in the England team
for the three Group stage games. In the last of these games, against France,
Greaves sustained a laceration to his left leg that put him on the injury list for
at least the next game, the quarter-final against Argentina. A photograph shows
a despondent and solitary Greaves in the bathtub after the match, his bandaged
leg rested on a chair to elevate it above the water. Upon seeing this image I was
reminded of Jacques-Louis David's painting, *The Death of Marat*, in which the
assassinated French revolutionary leader lies prone in his bathtub just seconds
after taking his last breath.[5] David was an ally of Marat and the painting depicts

1 A dejected Jimmy Greaves in the bathtub ponders the implications of his leg injury.

Marat's martyrdom to the revolutionary cause. We cannot assume an ambition for the photograph of Greaves at the time it was taken, but can now see it as prescient of Greaves's fall from favour under Ramsey in the England team and, even as a first step towards his declining fortunes in club football. The injury sidelined Greaves for both the quarter-final against Argentina and the semi-final against Portugal. He was declared fit for the Final against West Germany, but Ramsey preferred to stick with Geoff Hurst, the player who had replaced Greaves for the games against Argentina and Portugal. Journalists debated ahead of the Final as to whether or not Greaves should return to the team at the expense of either Hurst or the other forward player Roger Hunt. With England going on to win the World Cup, one might assume the matter to be settled in admission that Ramsey made the correct decision. However, this has not been so. With the passing of time the World Cup win has become incidental to the critics' bigger concern over the Greaves absence from the England team symbolising the death of English football in 1966 and, in this light, the image of Greaves in the bathtub becomes all the more poignant.[6]

The creatively gifted Greaves appeared to provide a link with the best of a heroic past that Ramsey was willing to overlook in his single-minded quest to have England win the Jules Rimet trophy. But Greaves was no old-fashioned hero. He was a hero well-suited to the bright lights of the 1960s. He appealed to a 'modern romantic' sensibility of the time. His face was prominent in commercial advertisements in newspapers and magazines, giving him a celebrity profile that extended beyond football. Greaves's orientation to life and football was the diametrical opposite of Ramsey's. Ramsey was uninterested in and wary of activities extraneous to football. He believed professional football players should be fully focussed on football and, if they were, there was time for little else. Ramsey's modern outlook applied only to football. In other ways he was quite traditionally English. This may seem at odds with claiming Ramsey as a modernist, but not when considered in relation to Alexandra Harris's compelling thesis on the tendency for English modernists to retain romantic attachments to idealised aspects of English life.[7] Ramsey did just this and, like the writers, architects, designers and artists Harris discusses, he too may be regarded as a 'romantic modern'.

In a country where modernism has struggled to gain popular appeal – especially in architecture – it is not so surprising that the sharp-lined geometry of Ramsey's playing 'system' has had its critics. Remarks about the aesthetics of football being made via seemingly exclusive reference to a romanticised 'beautiful game', suggest little appreciation for the type of football that Ramsey fostered. Ramsey's preoccupation with winning the World Cup has also been a sign, for some, of his lack in aesthetic vision. Yet I would argue that the unswerving ambition to win the tournament provided the framework within which his aesthetic vision was developed. Baudelaire predicted the modernist aesthetic in art when he wrote of the possibility of beauty residing in 'the essential quality of being the present'.[8] Ramsey understood this in relation to football. He did so because he understood the very nature of football as a modern activity, circumscribed by the present, in terms of 'seasons' and tournaments. I argue that the playing 'system' developed by Ramsey to win the 1966 World Cup was guided by an aesthetic awareness of related functionalist priority and that the result is comparable to a constructivist art project. This may present a challenge to more conventional ways of seeing football, but, for that, no apology should need to be made.

England's winning of the 1966 World Cup makes for a rather different book than one that would have involved a discussion of England hosting the World Cup finals without its national team going on to win the Jules Rimet trophy.[9] Inevitably, in an academic book concerned with questions related to English identity, the implications of the World Cup victory become the focus of enquiry.

This becomes most explicit in the final chapters of this book as discussion turns to themes of memory – how the World Cup win is remembered, commemorated and, indeed, criticised. Discussion of the World Cup Final on 30 July 1966 occurs, in one way or another, in all chapters. Discussion of the World Cup finals, as an overall event, occurs in the first two full-length chapters as well as a later chapter concerned with locating the World Cup tournament coming to England within the cultural mood of the mid-1960s. This discussion is thankfully spared the contemporary demand for referring to football World Cup finals as mega-events. 'Mega-event' was not on the terminological radar in the 1960s and a now quainter term such as tournament still seems to suffice as a descriptor of the World Cup as an event in 1966.

Prominent within the lexicon of jargon that accompanies 'mega-events' is the term 'legacy'. Promising a 'legacy' is now a core component of any city's bid to host the Olympic Games, and the assessment of post-Games' legacy delivery has emerged as an academic cottage industry. Compared to the Olympic Games, World Cup 'legacy management' is still at an early stage of development.[10] In 1966 there was no requirement for a legacy plan to be set out in advance. Legacy, without being explicitly referred to at the time, came on to the agenda in regard to the expectations accompanying government funding of stadia improvements ahead of the World Cup. This issue is discussed in Chapter 3. Apart from this understanding of legacy, it can also be considered in relation to unexpected outcomes from the 1966 World Cup. As such, legacy pertained to matters either directly related to football or to off-field events. A controversy that occurred in the Final provides an example of the former. Disputation remains to this day as to whether or not the ball actually crossed the line for England, and whether Geoff Hurst was rightly awarded the goal granted to them by referee Dienst in the first half of extra time. As such, the incident has provided a legacy by way of its influence to subsequent debates over the usage of goal line technology in international football. An off-field example of legacy relates to what can reasonably be recalled as the 1966 World Cup's most unusual sideshow occurrence. In March 1966, the Jules Rimet trophy was stolen from a rare stamp exhibition at Westminster Central Hall, where it was on display as publicity for the forthcoming World Cup finals tournament. In a happening of incredibly good fortune, which rescued the Football Association (FA) from extreme embarrassment, the trophy was found by Pickles the dog while out walking with his owner David Corbett in their south London neighbourhood. Pickles earned a sizeable reward for Mr Corbett and, for himself, an invitation to the celebration banquet following the World Cup Final.[11] The legacy of the episode was a lesson in the need for greater security. The FA commissioned the making of a replica trophy that was used for public exhibition purposes with the real trophy being kept under lock and key until the conclusion of the tournament. Despite greater care with security being taken over the years, the Jules Rimet trophy was again stolen, seemingly for good, in Brazil in 1983.[12]

In broadest intention *England and the 1966 World Cup* is offered as a contribution to the academic study of English cultural life. I maintain a long-held view that sport is a 'form' of culture and for this reason warrants scholarly attention. In *The Making of Sporting Cultures* I argued that some sports are so prominent within particular national contexts that they require mentioning in any reference to the 'common culture' of those nations. Accordingly, I so identified football within an English common culture.[13] This understanding underpins my interest in the subject matter of the present book. The theme of football and an English common culture is addressed most obviously in the next chapter and it remains influential to the discussion in other chapters throughout the book. A focus on the English experience of the World Cup leaves little room for attention to how the World Cup in England was experienced by other participant nations, not only the teams and supporters that visited in 1966, but supporters who observed the World Cup from abroad. There are a host of studies that could be written, and hopefully the approaching fiftieth anniversary year will serve as a prompt to scholars with the requisite language skills and access to vernacular materials to undertake such work.[14] Historical research is necessarily ambitious. According to Raymond Williams:

> It is only … our own time and place that we can expect to know, in any substantial way. We can learn a great deal of the life of other places and times, but certain elements, it seems to me, will always be irrecoverable … The most difficult thing to get hold of, in studying any past period is this felt sense of the quality of life at a particular place and time: a sense of the ways in which the particular activities combined into a way of thinking and living.[15]

Williams's modest approach to 'cultural history' remains influential to the study undertaken for and presented in this book. The related challenge has been to connect the 1966 World Cup in England to what Williams refers to as the 'structure of feeling' relevant to a given place and time. In this case it has required dealing with certain mythologies, such as the 'Swinging Sixties', not in a dismissive but a negotiated way, in an attempt to understand how the World Cup has been the subject of intertwining interpretations between reality and imagination. Although records and materials from a time do not reveal hidden truths, examination of them remains pertinent to meaningful cultural historical analysis and being able to verify matters as much as possible. In this belief I have consulted a number of archival repositories during the course of researching this book, the archive of the National Football Museum being especially significant, given its holdings of primary documentation relevant to the topic. Material accessed in the British Newspaper Archive, the British

Library and the Liverpool Records Office (the Everton Collection) has also been indispensable to the research.

The book's bibliography reveals, at a glimpse, an eclectic use of written material ranging from scholarly to popular publications. This is now familiar practice for research straddling old boundaries between 'high' and 'low' culture and will surprise few readers. Some may, though, baulk upon seeing the listing of a number of football player autobiographies, a genre proposed by David Goldblatt to be of the most 'debased literary currency'.[16] However, as tedious as some of the yarns may be, player autobiographies are valuable to historical research because they offer an insider's subjective reflection upon the particular sporting milieu the researcher is investigating.[17] Due to the fame afforded by the 1966 World Cup victory, a number of England players had autobiographies published within a few years of the tournament. Most have also had autobiographies published after or towards the end of their playing careers. The way in which recollections differ or emphases are made between two autobiographies written by the same player becomes a point of interest in this study. In most cases, if not all, the player autobiographies cited in the bibliography have been ghost written by football journalists. In cases where this has been declared on the title page, I cite the ghost writer in the respective entry. In cases where a ghost writer is not clearly acknowledged, the footballer is cited as sole author of his autobiography.

As much as I am interested in football-related information about the 1966 World Cup, I do not in this book systematically set out tournament- and match-related details in a manner that might be expected of a more descriptive historical account. For such details the *World Cup Report* by Harold Mayes, commissioned by the Football Association, remains the official reference source. Of internet sites available at the time of publication, England Football Online www.englandfootballonline.com provides a useful reference source for information pertaining to the England team at the 1966 World Cup.

This brief introductory chapter is followed by seven full-length chapters and then a brief concluding chapter, which considers the commemoration of England's World Cup victory. The chapters proceed thematically. Chapter 2 opens the encounter between post-war modernity and tradition, by examining the relationship between the World Cup and the FA Cup. The particular reason for looking at the relationship between the two is to understand how the World Cup victory was able to acquire such importance within a national context and football culture in which the World Cup competition struggled to gain significance. The symbolic conferment of prestige upon the World Cup by Queen Elizabeth II – like that given to the FA Cup – is seen as crucial to the cultural signification process. Politics of a cruder kind are discussed in

Chapter 3. Prime Minister Harold Wilson seemed to have little idea about the World Cup in the year prior to the finals coming to England, but by the time of England's victory he was so drawn to the golden glow of the Jules Rimet trophy as to create a 'legacy' for the way in which politicians would regard the World Cup into the future. His Government provided some funding for infrastructure and became involved in planning ahead of the tournament. The chapter addresses hosting issues and adopts a case study approach by focussing on Liverpool and Goodison Park. The concentrated study draws on a range of materials to provide insight into the cultural particularity of Liverpool's hosting experience.

Although somewhat mythologised, the mid-1960s was, nevertheless, a time of considerable change in social and cultural identity. Traditional masculinity was undoubtedly affected by the emergent rock'n'roll era. Football was not especially quick to respond, but the young men moving through its professional ranks could hardly ignore the behaviour of peers in other fields. The England squad in 1966 did not contain any players in the Beatlesque guise of George Best, and even its younger members have been regarded as conservatively conformist. Chapter 4 examines the masculinity of the 1966 England team via a parallel analysis of the masculinity of Alf Ramsey. Consideration of the complicated organisational circumstances which surrounded the players and, in particular, Ramsey, gives caution against accepting simplistic assessments of the manager and his players as embourgeoised establishmentarians. Ramsey was certainly not conventional or unoriginal when it came to playing tactics and strategy. The case for Ramsey being a football modernist, foreshadowed in the first part of this chapter, is developed and set out in chapter 5. This is possibly the most provocative chapter in the book. Its argument may or may not find favour with readers, but it should at least reopen the discussion of Ramsey and encourage an alternative consideration of his football tactics to that which presently predominates in relevant literature and discourse. Understandably, the World Cup does not tend to be regarded as an event that has offered much culturally beyond the football. Culturally related discussion has mostly favoured a populist imagining of the World Cup occurring against the colourful backdrop of swinging mid-1960s' England. Stereotypes notwithstanding, related considerations are relevant to more serious study and this is part of the story taken up in Chapter 6. Apart from pop culture associations the chapter also examines the cultural creativity directly sponsored by the World Cup, including posters, stamps, World Cup Willie the mascot and *Goal!*, the World Cup film. In differing ways each of these items offered something distinct, leaving (dare we say) a unique cultural legacy.

The final three chapters reflect upon the World Cup that was. Scholarly attention has, reasonably enough, been concerned with criticising ongoing celebratory representations of England's victory within the mass media. A number of academics refer to a 'myth of 1966', which they claim presents a glorious tale of England's victory, minus consideration of queries that might disturb a praiseful narrative of linkage back to a lost Albion. The logical extension for some is that the World Cup win is successfully deployed by the media to bolster popular adherence to a nationalistic ideology beneficial to both capitalist and politically conservative interests. In critique of these views, Chapter 7 offers an against the grain reading of evidence used by academics in their arguments. I suggest that the determined effort to be critical has resulted in a counter bias, involving, in some instances, a selective interpretation of events. I also contend that the public response to the so-called 'myth of 1966' risks being overstated in two ways. Firstly, in presumption that the public readily buy into media discourse on the World Cup victory and, secondly, that subsequent football-related festivities drawing on 1966-related imagery are necessarily an expression of the type of nationalistic sentiment assumed by critics. A notion of 'collective memory' underpins belief in the existence of a shared pubic view of historical episodes, such as England's World Cup victory. Chapter 8 moves into a dedicated discussion of how we grapple to make sense of memory in this way, even to query the possibility and usefulness to talk meaningfully of a collective memory. A concern is that individual memories, and their significance, are subsumed by efforts to build a bigger memory map. Accordingly, this chapter gives voice to 'autobiographical memories' of the 1966 World Cup Final. Given the dearth of primary field-based research, use is made of memory statements provided in the non-academic volume *Voices of '66*. The statements raise themes that could be drawn out in a more focussed and substantial oral history research project. The latter half of the chapter switches attention to autobiographical memories of the World Cup Final provided within fictional texts. Here we see rare evidence, allegorical perhaps, of the World Cup Final as a milestone moment in personal lives and as a connecting point in generational relationships.

Popular pessimism has it that England may never again host a World Cup finals tournament or its national men's team win a World Cup Final, wherever it might be played. Whatever the future may ultimately bring in these regards, it does seem fair to say that hosting and/or winning the men's football World Cup will be some way off for England. Resignation to the inevitability of future failure has gained momentum in tabloid forums as each year passes since the 1966 World Cup victory. Such resignation betrays the double-edged pessimism over England's World Cup prospects, whereby England's unlikelihood to ever win the World Cup again is believed as a denial of true destiny. However, the view taken in this book is that commemoration need not be given over to historical negativity. I believe it best to regard the 1966 World Cup and England's winning of its Final as a 'moment in modernity'. This is not to suggest a freezing in time, but a belief in the importance of understanding episodes within their own present. The concluding chapter recommends such an approach to the commemoration of the cultural significance of the 1966 World Cup in 'public memory' projects such as museum exhibitions. This book has been completed in the year ahead of the fiftieth anniversary year of the occasion, its publication timed to coincide with that golden anniversary. However, *England and the 1966 World Cup* is intended as more than an anniversary volume. I dare to imagine these very words being read in some years to come from this moment, and that you, the reader, will be encouraged to read on. If its pages can provide something of a 'felt sense' for the 1966 World Cup, within the cultural life of its 'particular place and time', then my ambition will have been fulfilled.

Notes

1 Clarke and Critcher, '1966 and All That'.

2 This chapter is written in the first person voice to offer a personal tone to the book's introduction. A more conventional third person voice is used in subsequent chapters throughout the book.

3 The photographs I got to see of Ramsey would have been in books about sport and boy's annuals kept in my school library. Such books and football magazines, like *Charles Buchan's Football Monthly*, would have been a key source of information about football for young people in Britain (mainly boys, given the gendered presentation of the publications) during the mid-1960s. The following excerpt from *The Boys' Book of Soccer 1966*, observing the World Cup victory, is typically respectful: 'England's display in winning the World Cup was a personal triumph for Alf Ramsey, their team manager, who planned it for three years. Dedicated to the game and to his players and impervious to all criticism, he moulded eleven individuals into a team, decided its tactics and brought the side to its peak fitness at just the right moment.' See Smith, 'England's Victory in the World Cup', p. 16.

4 The biographies by McKinstry (*Sir Alf*) and Bowler (*Winning Isn't Everything*) provide fair, while not uncritical, accounts of Ramsey's life and career in football. McKinstry's book benefits from privileged access to materials related to Ramsey held by Ipswich Town Football Club, where Ramsey was manager from 1955 to 1963. The only autobiographical work by Ramsey is *Talking Football*, published in 1952 towards the end of his time as a player.

5 *The Death of Marat (La Mort de Marat)* is located in the Royal Museums of Fine Arts Belgium, Brussels.

6 Greaves claims that he knew straight after the match against France that the leg injury would end his chances of playing again in the World Cup. He accepted that should the team advance to the Final without him, then Ramsey would be quite right to retain the successful line-up for the Final. See Greaves, *The Heart of the Game*, pp. 36–7. However, Greaves's defence of Ramsey's decision has tended to be double-edged. For example, he has also claimed, without explicit reference to Ramsey, that the injury against France 'provided the excuse for my exit from the tournament'. See Greaves, *This One's on Me*, p. 22.

7 Harris, *Romantic Moderns*.
8 Baudelaire, 'The Painter of Modern Life', p. 391.
9 An appropriate distinction is made within contemporary scholarship between men's and women's national football teams and respective tournaments. However, as an official England women's team was not formed until the early 1970s and the FIFA (Fédération Internationale de Football Association) Women's World Cup was inaugurated in 1991, the England national team and the World Cup competition are referred to throughout this book without gender distinction being made and references can, accordingly, be taken to mean the England men's national football team and the FIFA World Cup played by men.
10 Horne, 'Managing World Cup Legacy', p. 9.
11 For a thoroughgoing study of the episode see Atherton, *The Theft of the Jules Rimet Trophy*. Pickles went on, later in the year, to star in the comedy film *The Spy with a Cold Nose*. Sadly, he is reported to have died while chasing a cat in 1967.
12 When Brazil won the World Cup in 1970, a prerogative for a third-time competition winning country was exercised and the Jules Rimet trophy remained from then, until its disappearance, in the care of the Brazilian Football Federation. The replica trophy commissioned by the FA is one of the 1966 World Cup related items displayed at the National Football Museum, Manchester. Pickles' collar is also on display at the museum.
13 Hughson, *The Making of Sporting Cultures*.
14 For a current example of such research, see Meyer's essay on reportage and interpretation of the controversial third England goal from the 1966 World Cup Final. Meyer, 'Erecting a European Lieu de *Mémoire*'.
15 Williams, *The Long Revolution*, p. 47.
16 This phrase has been attributed to Goldblatt in a number of web-based citations. David Goldblatt has confirmed in personal correspondence to the author (7 July 2015) that he used this description of footballer autobiographies at a 'conference in Toronto in 2009'.
17 A similar point about the value of sportsperson autobiographies to historical research is made by Taylor, 'From Source to Subject', p. 485–6.

2

The Cup tradition and England 1966

The common culture of the English people in the twentieth century lay not in folk culture ... but in ... association football, home grown and as close as you could get. (Ross McKibbon)

By the time the World Cup came to England in 1966, the team of the host nation had competed in the four previous competitions, commencing with the 1950 World Cup in Brazil, which was the first post-war World Cup. Three other World Cup competitions had been played during the 1930s (1930, 1934 and 1938), in which England did not participate. Unsuccessful outcomes for the national team in the post-war World Cups seemed unpromising to a groundswell in public interest occurring ahead of England hosting the 1966 tournament. Yet, confident that playing at home would be in England's favour, Bobby Charlton believed the advantage would be maximised once the English people 'throw off detachment' and got behind the team. Charlton was effectively hoping for people to develop the type of committed interest in the World Cup which he knew them to have for the FA Cup. He noted that 'Cup Final Day' is an occasion when 'all over the country people stay close to their television and radio sets ... bring[ing] life to a stop for ninety minutes'.[1] Charlton's comment shows awareness that the FA Cup, particularly the Final, was an occasion of national significance, which fascinated not only dedicated football followers, but also others, who, while not so regularly interested in football, embraced its festive spirit. The World Cup, by its very nature, is a completely different tournament to the FA Cup, yet, while surely appreciative of the essential dissimilarity, Charlton was right to suggest that the World Cup required something of the same allure and collective mood to succeed as a public occasion in England. The purpose of this chapter is to look at the relationship between the 1966 World Cup and the cup tradition in England, and how, and to what extent, the World Cup melded within this tradition in the restless age of post-war modernity.

In his introduction to the 'official' history of the competition, Tony Pawson notes:

> There has never been any necessity to define 'the Cup'. For everyone in England that brief reference automatically implies The Football Association Challenge Cup.[2]

Pawson goes on to declare that the FA Cup has given rise to a 'host of imitators', including the World Cup. This rather reinforces Brian Glanville's emphasis on the FA Cup as 'beyond all doubt ... the mother of all football competitions' and somewhat detracts, at least in a historical sense, from the claim by anthropologist Desmond Morris that the World Cup is 'the greatest of all soccer contests'.[3] When it was inaugurated in 1871 the FA Cup competition very much reflected the public school amateur sportsman backgrounds of the FA hierarchy, but this soon changed as leading professional regionally based clubs came to dominate the competition. With this broadening of participation and the holding of the FA Cup Final in London, especially from 1923 when Wembley Stadium became the permanent venue, the deciding match of the competition acquired a status of annual national significance. The possibility of winning the Cup soon came to provide a rare type of unity in 'civic pride' between town leaders and the local citizenry.[4] For the latter, an annual pilgrimage was made to London, when working-class men from the North and Midlands came to see the Final if it involved their team. This ritual was sometimes referred to insultingly, by journalists, as hordes from the North descending upon the national capital.[5]

Resident in that capital from 1915, when he took up a teaching post at Birkbeck College, was the poet T.S. Eliot. A keen social observer, it is likely that Eliot – who was interested in the sport of boxing, if not football[6] – became aware of the fanfare surrounding the FA Cup Final. In his 1948 book *Notes Towards the Definition of Culture* Eliot provided a list, admittedly rather random, of activities and items indicative of a lived English culture. Among these were a number of annual events on the national register, 'Derby Day, Henley Regatta, Cowes [sailing regatta], the twelfth of August [opening day in the shooting season for Red Grouse], a cup final'.[7] The preponderance of events more associated with middle-class than working-class people may suggest that Eliot included mention of a cup final in belated recognition of the need for balance in his snapshot representation of a 'whole way of life'. If so, generic reference to 'a cup final' provided pertinent correction. A cup final, so mentioned, may well be that of a local competition, but the evocation invariably relates to the FA Cup Final.

Raymond Williams suggested that Eliot slid between definitions of culture, ultimately imposing his high culture definition on to that of popular culture.[8] Williams demanded a clearer statement on how distinctions of the kind we make within fields of high culture, such as art and classical music can be made within popular culture. Only by doing so may we truly appreciate the human value invested in a full range of cultural items and happenings. Williams defended some forms of popular culture, including football and jazz music, by distinguishing them from less worthy forms such as red-top newspapers, cheap thrill horror films and contrived pop music.[9] He recognised football's authenticity, as a cultural form, residing in its grassroots attachments to working-class communities. Despite the commercial dimension to professional football, the sport's popularity and viability depended, certainly still in the 1960s, upon traditional supporter affiliations. Accordingly, football requires a different kind of appreciation from high culture forms; it is appreciated with passion and close up, rather than dispassionately from a considered distance. Williams was a publicly engaged academic who wrote television criticism for *The Listener*. He personally enjoyed watching football via this medium and was keenly aware that other people did too, especially key matches that were broadcast live, such as the FA Cup Final.[10] Watching football live on television, rather than in replay, allowed for a connection between the fans in the stadium and those in the living room and, for this reason, Williams would advocate the rightfulness of football matches with a national interest being available live to air, as television emerged as the dominant means of visual communication.

Williams's advocacy for the cultural significance of football connects to his earlier rejection of the tendency by intellectuals to deride what they perceive as 'mass culture'. Indeed, Williams contended, 'there are in fact no masses; there are only ways of seeing people as masses'.[11] He believed the term masses to be an intellectual invention, by which people of the working class are objectified and effectively caricatured. Once such terms are questioned, the underlying intellectual snobbery exposed and the conventional restrictions on what counts as culture challenged, then a genuinely democratic understanding of cultural life can prevail. As this occurs, football, a sport with widespread popularity, can be properly regarded as a significant and legitimate cultural activity. Legitimate in the sense that it involves an aesthetic appreciation for many of its enthusiasts, in the same manner as activities more customarily regarded as being 'cultural', say attending the ballet or visiting an art gallery.

Accepting football as a form or element of culture also militates against a facile acceptance of the sport as being socially and economically democratic. Terms such as the 'people's game', as used by the historian James Walvin, should not be taken to mean that the working class has been the traditional owners of football in an economic sense. In using this term, Walvin had in mind the long grassroots and localised history of football, from the unruly free-for-all medieval games played across or between townships to the few-in-number street matches played by boys on cobble-stoned working-class streets in the suburbs of industrial cities.[12] As football became formalised into clubs, and the league competition system developed in the latter 1800s, working-class supporters could hold shares in their local clubs, but even at this early stage of professional development their dividend holdings were minimal, the great proportion of shares being held by businessman, who also had the far greater say in club management issues.[13] As Richard Holt suggests, working-class spectators traditionally enjoyed *cultural* ownership, rather than economic ownership, of clubs and the sport of football more generally.[14]

When the FA Challenge Cup was inaugurated in 1871 it reflected the FA's background in a way that soon came to sit incongruously against the local loyalties of working-class supported regional clubs.[15] Any semblance of Corinthian spirited amateurism faded rather quickly as the FA Cup transformed to take in professional clubs dotted around the country. The possibility of winning the Cup soon came to provide for a rare type of unity in 'civic pride' shared by town leaders and the local citizenry.[16] From the mid-1880s powerful regional clubs came to dominate the FA Cup competition. The victory of Blackburn Rovers over West Bromwich Albion in the replayed Cup Final of 1885/86 reflected the trend of success by professional clubs located above the south of England. Apart from Tottenham Hotspur winning in 1901 and 1921, and Chelsea being runners-up in 1915, the FA Cup Final did not feature a professional London club until West Ham United lost the first Wembley Stadium based Final to Bolton Wanderers in 1923. However, despite a shift in cup-winning fortunes away from amateurism and towards the North, the FA remained a staid organisation, which kept largely true, over time, to its origins, formed, as it was, by 'a small band of public school enthusiasts', in London in 1863.[17] Writing in 1973, David Triesman observed the FA Council to be made up of aristocrats and 'military gentlemen' of the highest rank. Representation from within football, let alone supporters from clubs, was a non-issue.[18] As will be discussed further on, the public school style elitism, in tandem with the non-professional footballing background of the FA leadership, was a source of irritation to Alf Ramsey during his tenure as England team manager.

Elitist arrogance seemingly characterised the FA's response when the starting of a world cup competition for national representative teams was touted. With rather lofty condescension the FA regarded such a competition as unnecessary, and FIFA's proposing it as an act of impudence. A view of the competition as irrelevant prevailed during the 1930s, and, accordingly, the FA withheld participation by the England national team from the first three World Cups held during that decade. The disdainful attitude towards FIFA and its proposed tournament was compounded by the existence of a football competition within the Olympic Games. The Olympic football competition was ostensibly an amateur gathering, and the FA wanted this status preserved for international football matches played between countries. However, the case was made somewhat tenuous in that the understanding of amateurism within Olympic football competition differed from one competing nation to another. This became most apparent when London hosted the Olympic Games in 1948 and the home football team – Great Britain (rather than England) – was eliminated in the semi-finals by Yugoslavia. The Great Britain team manager, Matt Busby of Manchester United, expressed the prevailing view within Britain that the football team representing Yugoslavia consisted entirely of 'virtual professionals'.[19] While it would be unreasonable to accuse countries with political systems that did not differentiate between sporting amateurs and professionals – in the supposed British way of sporting rightness – of cheating, the Olympic football competition rather obviously resulted in some uneven matchups. Thus, although the Olympic Games' football competition provided some reason for the FA's reluctance to involve an England team in the World Cup, it hardly stood as a completely amateur alternative to challenge the relevance of the World Cup's existence.

In organisational status the FA spent much of the 1930s disaffiliated from FIFA.[20] This was to the displeasure of the man who became Secretary of the FA in 1934, Stanley Rous. Rous, who went on to become the President of FIFA between 1961 and 1974, maintained a personal working relationship with FIFA in the 1930s, in defiance of what he referred to ironically as the 'splendid isolation' of the FA.[21] By the end of the Second World War, owing considerably to the efforts of Rous and Arthur Drewry, President of the Football League, England's insularity from the world football stage was breaking down. Drewry's appointment as Vice President of FIFA in 1946 almost ensured England's entry into the forthcoming 1950 World Cup; Rous's coinciding appointment to the World Cup Organising Committee guaranteed it would happen. The England national team duly qualified for the final series in Brazil via the then easy qualification path of the Home International Championship series of 1949/50, which it won.[22] However, the World Cup tournament yielded little more than disappointment and embarrassment for a team that commenced the finals as the most favoured team from Europe. England prevailed in the first qualifying group match against Chile 2–0, but in an upset of folkloric proportion was beaten 1–0 by the United States team in the next game.[23] From various reports it seems that this was an occasion when luck entirely deserted one team and favoured another. In the latter regard the game's only goal was scored by a miscued diving header by US player Joe Gaetjens, which deceived England keeper Bert Williams only because it came off the back of the attacker's head. There were also suggestions that the referee was partial towards the US team. For example, Stan Mortensen appeared to score legitimately with a header towards the end of the game, only for the goal to be disallowed.[24] The cross for that non-goal was supplied by none other than Alf Ramsey, England's right-back during the game. A specialist dead-ball kicker, Ramsey suffered the frustration of seeing a number of his free-kicks foiled by unorthodox goalkeeping or defensive play, which he regarded as pure luck on the part of his opponents. In his own words: 'So far as we were concerned there was a gremlin upon that football and it was not our day, the United States running out winners by that "streaky" goal in a match which I shall always remember for its many extraordinary incidents'.[25]

Ramsey, writing in 1952, so not very long after the defeat by the US, regarded the result as 'the biggest soccer upset of all time'. Yet, despite remarking on the unluckiness experienced by England during the game with a degree of magnanimity, he concluded, 'I have no alibis to offer for England's defeat'.[26] The chance for quick redemption did not go England's way, as the team was defeated in the next and final match of the qualifying round 1–0 by Spain, meaning Spain's advancement to the second qualifying round and England's elimination from the tournament. While the press in England helped to perpetuate the bad luck on the pitch story, especially in regard to the game against the US, responsibility for the overall failure at the tournament in Brazil was nevertheless sought. Yet, rather than being levelled at the players, blame was more readily attributed to the inadequacy of administrative planning and preparation ahead of the final series.[27] However, whatever excuses could be made, there was no escaping the fact that the England team had failed on the pitch to live up to their reputation and public expectation. The eventual participation in the World Cup indicated that other 'footballing nations had erased the gap ... and that England had much to learn' from international competition.[28] England qualified for the subsequent 1954 World Cup finals in Switzerland, again by winning the Home International series but, between qualification matches, suffered a 6–3 defeat in a 'friendly' game against Hungary at Wembley on 25 November 1953 – a profound loss that jolted the collective ego more than the 1950 World Cup embarrassment experienced against the United States. This was the first defeat of an England team at home by a non-British international team, a loss still highlighted in critical interpretations as the first deep puncturing of England's hubristic claim to international footballing superiority.[29]

Alf Ramsey was again England's right-back in the calamitous game against Hungary, the last Ramsey played for England. Although seeing the Hungarians at closest possible range, rather than openly recognising the opponents' outstanding play, Ramsey suggested that the high scorecard against England was down to poor goalkeeping by Gil Merrick of Birmingham City.[30] Although the criticism of Merrick is somewhat supported by video footage of the goals, this does not account for the highly developed skills of Hungarian players such as Ferenc Puskás, Nándor Hidegkuti and Sándor Kocsis, which seemed to bedazzle the England team throughout the game. Any chance of the resounding defeat being recorded as an aberration was lost on 23 May 1954 when England was beaten 7–1 by Hungary in a rematch played in Budapest. In the soon to follow World Cup finals, which commenced in June, England was unable to find redemption. England topped its qualifying group, but was then eliminated in the quarter-final by reigning champions Uruguay in a 4–2 loss, to a team again deemed to have players much more technically advanced than those representing England.[31]

England's hopes of improvement in the 1958 World Cup finals, held in Sweden, were dented by the Munich air tragedy of 6 February 1958, which claimed the lives of eight Manchester United players, four of whom – Roger Byrne, Duncan Edwards, David Pegg and Tommy Taylor – had featured in the 'qualifying zone' games against Belgium and Éire. The Home International Championship was not used as a qualification stage for this World Cup or from then on.[32] The 21-year-old Edwards was predicted to be a star of the 1958 tournament and England's most important player going into the next decade. The loss of him and his three club mates no doubt came to bear on the England team, which managed only third place in the qualifying group, finishing behind Brazil and the Soviet Union.[33] So, as in finals of the 1950 World Cup, England was eliminated in the initial stage of the tournament.

England again qualified for the subsequent finals, held in Chile in 1962, by winning its European zone grouping against Portugal and Luxembourg. A loss to Hungary, a win over Argentina and a draw against Bulgaria was enough to advance England to a quarter-final rendezvous with defending champions Brazil, which England lost 3–1. Given that Brazil went on to win the World Cup, this result might have appeared to be not too bad, but, despite a few players receiving praise, especially winger Bobby Charlton, England's performance in the 1962 tournament was reportedly lacklustre.[34] Upon return home, team manager Walter Winterbottom resigned his post, thus ending a long first phase of active engagement by England in FIFA's international competition.[35]

From a contemporary standpoint it is difficult to conceive how remote an event the World Cup was for people in Britain prior to its holding in England in 1966. The blanket free-to-air television coverage of the World Cup in Britain whether played as far away as Japan or as close as France ensures a keen interest in the fortunes of not only Home Nation teams, but also those of other countries. However, the relatively low level of television ownership and live-to-air coverage of World Cups meant that the tournament did not enjoy widespread popularity prior to 1966. The first World Cup finals series to be televised was that from Switzerland in 1954. In total, thirteen hours of football from this tournament were broadcast on television in Britain by the BBC. This increased to over twenty hours of match time coverage for the 1958 World Cup. Live television transmission from Chile was not possible in 1962, so the World Cup of that year was watchable only via recorded highlights, eighteen hours of which were shown by the BBC. Aware that the 1962 World Cup would not offer much of a financial return FIFA struck a deal with the European Broadcasting Union (EBU) for a combined payment for this tournament with that for the next in England in 1966. The 1966 finals eventuated as the first major televised World Cup with an estimated international audience in excess of four hundred million people.[36]

A significant portion of this number was made up of the television viewing audience in Britain. The 1966 World Cup Final match is reported to have been watched on television by more than thirty-two million people, probably an underestimation because, as Moran notes, this is unlikely to adequately account for the full number of people who watched on television in large public gatherings.[37] Respondents in Norman Shiel's book *Voices of '66*, an oral history of personal World Cup memories, bear testimony to such collective viewing experiences in pubs and clubs.[38] Without such gatherings it is unlikely that neighbourhood streets could have been reported as deserted during the time that England played West Germany in the Final. One respondent claims to have driven all over Guernsey during the game and declares 'the whole place was like a ghost town'.[39] Given that the commentaries in *Voices of '66* appear to have been gathered by Shiel more than thirty years after the World Cup, it is not surprising that many are from individuals who were either children or teenagers in 1966 and that those who watched the Final on television did so in the family home, rather than in a public space. Nevertheless, in accumulation, comments such as, 'I covered every blade of grass with the team as I watched them make their black and white progress to the final on the family's Ultra Bermuda television set', give a certain contextual justification to the claim, 'this … was the first time football was important to the nation as a whole'.[40]

Classified under the Broadcasting Act as 'Listed Events' World Cup matches remain one of the major sporting occasions available on free-to-air television in Britain. The 1966 World Cup established the precedent of popularity to validate such a status. In terms more specific to Britain, the World Cup was treated as a matter of 'public service broadcasting', in keeping with the notion of broadcasting responsibility embedded into the BBC by its first Director-General, Sir John Reith. Reith believed the public had the right to experience live broadcasting of key sporting events, including the FA Cup Final. During Reith's tenure at the BBC, the first live radio broadcast of an FA Cup Final occurred in 1930 and the first television broadcast in 1938. However, televising of FA Cup finals did not occur regularly until after the Second World War.[41] The first major sporting event to be televised by the BBC following the Second World War was the London Olympic Games of 1948. Indeed, the 1948 Olympics provided a landmark moment in British media history, whereby television came to the fore as a broadcasting form for sport. The Games provided an especially important experimental exercise in the televising of large open air events, a legacy from which the televising of the 1966 World Cup finals tournament was to benefit.[42]

Although when the 1966 World Cup came to England, its television presence was received with caution. The announcement in June of blanket television coverage of the tournament – 50 hours on the BBC and 16 hours on ITV – was reported sardonically in the British press. For example, *Daily Mail* reports featured the headlines, 'BBC puts viewers on a soccer diet' and 'You lucky people you'.[43] There was a strongly gendered dimension to such reports, suggesting that female viewers, in particular, would be dismayed by the displacement of regular primetime programming to accommodate World Cup matches. Towards the conclusion of the tournament newspaper reports had shifted in position to suggest that the comprehensive television coverage of World Cup matches in 1966 had won over women who were previously uninterested in football.[44] Sexist assumptions notwithstanding, as Pope suggests, this type of claim warrants the investigation it has yet to receive from researchers.[45]

Ahead of the 1966 World Cup Final, the BBC management reportedly predicted that the match would attract a record international television audience of 400 million, approximately 50 million more than that for the funeral of Sir Winston Churchill in January of the previous year.[46] Given his reticence about the televising of state ceremonial events, the late Prime Minister might well have been grateful for such a trumping. Churchill had been quite opposed to the televising of young Queen Elizabeth's Coronation in June 1953, which went ahead despite the Prime Minister's stated objection.[47] The televising of the Coronation provided a defining moment in the visibility of the new monarch to the people in a changing media age. In an essay written at the time, the prominent sociologists Edwards Shils and Michael Young presented a pro-monarchy case, arguing that the Coronation was a 'great act of national communion'.[48] Coronations might have always been thus regarded, but in 1953 television recast the protocol by which the Coronation takes place 'in view of the people', by giving them an immediate audience to the Queen's crowning. As some writers have suggested, there was something ironic about this most traditional of British occasions serving to highlight the dawning significance of television within this new age of post-war modernity.[49]

In the month before her Coronation, Queen Elizabeth had been seen on television in attendance at the 1953 FA Cup Final. The first monarch to attend an FA Cup Final was Queen Elizabeth's grandfather, King George V, in 1914. The King's attendance was a sign that his advisers had come to recognise football as a major social bonding activity for the common people and that the monarch should be seen to show an interest in the sport.[50] It cannot be certain that television has strengthened the bond between the monarch and the people, but it has certainly made Queen Elizabeth highly visible, the televising of her presence in a ceremonial role at the 1953 FA Cup Final, followed soon after by the televising of her Coronation, gave an appearance of more personal contact than people had with previous monarchs. The 1953 FA Cup Final has gone down in the history of the sport as one of English football's most famous matches. It was the game in which Stanley Matthews starred for Blackpool in a final minute 4–3 win over Bolton Wanderers. This was the first FA Cup Final to receive a mass television audience, largely due to the widespread sale of television sets ahead of the Queen's Coronation on 2 June 1953. Johnes and Mellor thus refer to the Coronation and the Cup Final (along with the Ashes cricket series, played in and won by England in the summer of 1953) as 'intertwined' episodes of 'national celebration'.[51] Indeed, the visual connection between the FA Cup Final and the Coronation must have been inescapable for those who watched both events on television, even extending to the possibility of the then recent memory of the Queen presenting the FA Cup to the Blackpool captain Harry Johnston flashing through the minds of some viewers when watching the Coronation on television one month later.

Between the 1953 FA Cup Final and the 1966 World Cup, Queen Elizabeth presented the FA Cup to winning captains on another six occasions, taking her position in the Royal Box at Wembley in 1955, 1956, 1957, 1959, 1963 and 1965. Had the Queen been in attendance for the 1964 FA Cup Final, on 2 May that year, she would have presented the Cup to West Ham United's captain Bobby Moore, following his team's 3–2 victory over Preston North End. However, as the match coincided with the christening of Prince Edward at Windsor Castle, the Queen was absent on that occasion, the ceremonial honours at Wembley performed by her cousin Lord Harewood, who was president of the FA at the time. A cup presentation to Moore had to wait for another two years, when Her Majesty handed the Jules Rimet trophy to him as England captain on 30 July 1966. The presentation of the trophy has become one of the key images of the 1966 World Cup Final. It remains available in a sequence of photographs, from the Queen holding the trophy, then through various stages of the trophy being passed to Moore, the Queen shaking hands with Moore, to Moore walking away with the trophy, kissing and then raising it. The television footage also shows Moore cleaning his hands before meeting the Queen. First he wiped them on the back of his shorts, then on the front of his shirt, before giving each hand in turn a quick wipe on the velvet draping covering the parapet in front of the Queen. Moore later remarked, that upon seeing the Queen's 'lilywhite gloves' as he approached, he realised his hands were filthy and thus concentrated on getting them clean rather than on 'getting hold of the World Cup'.[52] The story of Sir Walter Raleigh's cloak springs to mind, Moore's keenness to prevent the Queen from being exposed to dirt reminiscent of Raleigh's courtier gallantry in covering a puddle ahead of Queen Elizabeth I's impending step.

A young man of aristocratic-sounding name, Robert Frederick Chelsea Moore hailed from a working-class background in Barking, Essex. While intellectually gifted enough to gain entry to grammar school, Moore's passion was sport and he recalled harbouring a desire to represent England in football since his earliest experiences playing for the Barking Primary School team.[53] A special relationship between the Monarchy and the East End was started by Queen Elizabeth's parents during the Blitz, when they famously visited the area to meet people whose homes had been destroyed and those who remained under threat from continuing bombing. Moore's appearance before the Queen in the Royal Box at Wembley in 1966 is interestingly read against this historical backdrop.[54] Moore was born in April 1941 towards the end of the Blitz, during a month when East London was heavily bombed. Twenty-five years later, like her parents before her, Queen Elizabeth, 'looked the East End in the eye', when she honoured the young captain of West Ham United, as the victorious captain of England's winning World Cup team at Wembley. Yet the Queen was not in attendance of the 1966 World Cup Final for the express purpose of presenting the trophy to the captain of England. Her role, as head of state, was to make the presentation to the team captain of the victorious country, and this might well have been Uwe Seeler of West Germany.[55] Indeed, it was quite feasible that England would not have been in the Final at all, yet the Queen would have taken her seat for the game and made the trophy presentation nonetheless.

What the Queen made of the experience of attending the 1966 World Cup Final and England's victory we are unlikely to ever know. Sir Stanley Rous, who sat to the left of Queen Elizabeth during the Final, has commented, 'the Queen enjoyed it enormously and was obviously thrilled during the final point of extra time. She kept saying, "How much longer to go?"'[56] However, Rous might have completely misinterpreted the Queen's comment. Perhaps she was finding the extended match tedious and merely wondering when it would be over. Although, her experience of watching FA Cup finals had already exposed the Queen to the protraction of football extra time, as her last match in attendance, the 1965 FA Cup Final between Liverpool and Leeds United, had gone beyond the customary ninety minutes when the regular time score remained 0–0. Rous, then, may have been right in his assumption that the Queen was caught up in the excitement of rooting for England in the unquestionably dramatic extended stage of the match. Perhaps Lord Harewood had briefed her prior to the match, letting her know that despite most of the predictions made in advance of the tournament, Ramsey's team, having now made it to the Final, had a good chance of winning the World Cup.[57] Whatever the case might be in regard to the Queen's private thoughts, her relationship to football, and the relationship to football of the British monarchy more generally, changed on the afternoon of 30 July 1966 when she handed the Jules Rimet trophy to Bobby Moore.

By the time Queen Elizabeth attended the 1966 World Cup Final she had presided as the trophy-awarding Monarch over seven FA Cup finals. Each of those

2 Queen Elizabeth presents the Jules Rimet trophy to Bobby Moore.

occasions may be said to have been, to a certain extent, an occasion of British and not just English football. The professionalisation of football that occurred towards the end of the nineteenth century resulted in English club teams look-ing beyond England for their playing personnel. Prominent in this regard was Preston North End, winners of the first Football League Championship in the 1888–89 season, their undefeated team becoming known as the 'Invincibles'. This team did the first 'double' by also winning the 1889 FA Cup with a team including a Welsh goalkeeper and six Scottish outfield players. The number of non-English players in any particular English professional club differed over the years from one to another, but each of the FA Cup finals watched at Wembley by Queen Elizabeth featured a number of non-English players, who were eligible to play for either Scotland, Wales or the Republic of Ireland (the German national Bert Trautmann played for Manchester City in the 1955 and 1956 FA Cup finals and South African Albert Johanneson for Leeds in the 1965 Final). On four of the seven occasions, Queen Elizabeth presented the FA Cup Final trophy to non-English captains of the winning team – Jimmy Scoular (Scotland and Newcastle United) in 1955, Roy Paul (Wales and Manchester City) in 1956, Noel Cantwell (Republic of Ireland and Manchester United) in 1963, and Ron Yeats (Scotland and Liverpool) in 1965. The 1965 FA Cup

Final, the last the Queen attended before the 1966 World Cup finals was split between eleven English and eleven non-English participating players.

When watching the 1963 FA Cup Final from the Royal Box at Wembley, Queen Elizabeth witnessed a well-known Scottish player score the opening goal for Manchester United in that club's victory over Leicester City. Three years later, Denis Law was still with Manchester United and thus was a teammate in club football with Bobby Charlton and Nobby Stiles when they were victorious World Cup players for England. However, unlike the Queen, Law did not see the England win over West Germany, not even on television. He reports in his autobiography that he deliberately spent the afternoon of 30 July 1966 playing golf to avoid watching the Final at all. Members of the Cheshire located golf club, aware of Law's snubbing of the game and hope for an England loss, relished their chance to tell him the result by raising four fingers on one hand (to signify England's four goals) and their pint glasses in the other.[58] As a Scotland international player, Law understandably had a keen sense of rivalry towards England. Law represented Scotland throughout Alf Ramsey's reign as England manager, and on four occasions ahead of the 1966 World Cup. He also played, and scored the only goal, for a stellar Rest of the World team defeated 2–1 by England at Wembley in 1963 in an anniversary match to mark the 100th year since the establishment of the Football Association. Despite this personal history, Law's declared opposition to an England World Cup victory might have surprised some at the time. With two of his Manchester United teammates playing for England in the Final, a truce might have seemed appropriate on the occasion. However, Law's view is by now well-known and often cited with the intention of it typifying the depth of Scottish resentment over the England win and the general dislike the Scots have for the English when it comes to matters of football. Obviously enough, the pudding is deliberately overegged for journalistic effect, as serious argument cannot assume that all supporters of the Scotland football team dislike England to such a strong extent, or that they suffered the England victory in 1966 as miserably as Denis Law is claimed to have done. However, the Law anecdote and the tendency for its overstretching provide a useful reminder against any lingering temptation for English people to claim England's World Cup victory uncomplicatedly as a British sporting success; i.e. as a corrective to the seemingly prevalent assumption in England in 1966 that the England team was effectively representing all of Britain and that Scots would naturally lend their support to the cause.

Of course, not all English people revelled in England's victory. Those not so interested in football may have shared the opinion of social critics such as Bernard Levin that the World Cup hoopla was a distraction from more serious matters. In his lengthy cultural history of the 1960s, titled *The Pendulum Years*, Levin gives best part of two pages to discussing the World Cup, aimed towards his conclusion that celebratory shouts of 'Eng-land' rang hollow at a time of pending economic crisis and a loss of meaningful national purpose and identity. Irrespective of the victory, Levin contended, 'nothing had changed ... nothing was better for England just because the World Cup had been won'.[59] But surely, this criticism does little more than state the obvious; the nation's economic difficulties were always going to be there on the day after the Final, just as they were on the day before it was played. As discussed in the next chapter, the governing Labour Party was certainly seen as attempting to bask in the reflected glow of the Cup victory, but cynicism towards an apparent populist political positioning need not carry over to a criticism of England's football victory in its own right, or of the World Cup as a cultural event. Yet it is in this latter regard that Levin takes keenest critical aim by challenging the cultural merit of the World Cup victory. According to Levin, at a time when art in Britain was becoming trivialised and, hence pushed to the margins of public cultural life, 'a keenly contested football match was not a very great achievement'.[60]

Levin's viewpoint betrays a familiar snobbery, whereby sport is denied the status of culture and is placed in hostile relation to the arts.[61] Such tension has continued over the years, especially when scarce public funding for the arts is feared to be imperilled by the diversion of such funds into sport. Some of the leading figures within arts organisations spoke out in this regard ahead of London's hosting of the 2012 Olympic Games.[62] However, this was not so much the concern in 1966. The relatively small amount of money allocated from the public purse towards the staging of the World Cup, mainly for the improvement of stadium facilities, did not represent any significant threat to the arts, or, for that matter, to other areas of government spending.[63] Levin's criticism is ultimately an assertion about football needing to be put in its proper place, that place being of inferior significance to the genuine matters of cultural life. This is not only an elitist, but a narrow view of culture, one even at odds with that of the conservative view of common culture held by the likes of T.S. Eliot, within which football was acknowledged to be important. What Eliot might have made of the 1966 World Cup is another matter – he died in 1965 – but, given his explicit reference to 'a cup final' within his attempt to define culture, he would no doubt have encouraged consideration of its relationship to the cup tradition in England.

A broader view, taking in football as part of the cultural scene, also allows for the World Cup to be discussed in comparison to preceding post-war cultural events such as the Festival of Britain in 1951. As part of a sporting programme, during May 1951, the Festival of Britain featured a series of football matches between British club teams (from First Division to Amateur clubs) and visiting clubs from Europe. During the same month, also in association with the Festival, England played matches against Argentina at Wembley, and Portugal at Goodison Park. But football and sport was a mere sideshow; the

Festival of Britain is best remembered for the dazzlingly new architecture and design it featured, especially in the key exhibition site on the South Bank of the Thames.[64] The festival, heralded by its Director-General, Gerald Barry, as 'a tonic to the nation', projected a stark contrast to the image of austerity associated with the London Olympics of 1948.[65] Some critics have suggested that the architecture and design presented a merely decorative layer of gloss over more conventional ideas that underpinned the Festival's purpose. Against such scepticism, Conekin maintains the festival was genuinely committed to modernism and an ethos of change.[66] Her related point, 'that the festival betrayed surprisingly little nostalgia', bears especially interesting comparison to the 1966 World Cup. Given the nature of the World Cup competition, and especially England's fairly recent involvement in its tournaments, nostalgia had little role to play in 1966. The World Cup, in this significant way, differed from the FA Cup competition. Furthermore, while Alf Ramsey remained respectful of tradition, his modern approach to managing the England team (discussed in detail in subsequent chapters) gave little acknowledgement to the nostalgic tendencies of English football. The architecture within which the 1966 World Cup was played did not, despite some rebuilding and refurbishment, offer a new style. Ramsey's match strategy did. Ramsey may have known little about what occurred on the South Bank in 1953, as, at that time, he concentrated on the last years of his playing career. However, his subsequent move into football management marked a late modern turn, innovative enough to prompt an awakening of the sport in Britain from its long romantic slumber.

As indicated, there was very little shiny or new about the stadiums around England in which the World Cup matches were played, and however significant the change to football playing culture brought by Ramsey may have been, the stadiums provided a most obvious material reminder that the World Cup was coming to the historical home of football. This homecoming in itself, as Tony Mason notes, provided a most apparent link to a sporting past.[67] An understated Britishness of the occasion was evident in the opening ceremony. Compared to the colourfully energetic opening ceremonies of the forerunning Olympic Games in Rome (1960) and Tokyo (1964), the opening ceremony for the 1966 World Cup was more reminiscent of that from the Olympic Games held in the most British of colonial cities, Melbourne (1956). Yet even in Melbourne, the athletes themselves marched for their countries as the Games were officially opened. At Wembley in 1966, schoolboys took the place of the players from the sixteen competing nations. Both Stanley Rous and the minister with responsibility for sport, Denis Howell, were wary of fanfare, partly owing to a concern of facing embarrassment in the case of overseas visitor numbers being low.[68]

This administrative cautiousness was not shared by the England team manager. Indeed, much of the confidence given to the event came from Alf Ramsey's prediction that England would win. What seemed like an idle and uncharacteristic boast took on significance beyond Ramsey's intention. If the host nation's team manager was prepared to talk up prospects of winning the cup, then this must be a country looking forward to holding the tournament and receiving visitors in support of competing teams. Ramsey's positivity provided buoyancy in spirit, necessary for a competition heralded as a 'festival of football'. Had he shared and conceded pessimism for England's chances, this would only have added to a general flatness of mood in England as the tournament commenced, and thus encouraged a listless rather than festive atmosphere. Yet, although Ramsey's prediction gathered credibility and growing acceptance as England moved towards the Final, it did not mean that the World Cup became all important to England or to the football person's way of life. As Mason notes, via the observation of Jimmy Greaves, relative to the likely present-day response, the reception of the cup victory in England was quite low key. According to Greaves, 'If we won it now, the country would come to a stop for a week'. Greaves goes on to comment that within a week the focus on football had switched to the new League season.[69]

Based on recent performances, England may not be expected to win the World Cup for some time to come. Thus, furthering forecasting on a present-day public response to a World Cup victory seems rather moot. And, given the failure of the FA-led bid for England to hold the World Cup finals of 2018, and the resultant souring of relations with FIFA, it seems unlikely that the tournament will be hosted by England in the foreseeable future. On that note, much publicity was given to Prince William's representation before FIFA as President of the Football Association, in the company of David Beckham (royalty once again 'looking the East End in the eye') and Prime Minister David Cameron. While we might say that his grandmother was somewhat circumstantially drawn into a symbolic association with the England team in 1966, the Duke of Cambridge's enlistment to England's national football cause was fully volitional and enthusiastic. And it would be naive to suggest that his support extended merely to putting forward the case for England hosting the World Cup. His active executive status with the FA is as obvious a commitment to being a supporter of the on-field fortunes of the England team as one could make.[70] Although her cousin was President of the Football Association at the time, Queen Elizabeth did not attend the opening ceremony of the 1966 World Cup or hand the Jules Rimet trophy to Bobby Moore as a supporter of the England team. But the photographic image of her presenting the trophy to Moore is one of the indelible visual memories of the World Cup and its significance to England's post-war cultural history. The same cannot be said for photographic images of the Queen presenting FA Cups. Although unrealised at the time, and although some subsequent FA Cup finals have been heralded as amongst the most important within the history of English football, the FA Cup does not retain the symbolic value today that it had in 1966. It does retain a place on the national sporting calendar, but not on the cultural calendar in the manner meant by T.S. Eliot. That certain day in May is not FA Cup day as it once was and life is no longer brought to a stop for ninety minutes in the way referred to by Bobby Charlton.

The decline in interest in the FA Cup is attributable to a number of factors – clubs' obsession with results in the Premier League and the chase for qualification to the European Champions League being at the forefront. Although the World Cup comes around every four years, when regarded in connection with the UEFA European Football Championship, it provides a constant round of competitive engagement for the England team. In terms of an overall calendar for elite football, the Premier League (and higher echelons of the Football League) exists in interrelationship with the international commitments of leading players to England's games. In the worst of interpretations, the FA Cup now exists as an irritant in coexistence with the other, more highly valued, competitions. Despite pessimistic forecasts, reverse psychological downplaying of chances and England's failure to qualify for a number of subsequent World Cup finals tournaments, winning the World Cup has remained prominent within the imagination of England's football supporting public since the summer of 1966. Although some issue is taken in a subsequent chapter with what has been called the 'myth of 1966', it is the case that the cup tradition, as known to English football, changed on the afternoon that Queen Elizabeth declared the captain of her country to be the captain of the world.

Notes

1 Charlton, *Forward for England*, pp. 100–1.
2 Pawson, *100 Years of the FA Cup*, p. 1.
3 Glanville, 'The FA Cup Final', p. 51; Morris, *The Soccer Tribe*, p. 214.
4 Holt, *Sport and the British*, pp. 159–73.
5 Walvin, *The People's Game*, p. 65.
6 Chinitz, *T.S. Eliot*, p. 228 (n. 58).
7 Eliot, *Notes Towards the Definition of Culture*, p. 31.
8 Hughson et al., *The Uses of Sport*, p. 20.
9 Williams, *The Long Revolution*, p. 336.
10 Hughson, 'Watching the Football with Raymond Williams'.
11 Williams, *Culture and Society*, p. 300.
12 Walvin, *The People's Game*, p. 6.
13 Hill, *Sport, Leisure and Culture in Twentieth-Century Britain*, p. 27.
14 Holt, *Sport and the British*, p. 165.
15 Walvin, *The People's Game*, p. 47.
16 Holt, *Sport and the British*, pp. 159–73.
17 *Ibid.*, p. 165.

18 Triesman, 'Introduction' to Vinnai, *Football Mania*, pp. 15–16.

19 Hampton, *The Austerity Olympics*, p. 296.

20 Leatherdale, *England's Quest for the World Cup*, p. xi.

21 Rous, *Football Worlds*, p. 92.

22 Leatherdale, *England's Quest for the World Cup*, pp. 4–12.

23 Shaoul and Williamson, *Forever England*, p. 61.

24 McKinstry, *Sir Alf*, p. 111.

25 Ramsey, *Talking Football*, p. 72.

26 *Ibid.*

27 Shaoul and Williamson, *Forever England*, p. 63.

28 Leatherdale, *England's Quest for the World Cup*, p. 26.

29 For example, see Wilson, *Inverting the Pyramid*, pp. 87–91; and Featherstone, *Englishness*, pp. 129–31.

30 McKinstry, *Sir Alf*, p. 126.

31 Leatherdale, *England's Quest for the World Cup*, p. 56.

32 *Ibid.*, pp. 72–3.

33 Jimmy Armfield, who played right back for England in the 1962 World Cup and was a member of the twenty-two man squad in 1966, goes as far as to claim that had England not been denied the Manchester United players lost in the Munich air crash then it would have won the World Cup in 1958. Armfield, *Right Back to the Beginning*, pp. 53–4.

34 Leatherdale, *England's Quest for the World Cup*, pp. 118–19.

35 Shaoul and Williamson, *Forever England*, p. 85.Winterbottom's reign as the manager of the England team, from 1946 to 1962 has been interestingly referred to by Roger Hutchinson ('… *It Is Now*') as 'the Age of Innocence'. The same author refers to the subsequent period, into which Alf Ramsey stepped as England manager, as the 'Modern Era'.

36 Mason, 'England 1966', pp. 83–4. Detailed research on the televising of and the televisual arrangements for the 1966 World Cup has been undertaken by Fabio Chisari. See Chisari, 'When Football Went Global' and Chisari, 'Shouting Housewives!'

37 Moran, *Armchair Nation*, p. 295.

38 Shiel, *Voices of '66*.

39 *Ibid.*, p. 139.

40 *Ibid.*, pp. 121 & 110. The final series from Mexico in 1970 was the first World Cup to be broadcast on television in colour. 'Autobiographical memories' provided in Shiel's *Voices of '66* are further discussed in chapter 8 of the present book.

41 Hughson, 'Watching the Football with Raymond Williams', pp. 283–4.

42 Haynes, 'The BBC and the 1948 Olympic Games'.

43 Brian Dean, 'BBC puts viewers on soccer diet', *Daily Mail*, 1 June 1966, p. 11; Barry Norman, 'You lucky people you', *Daily Mail*, 2 June 1966, p. 8.

44 Richard Last, 'How England converted women to the World Cup', *The Sun*, 28 July 1966, p. 12.

45 Pope, 'Female Fan Experiences'. Within a month of the 1966 World Cup concluding, a number of women's football teams were formed in the Southampton area. Personal testimonies indicate that female players were directly inspired by the

victory of the England men's team in the Final. See, Lopez, *Women on the Ball*, p. 37 and Ward and Williams, *Football Nation*, pp. 120–3. Thus, while the impact of the World Cup on female fandom is rather uncertain, a fairly immediate 'legacy' is noticeable in regard to female participation in football.

46 John Parsons 'Record TV audience will see Final', *Daily Mail*, 29 July 1966, p. 12.
47 Hewison, *Culture and Consensus*, p. 67.
48 Shils and Young, 'The Meaning of the Coronation'.
49 Conekin et al., 'Introduction', *Moments of Modernity*, p. 2.
50 Russell, *Football and the English*, p. 74.
51 Johnes and Mellor, 'The 1953 FA Cup Final', p. 264.
52 Powell, *Bobby Moore*, p. 107–8.
53 *Ibid.*, p. 26.
54 Cf. Weight, *Patriots*, p. 460.
55 At the Wembley-held final of the 1996 UEFA European Football Championship, Queen Elizabeth II presented the trophy to the winning captain of Germany, Jürgen Klinsmann. In this final series – the only other major international football tournament ever to be held in England – the host team was eliminated at the semi-final stage by Germany.
56 Rous, quoted in *World Cup Winners 1966*, p. 38.
57 In his autobiography Lord Harewood makes brief mention of his role with the FA, including his responsibilities in the lead up to the 1966 World Cup finals. He makes no mention of any discussion with Queen Elizabeth about the topic of football. See Laselles, *The Tongs and the Bones*, p. 300.
58 Law, *The King*, p. 172.
59 Levin, *The Pendulum Years*, p. 236.
60 *Ibid.*, p. 234.
61 Levin was not always so antagonistic to football. Having attended the 1966 FA Cup final at Wembley (Everton v Sheffield Wednesday) as a football watching novice (and admitting to having no prior interest in the sport), Levin expressed pleasant surprise at the spectacle he encountered and, subsequently, wrote in praise of football artistry: 'This is a skill of an order so high that admiration for it enables one almost to understand what the sports writers are talking about when they chatter of ballet, and poetry-in-motion'. See, Levin, 'At the Cup Final'.
62 A particularly vocal critic in this regard has been John Tusa, former Director of the Barbican Arts Centre in London. See for example his criticism of the Cultural Olympiad associated with London 2012, www.theguardian.com/artanddesign/2007/aug/05/art.artsfunding. Accessed 14 April 2015.
63 Although, as Mason ('England 1966' p. 86) notes, this did not stop the Treasury from quibbling over the suggestion of public money being allocated to World Cup infrastructure. See also the related discussion in the next chapter of the present book.
64 Conekin, '*The Autobiography of a Nation*', pp. 49–57.
65 Turner, *Beacon for Change*, p. 7.
66 Conekin, 'Here is the Modern World Itself', p. 228.
67 Mason, 'England 1966'.

68 *Ibid.*, pp. 87–9.

69 *Ibid.*, p. 95. Greaves in *Guardian Sport*, 25 August 2003, p. 19. Of related interest, a comment by Kenneth Wolstoneholme during his BBC television commentary on the Final suggests that thoughts of the new season were present even before the World Cup had concluded. Following a very wayward long-range shot at goal by the England right full back, after about 23 minutes of play, Wolstoneholme remarked, 'George Cohen should probably get some shooting practice in before he starts the English season, which begins in three weeks, by the way'. *The World Cup Final 1966: England V West Germany* (BBC Worldwide Ltd) was released on DVD in 2002.

70 www.englandfootballonline.com/Seas1990–00/1997–98/M0749Col1998.html. Accessed 3 June 2015.

3

When football first came home: the World Cup in England

England, in 1966, had its own way of embracing and emphasising the universality of the World Cup. (Hugh McIlvanney)

Between 1959 and 1969 the Rank Organisation produced a regular series of short documentary films that were shown as curtain raisers before the screening of feature films at their Odeon and Gaumont cinemas. One such film, from 1966, was *Behind the World Cup*. This promotional film of sorts, which runs for a total of nine minutes, commences with footage of Italy's 3–0 defeat of Scotland at Naples' Stadio San Paolo in a World Cup qualifying match in December 1965, before switching to a dusty building site in front of a railway viaduct somewhere in England. The opening commentary, narrated by actor Tim Turner, which accompanies these contrasting scenes, is as follows:

Here in Naples, as in other cities all over the globe, top international soccer teams fought like gladiators to qualify for the greatest event in world football, the World Cup of 1966. In this year and for the first time in the Cup's short hectic history, the final rounds came to be played in Britain in the islands where the game, as we now know it, was born more than a century ago. Soccer rages from stadium to backyard and must surely be Britain's most successful export. It's played in more than 120 countries throughout the world.

Further into the documentary, the commentary reiterates:

In little more than a hundred years football has erupted like Vesuvius, a long way from the placid village greens of England it's now the national game of countries around the Mediterranean and in Latin America, it's crossed the frontiers of Europe to Russia and beyond, more than any other it's the global game played barefooted on tropical Pacific islands and fur clad near the poles. More than seventy countries competed for places to get into the last sixteen for the World Cup. To the fervent, frenzied supporters the matches had everything, football, patriotism, excitement and the march of the gladiators. These, indeed, were the Roman games of the modern world, played maybe from Ecuador to Glasgow and, as the preliminary games went on, so the excitement rose along with the thermometer of national fervour.

The commentary seems quite deliberately aimed at drawing a distinction between the World Cup and the Olympic Games, by explicitly associating the former with the legendary gladiatorial Roman games. This association is used to positively sanction a description of the World Cup arousing frenzied support of a patriotic kind. At the time the documentary was made, this would have presented quite a different media representation to that popularly known for the Olympic Games, in which rivalry along national grounds was discouraged more than it is today.[1] The keenness of national rivalry attributed to the World Cup in this commentary is seemingly justified by the claim of football being taken on as the 'national game' in so many countries, including most of those involved in the qualifying rounds for the 1966 finals. Reference to football as *the* 'global game', a rather early use of this now ubiquitous term, further implies a statement of claim for the World Cup being, at least, of equal importance to the Olympic Games in the 'modern world'.

A similar understanding was offered by J.L. Manning of the *Daily Mail*, who saw the 'fanatical interest it arouses … around the world', as setting the World Cup apart from the Olympic Games.

> The Olympic Games are softened by their almost religious pageantry and made exquisite by the supreme endeavour of the individual. They are all flags and gallantry and honour has to be satisfied with a medal and honest rewards. The World Cup unashamedly cares nothing for ritual and idealism. It strips sport of all pretence to present an out-and-out professional show of games-playing skill.[2]

The simple, not entirely accurate distinction, between the Olympic Games involving contest between individuals, and the World Cup a contest between teams, is taken by Manning as reason for the passion aroused by the latter. Further into the article he suggests that the one-sport nature of the World Cup makes for a particularly 'intense competition'. The other key distinction, to which he refers, one less relevant today in the case of some athletes, is between the amateurism of Olympians and the professionalism of World Cup football players. According to Manning, these statuses make for rather different motivations – Olympians satisfied with medals as a marker of their honour and commitment to the amateur ethos, footballers more ends driven and less idealistic about the conduct of their competitive process. This is to suggest that the cut-and-thrust, even cutthroat, mentality of professional football leagues is brought by players and managers into the World Cup competition. This is undeniable to an extent, but should not be allowed to obscure the fact that the World Cup is competed in as a matter of honour by most players, for a pittance in comparison to what they earn from playing club football. This was the case for England players in 1966, as it is for players today. However, while today's World Cup finals offer a player contractual rewards and a stage for showcasing themselves for higher market value in the top European leagues, the World Cup in 1966 offered no such opportunity.[3] Despite the talk of a modern Roman games, there was little clarity in any quarter about what to expect from the forthcoming event. This chapter focuses on the uncertainty and confusion surrounding the preliminary period and how respective parties – principally politicians, hosting locations, football clubs and, indeed, the Football Association – muddled their way through to deliver what can arguably be claimed as a rather successful World Cup occasion.

The ceremonial aspects of both the Olympic Games and the World Cup were, undoubtedly, much simpler half a century ago than they have more recently become. But it is a question of scale, as both events have engaged more elaborate sideshows over the years, marching bands giving way to pop stars, dancers and, especially in the case of the Olympic Games, themed theatrics ostentatious enough to embarrass Broadway at its boldest. The Olympics were, and remain, more ceremonial than the World Cup, if for no other reason than the host of medals awarded to winners and place getters throughout the occasion. But, as suggested by Manning, the historical connection to Greek antecedents is what primarily distinguishes the Olympic Games, which are, after all, an attempt by their 'founder', Baron de Coubertin, to replicate that ancient tradition within modern times.[4] As a product of modernity the World Cup bears no such burden or legacy. Whereas athletes come to the Olympic Games as representatives of modern nations, football teams play in the World Cup under the very name of those nations, and it is from this designation, in direct association with nationhood, that the World Cup acquires its combative air, rather than through an exaggerated link back to the Roman gladiatorial contest. Whether or not the World Cup is regarded as unacceptably nationalistic, as flagged by George Orwell in his essay 'The Sporting Spirit', or, more acceptably, as patriotic, in keeping with that same writer's distinction between patriotism and nationalism, is a still relevant matter for debate over the moral social suitability of international football competition.[5]

One way in which the World Cup compares favourably to the Olympic Games, according to J.L. Manning, is in regard to the relative simplicity of its organisational arrangements. The title of his article, 'Where has all the fussing gone?', is a reference to the complications that beset planning ahead of the Melbourne Olympic Games in 1956. Indeed, political bickering had halted progress with arrangements and the delivery on necessary infrastructure to the extent that the International Olympic Committee President, Avery Brundage, threatened to disqualify Melbourne as host city.[6] A lesser reliance on the public purse spared the World Cup in England the kind of 'fussing' to which Manning refers, but this cannot be taken to mean that organising the tournament came without hassle. Indeed, organising an event of this size, across a number of hosting cities, presented a different set of logistical problems; problems that reflected the core difference between the World Cup and the Olympic Games. The ancient Greek games were occasions which drew together athletes from city-states. In a parallel arrangement, the modern Olympic Games are hosted by large cities in different international locations, held firstly, and appropriately, in Athens in 1896. The World Cup was conceived within the context of FIFA's expansionist ambitions rather than from any sense of commitment to philosophy and history and, from this circumstance, the modern nation state became the organisational and hosting point for the finals of each tournament.

England's slow welcoming of the World Cup stemmed from troubled relations between the Football Association and FIFA, which dated to the years of the latter organisation's emergence in the early twentieth century. Fluctuating animosity came to a particular head in 1927 when FIFA, in the eyes of FA officials, was seen to work in cahoots with the International Olympic Committee (IOC) in regard to striking an agreement, mutually acceptable and beneficial to both organisations, about the 'amateur' status of part-time professional football players, regarding their participation in the forthcoming Olympic Games in Amsterdam.[7] The FA led an initiative, at a meeting in Sheffield in 1928, to withdraw British football associations from FIFA; re-entry to the federating body did not occur until 1946. This stance meant that England, as discussed in the previous chapter, effectively snubbed the first three World Cup tournaments (1930, 1934 and 1938) and did not compete until an inglorious involvement in and departure from the tournament in Brazil in 1950. The withdrawal from FIFA, based on the claim that British associations 'should be free to conduct their affairs in the way that their long experience has shown to be desirable'[8] gave a nod to the importance of tradition that the FA believed FIFA to be unconcerned about and prepared to violate. This positioning matched to an illusory image of English football being pre-modern and at odds with the contingencies of professionalism which FIFA was attempting to negotiate.

The image is attached to perceptions about the shaping of association football occurring within English public schools. Public schools were of undoubted historical significance to football, but when codification of playing rules occurred at a meeting in London in October 1863, criticism was actually made of the non-public school pedigree of some of the (nevertheless well educated) participants, including the Hull-born solicitor and first secretary of the FA, Ebenezer Cobb Morley.[9] Some five months before Morley and colleagues met at the Freemason's Tavern in Great Queen Street, London, for the stated purpose of regulating 'the game of football', a seemingly unrelated event transpired in Paris when, on 15 May, the painting *Déjeuner sur l'herbe* by Édouard Manet was exhibited at the Salon des Refusés, following its rejection by the official Salon. The painting caused controversy, not only because of its subject matter – a naked woman in the company of two dressed men – but also because of its unconventional style in Manet's denial of depth in favour of a confrontational presentation of his characters at the forefront of the image, the naked woman looking directly into the eye of the viewer, seemingly unconcerned by any moral condemnation that might be cast towards her. *Déjeuner sur l'herbe* is widely regarded as the first modern painting within the history of art, an identification based largely on Manet's rule breaking.[10] It would seemingly stand in contrast to the codifying of association football, an activity of rulemaking, yet that very act of regulation was a necessary intervention towards the development of football as a distinctly modern cultural practice.[11]

Perhaps unforeseen by Morley and colleagues, rule codification abetted the growth of professionalism and it soon became a key marker of the modernity of English football. As observed in the previous chapter, when Preston North End won the first full season of the English Football League in 1888/89, and achieved the 'double' by also winning the FA Cup of 1889, the team comprised a number of professional imports from Scotland.[12] So from the early period of organised competition, the amateur ethos was becoming largely irrelevant to both those who played and watched the game. The former wanted to escape the drudgery of the factory and coalmine by being paid to play football, while the latter wanted their clubs to be successful in the League and, on this basis, welcomed the addition of professional players who strengthened the on-field calibre of the local team. While London had provided a central gathering point for Cobb and his associates for their meeting to set the rules for football in 1863, the meeting in April 1888 that resulted in the formation of the Football League was held in the Royal Hotel, Manchester. Led by William McGregor of Aston Villa, the participants settled upon a competition comprised of not one southern located club, but six from the North and six from the English Midlands.[13] It was with the formation of the English Football League that McGregor and colleagues set the modern game of football in train, and it was to the history of this modern game, not the game of the placid village greens of England, that football came home in 1966.[14]

The hosting locations for the World Cup finals tournament were determined in the first half of 1963. The geographical spread deemed appropriate by the FA was two locations in the North West, two in the North East, two in the Midlands and two in London. The suitability and availability of grounds for World Cup matches became the overriding criteria: only grounds with a 50,000 spectator capacity were deemed adequate for the occasion.[15] Two grounds initially accepted as locations were withdrawn: St James's Park, Newcastle because of wrangling with local authorities and Arsenal's Highbury Stadium because it did not meet the pitch measurements required by FIFA rules (115 yards long and 75 yards wide).[16] White City Stadium in London became the replacement for Highbury and the problems in Newcastle brought Middlesbrough on to the agenda, with Ayresome Park replacing St James's Park as an approved venue.[17]

Other venues were Roker Park, Sunderland; Old Trafford, Manchester; Goodison Park, Liverpool; Hillsborough, Sheffield; Villa Park, Birmingham; and Wembley Stadium. The home ground of Yorkshire club Sheffield Wednesday, Hillsborough, was rather shoehorned into the arrangement to fit the bill as the second Midlands location. More limited capacity reserve venues were also named – uncalled upon as it turned out – as Ashton Gate, home ground of Bristol City and the Victoria Ground, Stoke.

The World Cup coming to England provided some placation to long-held begrudging, outside of London, to Wembley's almost monopoly on international football matches. The news was heralded by Horace Yates of the *Liverpool Daily Post* as 'atonement with a vengeance'.[18] Yates reported that Goodison Park well deserved the five games, including a quarter and semi-final, which it had been awarded, thus making it the number two venue for the World Cup occasion. Goodison shared, with the other non-London based 1966 World Cup venues, a connection in architectural history: each of them featured the work of Britain's most renowned football stadium architect, Archibald Leitch. Originally a designer of factories, Leitch turned to a new career specialism with the commission in 1899 to build Ibrox Park, home ground for Glasgow Rangers.[19] The previous haphazardness in the design aesthetics of football stadiums was replaced by a sense of pattern as Leitch became responsible for stands built at more than twenty stadiums around the country. Leitch's background as a mechanical engineer was reflected in his football architecture, which favoured two-tiers – the top tier with criss-crossing balustrades – full-side of the pitch length grandstands, with seats behind standing enclosures in the forefront.[20] Modernist in their functionalism, Leitch's stands, over time, garnered appreciation, especially for their one classical feature, a distinctive pediment bearing the home club's name. Only wealthier clubs could afford grandstands of Leitch's design, and the home grounds chosen as venues for 1966 World Cup matches reflected the economic history of the Football League in this regard. Along with Goodison Park, the home ground of one other foundation club in the Football League, Villa Park, was among the chosen venues. At Aston Villa, Leitch worked in conjunction with the club's ambitious chairman Fred Rinder. Together, in 1914, they laid out a blueprint for Villa Park's long-term development. While Leitch's structural design plan was followed, the decorative features of buildings at Villa Park, instigated by Rinder, were much more elaborate than the functionalism of Leitch would have conceived.[21] The truer mark of Leitch was said to be most evident at Goodison Park, where a two-tiered stand in 1907 was followed by something grander two years later.[22]

The new Main Stand opened in 1909 to accolades in the *Athletic News*: 'Visitors to Goodison Park will be astonished at the immensity of the new double-decker stand.'[23] And Leitch's work at Goodison continued, with further stands built in 1926 and 1938, the last of which, the Gladwys Street end stand,

came towards the conclusion of Leitch's career, by which time his son was possibly running his practice. Upon this completion, Goodison became the first
ground in Britain to have double-decker stands on all four of its sides.[24] Apart
from repairs caused by bomb damage during the War, the stadium looked
much the same in 1966 as it had done since Leitch's final intervention and,
even nearly thirty years on, must still have been quite a spectacle to those
visitors in attendance of the five matches played at Goodison Park during the
World Cup finals. Parochialism notwithstanding, Yates's lauding the merits
of Goodison as a football ground 'without superior' and another reference to
it as the 'Wembley of the North' had some justification.[25] However, despite
such claim, based on architectural merit, Goodison Park might well have been
passed over, had the FA stuck to the same criteria used to rule out Highbury
Stadium as a World Cup venue. Upon initial inspection – as early as September
1962 – the pitch at Goodison was found to be lacking by thirteen feet in length
and six feet in width, in regard to FIFA requirements.

Necessary alterations were made specifically for the World Cup matches at
Goodison, with a reversion to the former pitch size once the tournament had
concluded.[26] A more permanent intervention, with the World Cup in mind,
involved reconstruction on the Stanley Park End for the accommodation of
'foreign supporters', with an improvement to facilities including seating, lava-
tories and bars.[27] A cark park, built behind the stand, required the demolition
of terraced housing and the relocation of residents at the expense of Everton
Football Club. The row of terraces had to be purchased from Liverpool City
Council by Everton F.C. to enable the demolition to go ahead.[28] In a brief chapter on Goodison Park in his acclaimed book from the time, *Soccer Syndrome*,
John Moynihan addresses the housing issue by way of a door-step interview
conducted with one of the affected residents:

> He said he and his wife had been found alternative accommodation by Everton,
> near a cemetery a mile or so away. 'The club has been very nice about it …
> They've found us a handy little place with sanitation.'

The man's wife intervened in the conversation to inform Moynihan that her
husband had lived in the street for fifty-six years, during which time he had
been a neighbour to a number of Everton greats, including Dixie Dean. The
woman confirmed her husband's gratitude to Everton for providing them with
a 'nice house' as an alternative residence to the one they must leave.[29] But while
the woman had no complaint about the football club, the same did not apply to
football fans. She contended:

> The crowds aren't the same any more. They have no respect. They come by here
> and they would break the place up if they could. I'm not sorry to leave. You ought
> to smell the place on Saturday. They don't bother to use the toilets.[30]

The offenders in question might have been visitors to Goodison Park, but this type of remark from a local would only serve to increase the jaundice of those prepared to single out football fans from Liverpool for particular condemnation. In *The Other England* (a book in Penguin's *Britain in the Sixties* series) Geoffrey Moorhouse declared that football fans from Liverpool (either those of Everton or Liverpool F.C.) 'have acquired a reputation for atrocious behaviour' at both home and away matches'.[31] In a manner of casual ethnography, he draws upon his own experience as a supporter of Bolton Wanderers to speak of his mixture of 'trepidation and disapproval' in expectation of a visit from the fans of the two major Liverpool football clubs. An allusion by Moorhouse to J.B. Priestley seems appropriate given the former's connotation of Liverpool residents as constituting an uncivilised breed, a view expressed candidly by Priestley in one of the more obnoxious passages from his *English Journey*.[32] Moorhouse concluded, if England were to experience 'football crowd rioting' on a scale seen in one of the sport's more 'intemperate spots' – South America and Italy are named – the 'chances are it will be at Anfield or Goodison Park'. Given the expression of this view in 1964, it is unlikely Moorhouse would have welcomed the announcement of the latter as one of the 1966 World Cup venues.

However, such prejudice did not come to bear on the decision-making process. Indeed, Liverpool's 'fanatical football population' was hailed by Horace Yates

3 A World Cup street party celebration in Liverpool.

as a deserving quality to justify Goodison Park's selection as a World Cup staging arena.[33] The fans of both Everton and Liverpool had plenty to cheer about in the years preceding the World Cup. Liverpool won the FA Cup in 1965 and the First Division title in 1963/4. Everton were First Division champions in 1962/63. In the World Cup year, Liverpool won the First Division championship and Everton the FA Cup. As such, the latter club played in the last domestic competition game at Wembley ahead of the World Cup, the FA Cup Final against Sheffield Wednesday on 14 May 1966. Everton also played in the first domestic game subsequent to the World Cup tournament, in a 1–0 loss to Liverpool in the Charity Shield, played at Goodison Park on 13 August 1966. Spectators saw two England players from the World Cup Final winning team play in this match, Ray Wilson for Everton and, goal scorer on the afternoon, Roger Hunt for Liverpool. That they did not get to see these players at Goodison Park during the World Cup was a point of some contention.

Expectation had built that should England reach the semi-final stage, then their game would be played at Goodison Park. The eventual decision taken by FIFA to instead play the England/Portugal semi-final at Wembley was reported in the press as causing outrage on Merseyside. Horace Yates claimed that cries of betrayal were justified due to the failure of football officialdom to let the belief regarding Goodison hosting an England semi-final 'flourish unchecked'.[34] A subsequent, less sympathetic, interpretation was provided by Jack Rollin of the *Sunday Telegraph* who dismissed any objection to a presumed switch of the semi-final matches as a 'red herring', because it had never been laid down before the tournament that a decision on the semi-finalist venues would be taken before they were known.[35] The FA appears responsible for some of the confusion. Its monthly news bulletin was cited in an article in *The Liverpool Daily Post* as giving clear indication that the winners of quarter-finals 1 and 3 would play in the first semi-final at Everton on 25 July.[36] The winners of those respective quarter-finals were England and Portugal. However, contrary to this specification, the official World Cup handbook clearly stated that the particular semi-final allocations would not be made until the teams were known.[37] The Secretary-General of FIFA, Dr Helmut Käser, subsequently announced that the decision to play the England/Portugal game at Wembley was based on it being deemed the better crowd attractor of the two semi-finals.[38]

On bare numbers, Dr Käser's opinion was borne out. The official attendance figures were 94,493 and 43,921 for the England/Portugal and Soviet Union/West Germany semi-finals respectively. The crowd number at Goodison Park was reported in the press as a 'brush-off' from fans disgruntled by the allocation decision.[39] Tickets, pre-purchased well in advance, were said to have been thrown away by many people, prompting the claim that the attendance number 'was easily the lowest' recorded at Goodison Park.[40] The official attendance figure for the previous match at the ground, the quarter-final between Portugal and Korea, was 51,780. The highest attendance recorded at Goodison Park, 62,204, was for its final Group 3 game between Portugal and Brazil. The other figures were Brazil/Bulgaria 52,847 and Brazil/Hungary 54,475. The 3–1 victory over Brazil secured top place in the Group for Portugal and a matchup against a supposedly easy opponent in the quarter-final, which might also have had a bearing on the attendance figure for that game. Had fans been aware of the pluck and skill North Korea's under-rated team would bring to Goodison Park, they might well have turned up in greater number to watch them. The relatively high crowd attendance through the Group stage appears, though, to be explainable by Brazil's informal status as the home team, being the only team in the Group to play each of its three matches at Goodison Park.

Brazil's first match, a 2–0 victory over Bulgaria, was heralded 'King Pele Enters in Glory', and seen as a warm-up to the tougher games that would follow. The exotic appeal to the press of Pele's 'banana shot' free-kick was matched by the reportedly carnivalesque performance of Brazilian spectators. The beat of a 'big samba drum high up in the stands at Goodison Park' was accompanied by the chant 'Brazil, cha-cha-cha' from 'fever gripped Latin hordes', as they 'swayed, stomped and clapped their hands'.[41] By comparison the previous day's opening game between England and Uruguay was reported as having 'far less fervour despite the pomp', although the blame for this was put down to the negative and highly defensive play of the Uruguay team, which 'didn't give the London crowd much to crow about'. Brazil defeats in the next two Group games at Goodison Park to Hungary and Portugal meant an unexpected early exit from the tournament and, although much criticism was made of the failure of referees to protect Pele against foul play, particularly in the match against Portugal, the reigning champions from the past two World Cups were adjudged to have performed disappointingly as a team.[42] Had Brazil's fortunes gone differently and had they, rather than Portugal, ended up matched against England in the semi-finals, then the cry for the game to be played at Goodison Park might have been all the louder.

Protest against the semi-final allocations was evident in makeshift banners on display at Goodison Park during the Soviet Union/West Germany match. The target of criticism remained vaguely set between FIFA and the FA in banners worded 'Down with FIFA', 'England fix insults Liverpool' and 'England snubs Liverpool'.[43] An attempt to mollify the upset locally by Mr Sid Rudd of the World Cup Liaison Committee in Liverpool, reiterating FIFA's position on the semi-final scheduling, appears to have been ineffectual. He was not helped by the dignified but, nevertheless, parochial stance taken by the Everton club Chairman Edward Holland Hughes. Although accepting that the staging of a semi-final at Goodison Park involving England was not formally set, Holland Hughes stated that his club had 'been led to believe ... that if England got that far this privilege was to be ours'.[44] He also believed that despite Wembley's much larger attendance capacity, Goodison Park 'would have done full justice to the occasion'.[45] Of particular interest was his explicit evocation of the North/South divide in making the case for Goodison's overlooked deservingness:

> What is more disconcerting is that the football-loving public of the North of England have been ignored and deprived of seeing the England side in a single World Cup match, notwithstanding the North's significant contribution to the composition of the English team ... In Lancashire and Liverpool in particular, we have a football-loving public which would have rised [sic] to the opportunity in a manner which London certainly will not be able to excel.

The point about team composition is used to good effect. Only four of the eleven England players in the post-Group stage team played for London-based clubs; six played for Northern clubs, and one for a Midlands club. Eight of the players were born in the North; Lancashire-born Geoff Hurst moved to Essex at six years of age. While player backgrounds were not likely to have a bearing on official deliberations about semi-final locations, the example does flag a criticism of neglect for geo-historical particularities in the decision-making process. Holland Hughes rather stretches the case in claiming the 'football-loving public' of the North would have outdone Londoners in their manner of support for a semi-final. But the related implication about the cultural distinctiveness of football in the North suggests, reasonably enough, that a semi-final at Goodison Park would have provided a certain atmosphere in keeping with regional tradition. Considered beyond the context of local disgruntlement, Holland Hughes's lamentation on the England team not playing at least one of its World Cup matches in 1966 in the North has a continuing critical resonance.

While the Chairman of Everton may have felt every confidence in making a case for a semi-final to be held at Goodison Park, we can be confident in turn that disputing the rightfulness of Wembley Stadium as the venue for the World Cup Final would not have entered into his mind. Although his reference to the 'pomp' of the opening game suggested a slight tongue in cheek, it would not have been planted firmly enough to constitute serious mockery. Few in football officialdom would have challenged the ceremonial significance of the Queen's attendance at the opening and closing occasions of the tournament. And that her presence for these occasions would be at the noblest of stadiums in the national capital would have been generally taken for granted. Harry Gee refers to England winning the World Cup, 'with the Queen watching', in such an assumed way that we might picture Wembley as one of her palaces.[46] But Wembley made its own claim as the site for the tournament's denouement apart from the regality of its formal name, Empire Stadium. Indeed, Wembley grabbed its place within the history of football from its inception, with the staging of the famous 1923 FA Cup Final and the overwhelming enthusiasm of Northerners to make the trip to London to see Bolton Wanderers take on and defeat West Ham United. The stadium's capacity of 127,000 was proven woefully inadequate as a crowd of around 200,000 caused such an overflow as to spill on to the ends and sides of the playing area and partly on to the pitch to delay kick off for approximately forty-five minutes. Quelling of the crowd has been thanked to the legend of a white police horse and its mount, although a number of other horses, less conspicuous in photographs because of their darker coats, are believed to have played their part. According to Gee, King George V played a significant role too, his arrival at Wembley contributing to the 'steadying of the crowd and to their eventual control'.[47] If this is true, then it makes for a unique case in British modern history of a monarch having such a direct and immediate impact on his subjects.

Apart from hosting games between England and Scotland, Wembley did not really emerge as a venue for international football until the 1950s, once the frostiness of the FA's relationship with FIFA had partly thawed. So Wembley's claim to pre-eminence going into the 1966 World Cup was based on the strength of its historical reputation as a domestic rather than international arena, at least in regard to football (serving as the main arena for the 1948 Olympic Games was Wembley's main international achievement prior to the World Cup). And by 1966 London clubs had established enough success within the domestic history of professional club football to legitimate the selection of the capital city as a base for the national team. Particularly significant within this history was Arsenal Football Club, dominant as it was in the 1930s, winning the First Division title five times and the FA Cup twice. This period of great success led to architectural developments – best known are the Art Deco-styled stands designed by Charles Waterlow Ferrier – that gave Arsenal Stadium a distinctly post-Leitch look and stood it well for consideration as a World Cup venue in 1966.[48] However, the club's reluctance to meet the costs needed to make temporary ground alterations to satisfy FIFA requirements on pitch size was noted as a problem in FA meetings in 1963 and led to the scratching of Arsenal Stadium from the venue list and its replacement by the arena built for the 1908 Olympic Games, White City Stadium.[49] Thus, when the World Cup came to England, irrespective of Wembley's own football history pedigree, the North/South divide was marked by matches being played at two former Olympic Stadiums in London and at the dedicated home grounds of Football League clubs elsewhere in the country.

Only one World Cup match, Uruguay versus France on 15 July 1966, was played at White City Stadium, and only then because Wembley could not be used on the designated date, as it clashed with the regular Friday evening

4　Wembley Stadium on World Cup Final day.

dog-racing event. Apart from that one game, White City's role in connection with the tournament was given over to administrative affairs rather than football. As the demands of planning for the World Cup became too overwhelming for the FA staff at its Lancaster Gate office, a headquarters for what became named as the Football Association World Cup Organisation (WCO) was established in a purpose-built block to one of the external sides of the White City stadium.[50] As well as dealing with the undoubted complexities of ticketing arrangements, another of the WCO's tricky assignments was overseeing the concern that the World Cup provided a favourable experience for overseas visitors.[51] Holding the World Cup in England necessarily meant dealing with such matters, but when it came to facilitating practicalities, for example interpreter services in the locations where visitors would be gathered, the FA exhibited the uneasiness of a reluctant dinner host.[52] There appeared an internal tension in the FA's attitude, between reticence to deal with matters beyond football and the necessity to entrust responsibility to local organising bodies. The FA's Chairman, Joe Mears, objected to the idea of having an opening ceremony at each venue – this should remain Wembley's privilege only – but deemed that a civic dignitary of local choice be called upon to open the first match at the respective stadia.[53] Gauging from the example of Everton, the hosting clubs were cautious about how much responsibility they should take on in regard to World Cup organisation. Chairman John Moores wrote to the Liverpool County FA in April 1964 to declare that while his club was 'quite prepared to give any assistance … in connection with outside matters' it will 'have quite sufficient to deal with in staging the matches'. He thus saw the 'local liaison committees' as very much the responsibility of the FA and its county bodies.[54]

During the World Cup, the Liverpool local liaison committee established an Overseas Visitors' Lounge at Reeces Ballroom in the city centre. Mr George Elliot of the committee hailed the Lounge as a resounding success:

> Everyone has complimented us on the arrangements we made for them. They have been able to come here for a drink at any time of the day, with the television to watch, and their own national newspapers to read. We have fixed them up with accommodation, with sightseeing trips, special transport to the matches, and done all we can to make them feel at home. I am sure many of them will be back to see more of England in general and Liverpool in particular.[55]

Mr Elliot's opinion was generally shared, but a remark by the assistant manager of a Liverpool hotel – 'I think our guests were agreeably surprised at the tremendous welcome they received'[56] – gives an indication of local nervousness over whether or not overseas visitors would enjoy their time in Liverpool.

It was reported that £220,000 was 'poured into Goodison Park for the Group 3 games', but visitor expenditure beyond the stadium went unmeasured. Anecdotal evidence was mostly positive. High-street retailers believed their sales to have benefited from 'interest shown in British clothes, pop records and fancy goods'.[57] However, optimism about a good impression serving as an omen for the return of visitors in the future was not shared by all. One Liverpool-based hotelier spoke of expecting to receive 'coffee millionaires from Brazil' as guests, but, instead, patronage came from 'fans of modest means who had been paying for their tickets over the last two years'.[58] The hotelier suggested these visitors came specifically to attend Brazil's matches, spend as little as possible, and then depart. Hard-nosed as it might have sounded, his opinion raised critical reflection upon presumptions about the commercial benefits of the World Cup beyond the football-based economy.

Hotels inevitably experienced a spike in guest numbers during the Group stage. For example, the Piccadilly Hotel in Manchester reported that for the first two weeks of July 1966 its guest numbers were 40 per cent constituted by World Cup attendees. However, disappointment in the discretionary spending of tourists was noted, particularly in feedback from the North East, where it was reported that 'host city corporations' expended approximately £10,000 on overseas visitor centres, decorations and glossy brochures for a rather dubious return, as visitors did not 'hang about'.[59] But the bleak assessment from the North East, about the World Cup being 'over-sold in the provinces', was not verified elsewhere. News from Birmingham was closer to that from Liverpool; the overseas visitors' club in the Midlands' city was reportedly 'packed each night, usually with Germans and Spaniards'. Rackhams department store in Birmingham estimated that the daily sale of postcards increased from an average of twenty-five units to eight hundred units on World Cup match days.[60] The allocation of Groups was the main bearing on these respective tourist fortunes. For example, Aston Villa hosted West Germany, Spain and Argentina twice each for matches, and Birmingham appears to have benefited from the spending of visitors from the first two of these countries in particular. Meanwhile, Middlesbrough hosted North Korea for all three of its Group stage matches and, therefore, its rivals from the Soviet Union, Chile and Italy only once each. As North Korea was not followed by supporters in the manner of other teams, the tourism benefits of the World Cup were always likely to be slim on Teesside.

Yet Middlesbrough was hailed a success as a hosting location for a different reason, namely the way in which local fans warmly supported the team from North Korea during their games at Ayresome Park. Playing in shirts of a similar colour to Middlesbrough F.C. might have helped, as might North Korea's underdog status within the tournament.[61] The diminutive size of the players was also part of their appeal, but in this aspect the undoubted sincerity of local collective affection was matched with patronising exoticism. At the time, this was regarded as playful hospitality. Even one of English football's finest chroniclers, Arthur Hopcraft, could recall as his 'lasting memory' of North Korea's win over Italy, the sight of 'a tall British sailor lugging two Koreans off the pitch, one under each arm, like prizes'.[62] Read today, the condescending ethnocentrism in this passage by Hopcraft unfortunately all but undermines his subsequent observation of the relationship between the North Korea players and their hosts being emblematic of football's genuine cross-cultural bond. Unfortunate especially because the Teesside hosts did much to make up for the lack of welcome afforded to the North Korea entourage by the British Government, ahead of their trip to England to participate in the World Cup finals.

North Korea's qualification came as something of a surprise, eventuating from a play-off against Australia after a majority of countries in the Africa, Asia and Oceania FIFA regional configuration boycotted the playoffs because only one place at the finals was afforded to their entire number. The team's pending arrival in Britain gripped the Government with diplomatic discomfiture, primarily caused by a fear that allowing the team entry into the country might be read within the context of Cold War politics as proxy recognition of a communist regime. However, refusing the North Korean players entry visas was discounted, after being given fleeting consideration, as the resultant disruption to the World Cup tournament risked causing too much upset domestically. The popularity of football thus impinged upon political decision-making in a quite unexpected circumstance. But the politics of the moment did, in turn, impact upon the World Cup as FIFA and the FA agreed, without complaint, to the Government's request to literally lower the tone of national identity by restricting the playing of national anthems to the opening ceremony and the Final.[63] This meant the anthems of England and their opponents, Uruguay, would be played before the opening match and the anthems of the competing teams, as well as 'God Save the Queen', in respect of Her Majesty's presence, would be played ahead of the Final. Given the unlikelihood of North Korea reaching the World Cup Final, the Minister of Sport, Denis Howell, was able to satisfy the concerns of the Foreign Office and their NATO colleagues with this resolution. However, Howell confesses his anxiety upon hearing that North Korea was leading Portugal 3–0 in their quarter-final match. He nervously envisaged 'the dreaded national anthem' being played after all, despite his efforts to avoid such an outcome. His relief in hearing of Portugal's comeback and victory prompted an only half-joking exaggeration, 'disaster had been averted!'[64]

The official World Cup report notes politely that the first approach by the FA to Her Majesty's Government, in 1963, for financial assistance to improve facilities ahead of the tournament, 'met with no success'.[65] The subtext was that the Macmillan Conservative Government had no interest in the World Cup. When Labour came to office a renewed request received an initially disappointing response. Newly appointed as Minister of Sport, Denis Howell 'reiterated that Government help was unlikely to be forthcoming'. The report goes on to suggest that funding eventually came only because of the FA's persistence.[66] The memoirs of Denis Howell offer a different emphasis on events. Unable to resist the politician's perpetual temptation to disparage an opponent, he refers to a conversation in which the Secretary of the FA, Denis Follows, informed him that the Conservative Minister for Education, Quintin Hogg, offered nothing more by way of World Cup support, than 'police escorts for various teams as they drove around the country'.[67] Howell indicates this prompted him to approach Harold Wilson as a matter of some urgency. He claims to have told the Prime Minister, 'It is not much use having a Minister for Sport with a World Cup on his hands if he has no money to organize it.' Wilson appeared to be unaware of the forthcoming tournament and, to Howell's amazement, responded 'How much do you want?' Having no real idea on sums at that particular stage Howell simply guessed and asked Wilson for half a million pounds. Wilson replied, 'Right ... I will agree to that, but no more.'[68]

Even more surprised by the Prime Minister's pledge was Sir John Lang, principal advisor to Howell. Despite Wilson's handshake agreement with Howell, Lang remained unconvinced that the Treasury would accept such a financial commitment being made to football. Perhaps Howell allowed this

warning to temper his discussions with the FA, and downplay the probable financial commitment coming from the Government, at least until he saw
firsthand just what kind of investment might be required to bring the participating stadia up to a suitable standard for World Cup hosting. Compounding
uncertainty, according to Howell, neither the FA nor the clubs had much of an
idea about what these standards should be, so he and Lang set the standards
themselves, based on Howell's assumption that overseas visitors to the World
Cup, not only the official entourages, but also many of the supporters, 'would
be people of substance and they certainly would not tolerate the male-oriented
provision which was normal at English football grounds in the mid-1960s'.[69] In
a whirlwind tour between 12 and 15 February 1965, Howell and Lang, in the
company of Sir Stanley Rous, visited the regional club grounds at which World
Cup matches would be played. Resultantly, three key criteria were established:
1) the need to increase the number of seats; 2) the provision of reception
lounges at the ground and in the towns where games were to be played; 3) the
provision of good press facilities at the grounds and in the towns.[70]

With the grounds tour done and the criteria for facility provision established,
Howell tasked Lang to devise a funding formula to compensate clubs for the
improvements they needed to undertake. Lang's recommendation, which was
agreeable to Treasury and duly approved by Howell, was for a 'level of grant
at 50% for substantial work of a permanent nature and 90% for temporary
installations'.[71] Subsequent to the World Cup tournament, Howell reported
to Parliament the actual Government expenditure incurred. The breakup
between grants and loans and the particular allocations to clubs, made via the
FA, are given in Table 1.

Totalling a little under £400,000, this spending was a good £100,000 less
than the amount Howell had been granted. With this modest figure, shored up
by England's World Cup victory, Howell had every reason to be confident when
making his parliamentary speech and his conclusion – 'There was not a word of
criticism inside or outside the House – no one dared!' – need not be doubted.[72]
Howell's jovial narrative style does not betray his sincerity in achievement.
Properly titled Minister with Responsibility for Sport, Howell's was a junior

Table 1 FA grant and loan allocations

	Grants	*Loans*
Aston Villa	£46,100	£9,900
Everton	£48,360	£10,740
Manchester United	£39,940	£9,760
Middlesbrough	£42,900	£30,500
Sheffield Wednesday	£78,700	£17,700
Sunderland	£61,300	£3,600

portfolio in the first Wilson administration, similar to other portfolios, such as Jenny Lee's Minister with Responsibility for the Arts, both designations giving recognition to Labour's intended emphasis on areas of culture and society that had, hitherto, been more or less allowed to operate without the steering hand of government.[73] Howell was ambitious and eager to make his mark quickly. By the time of his appointment, the World Cup's arrival in England was an impending circumstance but, nevertheless, the funding of stadia facilitation by government, without Howell making it an imperative, might not have been forthcoming. At the same time as he was sorting out funding for the World Cup, Howell was dealing with the complications of establishing the Sports Council, not least of which was initial opposition from his advisor Lang.[74] Included in Labour's election manifesto, promise of a Sports Council was a signifier of Harold Wilson's belief as party leader that being seen to materially back sport would hold appeal across the electorate. The subsequent recommendation, when in office, of Stanley Matthews for a knighthood symbolised a continuing acknowledgement that sport had not been taken seriously enough in the past as a worthy cultural endeavour.[75]

In keeping with his reputation for opportunism, the genuineness of Wilson's commitment to sport has been challenged, his behaviour associated with the 1966 World Cup being used by both academic and popular historians of the period to expose his readiness to milk the cow of good fortune. Dominic Sandbrook highlights Howell's recollection of Wilson's initial ignorance of the World Cup against the Prime Minister's preparedness to be involved in the post-victory celebration with England players on the balcony of the Royal Gardens Hotel in Kensington. Christopher Booker describes the same episode as Wilson 'sneaking rather desperately into the limelight'.[76] But this is rather to place Wilson in a damned if he did, damned if he didn't situation. Had Wilson not become involved in the World Cup celebration he would have been depicted in the media as uninterested in this significant occasion of collective joyousness. It would have confirmed his reputation as an Oxford don, out of touch with the common person. The juxtaposition of Wilson's earlier unawareness of the World Cup with his presence at England's victory gives the impression of him knowing nothing about football, but being prepared to embrace it purely for political grandstanding. However, Wilson did have a background as a football enthusiast. Wilson (born 1916) was a schoolboy when Huddersfield Town won the First Division title over three consecutive seasons, 1923/24, 1924/25 and 1925/26 and the FA Cup in 1922. Wilson experienced these victories, along with those of Yorkshire in the county cricket championship, as a matter of great regional pride. Recalling Huddersfield Town's run of winning major football trophies, effectively four years in a row, Wilson declared, 'we felt we were the Lords of Creation'.[77]

To attend the World Cup Final at Wembley on 30 July 1966 Harold Wilson cut short a press conference he was giving in Ottawa with the Canadian Prime Minister Lester Pearson. Pearson joked with him in front of the cameras and bet the Prime Minister five pounds that England would not win, a challenge Wilson duly accepted. The main purpose of his North American trip was to hold discussions with Lyndon Johnson, a key ambition being to persuade the US President to encourage American companies into continuing investment in the UK economy despite a looming devaluation of the pound.[78] Prior to the trip, Wilson feared that his recent refusal to offer the US support in the Vietnam War would earn him 'a frozen mitt from the President'. However, to his surprise the greeting was 'as warm as ever'.[79] Richard Crossman, Minister for Housing, noted in his extensive diaries the lift in Wilson's mood upon return from the US. This coincided with Crossman seeing Wilson after the World Cup Final and he attributed the Prime Minister's perking up to a combination of a good reception from President Johnson and England's football victory. Although not a football enthusiast in the way of other Labour Ministers, including Wilson's Deputy, George Brown (who also rejoiced on the balcony of the Royal Gardens Hotel with England players), Denis Howell and, most of all, the Minister for Education, Anthony Crosland (reportedly a *Match of the Day* fanatic), Crossman believed the World Cup victory would give the economy a boost by invigorating confidence:

> It was a tremendous, gallant fight that England won. Our men showed real guts and the bankers, I suspect, will be influenced by this, and the position of the Government correspondingly strengthened.[80]

Crossman's reference to gallantry bears interesting comparison to part of a speech made by Lyndon Johnson at a lunch, on the day before the World Cup final, in honour of Prime Minister Wilson's visit to Washington. Wilson recalled being 'amazed ... by the hyperbole' Johnson used in 'proposing [his] health':

> England is not a country of amateurs. We know her as a country whose greatest resource is 'the strong heart of her sons'. That is why I am confident she will prevail ... [T]he courage of Churchill must always be a force for progress, an influence for good in these days ... I must say that England is blessed now, as it was then, with gallant and hardy leadership. In you, sir, she has a man of mettle ... She is blessed with a leader whose own enterprise and courage will show the way.[81]

Someone in England hearing these words at the time, without knowing the particular ascription, could have been forgiven for thinking they were directed at Bobby Moore, an interpretation not lost upon the *Daily Express* cartoonist Michael Cummings. On Monday 1 August the newspaper carried a cartoon by Cumming's captioned, 'If President Johnson can think I'm a Churchill *you* can think I won the World Cup', its image showing the shadowy figure of Churchill in background giving his famous two-fingered V sign, while, in the foreground, Harold Wilson, kitted-out as an England player, celebrates with football under one arm, the other raising the Jules Rimet trophy. That Wilson includes this very same cartoon in the lengthy memoir of his First Administration indicates his self-reflexivity and good natured response to the criticism he received for his appearance at England's World Cup celebrations.[82]

Harold Wilson was fourteen years old when the first FIFA World Cup was played in Uruguay in 1930. In that year Huddersfield Town was defeated in the FA Cup final by Arsenal, managed by Herbert Chapman, the same man who had steered Huddersfield to success in the 1920s. While the young Harold was no doubt focussed on his own team's fortunes in that season, he was not likely to have known of the event that kicked off in Montevideo in July 1930. Thirty years hence, Wilson, preoccupied with internal Labour Party politics – he unsuccessfully challenged Hugh Gaitskell's leadership in November 1960 – probably failed to notice press reports in August announcing that England was designated to host the World Cup in 1966. It is against this backdrop that Denis Howell's claim about Wilson's ignorance regarding the World Cup, when Prime Minister in 1965, needs to be understood. Howell possibly over-stated Wilson's response for effect, but that he would have known little to nothing about the planning of the World Cup at that time and what role, if any, the Government should play, was in keeping with the then status of the competition. Asking his Minister for Sport, 'what is it all about', was not as silly a sounding question as it would be today if asked by a Prime Minister eighteen months ahead of a football World Cup coming to their country.

The well-known saying, 'A week is a long time in politics', is attributed to Harold Wilson.[83] His namesake in the winning England team indicated much the same thought about World Cup football:

> World Cup matches are so different from the FA Cup, where you have two or three weeks between rounds … You have no time to relax between games in the World Cup. No sooner have you finished with one match, than you are ready for the next.[84]

After the World Cup, former Huddersfield Town player Ray Wilson returned, without fanfare, to his home in the Merseyside village of Lydiate. In less than two weeks he was back in action with Everton against Liverpool competing for the Charity Shield, and then into the lengthy, if less frantically paced, League season. For Harold Wilson – MP for the constituency of Huyton, near Liverpool – the headiness of the moment notwithstanding, the World Cup final was little more than an afternoon and evening away from normal duties. Immediately he returned to parliamentary sittings, longer than usual for the month of August to secure passage of the Government's Prices and Incomes Bill through the House of Commons.[85] But the populist appeal of the World Cup was not lost on Wilson and he reputedly believed England's defeat in the quarter-finals of the World Cup in Brazil, just five days before the election in June 1970, had been unhelpful to the Labour Party's declining favour with the electorate and subsequent loss of Government.[86] The 1966 World Cup left an indelible mark. While present political leaders may not be inclined to link England World Cup team performances to their political fortunes, they nevertheless, as exhibited by the current Prime Minister (David Cameron), remain very keen to have a World Cup finals tournament played in England once more.

Notes

1 Hughson, 'The Friendly Games'. A rather explicit symbolic connection to the Olympic Games was evident from the outset for the 1966 World Cup as the announcement of England as host nation was made at the 32nd FIFA Congress in Rome during the 1960 Olympics, *F.A. News*, X: 2 (September, 1960), p. 45.

2 J.L. Manning, 'Where has all the fussing gone?' (the Last Word column), *Daily Mail*, 8 July 1966, p. 16.

3 England players were reported to receive £60 for each match appearance, reserve players, £30 per match. Players were allowed £2 per day spending money, and their travelling and hotel expenses were arranged and paid for by the FA. This included a 'daily telephone call home to the wife'. The £22,000 bonus to be paid in the event of England winning the World Cup – determined by the FA's Finance and General Purposes Committee on 18 June 1966 (meeting minutes) – was left to Ramsey to distribute as he saw fit; Roy Peskett, *Daily Mail*, 28 July 1966, p. 6.

4 Hughson, 'The Cultural Legacy of Olympic Posters', p. 754; In an article in the FA's monthly magazine, journalist and author Geoffrey Green wrote, 'I do not suppose even the Olympic Games, with its symbolic flame and its cherished ethos of amateur idealism has more to offer than the concluding stages of the World Cup Tournament; Green, 'A Glorious Occasion for British Sport', p. 468.

5 Orwell, 'The Sporting Spirit'. In his essay 'Notes on Nationalism' (p. 411), Orwell defines patriotism as a 'devotion to a particular place and a particular way of life, which one believes to be best in the world but has no wish to force upon other people'.

6 Hughson, 'An Invitation to "Modern" Melbourne', p. 278.

7 Tomlinson, *FIFA*, p. 18.

8 *Ibid.*, p. 18.

9 Clayton, 'It's Only a Game', p. 153.

10 cf. Russell, *The Meanings of Modern Art*, p. 16.

11 cf. Leaver, 'Fútbol and Modernist Aesthetics', p. 3.

12 Hughson, *The Making of Sporting Cultures*, p. 106.

13 Butler, *The Football League*, p. 11.

14 This view is based on an outsider's (viz. the author) acceptance of endogenous

opinion, articulated so well by Percy Young in *Football Facts and Fancies* (p. 118) that: 'Football in the North, and the Midlands, has not been transplanted among us – in its modern form. It has grown up from amongst us, has often redeemed our existence in the cities of no great beauty, has relieved the mind in times of disastrous economic crisis.' On a similar note, see the passage by Hopcraft in *The Football Man* (p. 219) on the 1966 World Cup and 'the true England of the industrial provinces'.

However, an article in the FA's monthly journal at the time of the World Cup, written by Edward Grayson – 'England's Duty to the Past' – declares the primary indebtedness of England's World Cup team of 1966 to the Corinthian Football Club, formed in 1882. This was perhaps a way of the FA making a statement on what they regarded as the historical importance of amateurism. For a history of the Corinthians see Taylor, *On the Corinthian Spirit*.

15 Mayes, *World Cup Report 1966*, p. 19

16 The FA World Cup Organising Committee meeting minutes, 23 April 1963, p. 56; and the official handbook *World Championship Jules Rimet Cup 1966*, Section X1, Grounds and Footballs, Article 17.

17 The decision to replace St James's Park with Ayresome Park, Middlesbrough is recorded in the World Cup Organising Committee meeting minutes 22 September 1964, p. 78.

18 H. Yates, 'World Cup to Come to Goodison', *Liverpool Daily Post*, 18 October 1963.

19 Inglis, *Engineering Archie*, p. 64.

20 Bowden, 'Soccer', p. 117.

21 Inglis, *Football Grounds of Britain*, pp. 31–2.

22 *Ibid.*, p. 156.

23 *Ibid.*

24 *Ibid*; and Inglis, *Engineering Archie*, p. 103.

25 'Wembley of the North ready for K.O. day', unreferenced press clipping from *World Cup 1966, Goodison Park* scrapbook, Everton Collection (Liverpool Records Office) Reference number: EFC/21/47.

26 This was because the added pitch length was considered by Everton officials as not ideal for regular football competition, because it put players at risk of being unable to slow down enough to avoid going over the goal line and into the crowd. 'Everton's pitch is 13 ½ feet longer', from *World Cup 1966, Goodison Park* scrapbook.
This decision ran contrary to the initial hope of the Minister of Sport, Denis Howell who informed the FA of his view that any adjustments to football grounds might best remain as 'a permanent reminder of the World Cup after 1966'. See the FA World Cup Organising Committee meeting minutes for 9 March 1965. The view is confirmed in Howell's autobiography, *Made in Birmingham*, p. 163.

27 'Wembley of the North ready for K.O. day'.

28 Agreement to inform Liverpool City Council about these plans was reached at a meeting of the Everton Football Club board, on 20 April 1964. Minute Book number 25 (1959–64), item number 292, Everton Collection (Liverpool Records Office) Reference number: EFC/1/1/29.
The Everton board claimed the resultant alterations would be beneficial,

ensuring at least 50,000 in match attendance for each of the World Cup fixtures held at Goodison Park. 'House down – house full', unreferenced press clipping from *World Cup 1966, Goodison Park* scrapbook; see also, 'World Cup Football on ... Merseyside' by W. Dickinson, then Secretary of Everton F.C.

The minutes for the FA's World Cup Organising Committee meeting on 22 July 1965 record, under Item 12, Ground Alterations, that the Everton Football Club has taken responsibility for the re-housing of tenants evacuated from demolished residences.

No mention is made in accessible Everton F.C. records of the club needing to purchase the houses before demolition could go ahead. The point is raised in the autobiography of the Minister of Sport, Denis Howell, *Made in Birmingham* (p. 162), who claims to have played a mediating role on the club's behalf to ensure a hassle-free approval from Liverpool City Council.

29 Moynihan, *Soccer Syndrome*, p. 126; The demolished housing as having once been residences for players is referred to by Inglis, *Football Grounds of Britain*, p. 158.

30 Moynihan, *Soccer Syndrome*, p. 127.

31 Moorhouse, *The Other England*, p. 135.

32 Moorhouse's allusion, *Ibid.*, p. 136, is to a more favourably evocative description of football supporter passion in Priestley's novel *The Good Companions* (pp. 5–6). The non-football related unfavourable commentary on the people of Liverpool is made in Priestley, *English Journey*, pp. 248–50.

33 Yates, 'World Cup to Come to Goodison'.

34 H. Yates, 'Merseyside talks of betrayal', *Liverpool Daily Post*, 25 July 1966.

35 Rollin, *England's World Cup Triumph*, p. 17.

36 'A soccer snub, say angry fans of Merseyside', *Liverpool Daily Post*, undated press clipping from *World Cup 1966, Goodison Park* scrapbook. As evidence the article shows an unreferenced photographic snippet from the FA's monthly. The original can be found in the schedule of matches appearing in *F.A. News*, XV: 12 (July, 1966), p. 464.

37 *World Championship Jules Rimet Cup 1966*, p. 25; for similar confirmation see also the 'draw for the final competition' in the World Cup related issue of the *FIFA Official Bulletin*, Number 44, 1966.

38 'A soccer snub, say angry fans of Merseyside'.

39 'The big semi-final brush-off', unreferenced press clipping from *World Cup 1966, Goodison Park* scrapbook.

40 'Liverpool fans stay away', unreferenced press clipping from *World Cup 1966, Goodison Park* scrapbook.

41 'King Pele enters in glory', unreferenced press clipping from *World Cup 1966, Goodison Park* scrapbook.

42 McIlvanney, 'Portugal *v.* Brazil'.

43 Robinson et al., *1966 Uncovered*, p. 109; 'Liverpool fans stay away'.

44 Yates, 'Merseyside talks of betrayal'. An expectation at Everton F.C. of Goodison Park hosting England should the team make a semi-final appearance is not indicated in an article written prior to the tournament's commencement by the Club Secretary Mr W. Dickinson. Reference is made to the dates of matches, but the only

mention of England is made in suggestion that should the national team not play at Goodison, Merseysiders would, nevertheless, provide an eager audience for any game between visiting nations. Dickinson, 'World Cup on … Merseyside', p. 214.

45 Respective stadium crowd capacities announced ahead of the World Cup were given as Wembley 97,000 and Goodison Park 78,299. *Football Monthly's World Cup Souvenir, England 1966*, pp. 66 & 70.

46 Gee, *Wembley*, p. 162. While Wembley Stadium was not disputed as the main World Cup venue, related criticism was raised. For example, the *Daily Mail* ran an expose, with accompanying photographs, on the 'desolation and decay' of Wembley Hill and Wembley railway stations, only three days before the World Cup commenced. The office of London Midland Region, then responsible for these stations under the nationalised British Railways, was reported as being unconcerned about the condition of these stations, in regard to the World Cup, as it was anticipated that most fans would arrive via Wembley Park and Wembley Central stations. The newspaper article suggests this to be an unsatisfactory response, as the two stations under criticism were much closer in walking proximity to the Wembley Stadium turnstiles than the two stations proposed by the railway authority for maximum use. See, 'When the world comes to Wembley next week … this is what it will see', story John Spicer, pictures David Davies, *Daily Mail*, 8 July 1966, p. 11.

47 Gee, *Wembley*, p. 18.

48 Inglis, *Football Grounds of Britain*, p. 20.

49 FA World Cup Organising Committee meeting minutes for 11 March 1963 and 29 June 1963.

50 Mayes, *World Cup Report 1966*, p. 22.

51 A thorough explanation of the complexity in planning for ticket sales is provided by *Ibid.*, pp. 22–7.

52 The FA World Cup Organising Committee deemed that Her Majesty's Government should contribute to the costs of local interpreter services as this provision was arranged at the Government's 'insistence'. Meeting minutes, 18 April 1966.

53 FA World Cup Organising Committee meeting minutes for 28 September 1965, item 14, 'Other Business'.

54 The Everton F.C. board approved Mr Moores' letter to be sent to the Liverpool County FA at its meeting on 13 April 1964. Minute Book number 25 (1959–64), item number 283, Everton Collection (Liverpool Records Office) Reference number: EFC/1/1/29.

55 'City leaves its mark on World Cup visitors', *Liverpool Daily Post*, undated press clipping from *World Cup 1966, Goodison Park* scrapbook.

56 *Ibid.*

57 *Ibid.*

58 'Who's made money out of the World Cup?', *Financial Times*, 30 July 1966, p. 8.

59 *Ibid.* Whether the report came from Middlesbrough or Sunderland is not indicated, but a full report from the Sunderland Local Liaison Committee in the official *World Cup Report* by Mayes (pp. 297–9) – the only report of this kind included by way of an example in the volume – gives no clue to such adverse assessment. Indeed, the report concludes positively, 'If the views of the many visitors who reported their

enjoyment of Sunderland are shared by the remainder, then the town has been placed on the world map in an attractive way with its reputation enhanced.'

60 *Ibid.*

61 Robinson et al., *1966 Uncovered*, p. 17.

62 Hopcraft, *The Football Man*, p. 220. For a related critique of Hopcraft's unintentionally racist depiction of North Korea players see Bose, *The Sporting Alien*, p. 30.

63 An entry titled 'North Korea' in The FA World Cup Organising Committee meeting minutes for 10 November 1965 (item 5) notes a forthcoming meeting with the Foreign Office to discuss problems which may arise 'as this country has no Diplomatic Relations with Her Majesty's Government'.

     For a comprehensive discussion of the British Government's concerns about the participation of North Korea in the 1966 World Cup, see Polley, 'The Diplomatic Background to the 1966 Football World Cup'.

64 Howell, *Made in Birmingham*, pp. 171–2.

65 Mayes, *World Cup Report 1966*, p. 86.

66 *Ibid.*

67 Howell, *Made in Birmingham*, p. 142.

68 *Ibid.*

69 *Ibid.*, p. 160.

70 FA World Cup Organising Committee meeting minutes for 9 March 1965, item 4b, 'Government Support: Visits to Grounds'.

71 Howell, *Made in Birmingham*, p. 163.

72 *Ibid.*, p. 175.

73 Jefferys, *Sport and Politics in Modern Britain*, pp. 78–9.

74 *Ibid.*, p. 81.

75 *Ibid.*, Harold Wilson claims Matthews as 'a long overdue recommendation', from the fields of sport, entertainment and the arts, for a knighthood, one of 'the forgotten men of Conservative lists'. See Wilson, *The Labour Government*, p. 59.

     Alf Ramsey became the second person from football to receive a knighthood. The nomination, which again came from the Wilson Government, was conferred in the New Year's Honours list of 1967. See McKinstry, *Sir Alf*, p. 364.

76 Sandbrook, *White Heat*, pp. 309 & 323; Booker, *Neophiliacs*, p. 298.

77 Wilson, *Memoirs*, p. 9. Wilson actually overestimates Huddersfield Town's trophy successes, writing that the team won the FA Cup twice during their best years; in fact the FA Cup was won only once. The error, and fogginess of memory, is somewhat explained by near success. As well as winning the FA Cup in 1922, Huddersfield Town was runner-up in 1920, 1928, 1930 and 1938.

78 Colman, *'Special Relationship'*, p. 85.

79 Wilson, *The Labour Government*, pp. 263–4.

80 Crossman, *Diaries of a Cabinet Minister*, p. 594. Wilson, see *The Labour Government*, p. 266, gives a vivid description of Brown cavorting on the balcony and singing the praises of the West Ham players in the winning England team. Crosland's 'passionate love affair' with football and *Match of the Day* is recalled by his wife, Susan Crosland, in the biography *Tony Crosland*, p. 153.

     While Crossman hoped England's World Cup victory would lift the confidence of bankers in the state of the nation, the Editorial in the September 1966 issue of the *F.A. News* (XVI: 2, p. 47) claimed the player's efforts in victory would boost export industries and should serve as 'an example of the devotion and loyalty to the country which many others would do well to follow'. In his book *Patriots*, pp. 462 and 779, Richard Weight assumes this to be a 'thinly veiled attack on militant trade unionists and students', authored by Lord Harewood. There is no particular evidence to support this claim, although Lord Harewood did resort to jingoism in his 'Foreword' to the *World Cup Report* by Mears.

81 Wilson, *The Labour Government*, pp. 264–5.

82 *Ibid.*, p. 265. Wilson was Leader of the Opposition at the time *The Labour Government* was published in 1971. His inclusion of the *Daily Express* cartoon in the volume indicates that he did not regard jibing of his World Cup related behaviour to be of any serious damage to his political or personal reputation.

83 Possibly the most famous of sayings attributed to Wilson, 'A week is a long time in politics', is of uncertain origin. Questioned in 1977, Wilson could not remember when the comment was made or the precise wording. As is often the case, the quote on popular record is probably different from what was actually said and meant. See Rees, *Brewer's Famous Quotations*, p. 501.

84 'Quiet return for Ray Wilson', unreferenced press clipping from *World Cup 1966*, *Goodison Park* scrapbook.

85 Wilson, *The Labour Government*, p. 267.

86 Roy Jenkins is one Labour Party insider responsible for a possible exaggeration of Wilson's view in this regard. See Jenkins, *A Life at the Centre*, p. 301.

4

Alf Ramsey and the importance of being earnest: masculinity, modernity and the 1966 World Cup squad

Arms raised like gladiators, they embrace. Human emotions swamp them, child-
ishly even. For such protagonists of perfection … (Alan Ross)

One of the most memorable photographic images from the 1966 World Cup
Final, snapped as extra time concluded, shows the non-playing members of
the England squad exploding in joyous celebration, some cheering, others,
such as Wolverhampton Wanderers' veteran Ron Flowers, raising their arms
to the heavens. Within this scene only one person remains seated: Alfred
Ernest Ramsey. As Jimmy Armfield, former captain of the England team
and unofficial leader of the non-playing squad members, attempts to coax the
England manager to his feet, Ramsey sits stone-faced, seeming to look in the
direction of the photographer.[1] Throughout the victory rituals at Wembley,
Ramsey retained his staid countenance. As Bobby Moore climbed the stairs to
the Royal Box to receive the Jules Rimet trophy from the Queen, Bryon Butler
reports Ramsey sitting 'impassively at his moment of fulfilment'.[2] 'Impassive'
is one of the politer terms to have been used when describing Ramsey's general demeanour. As the years have passed, the references have become less
polite. Writing forty years on from the 1966 World Cup, David Goldblatt
referred to Ramsey as a 'tight-wired, emotionally constipated man' and regrets
as unfortunate the England manager's inability to 'publicly share his triumph
and glee with his players or nation'.[3] Reflecting upon his low-key behaviour
on the afternoon of the World Cup Final, a few years hence, Ramsey sounded
almost apologetic. He suggested a subsequent win of that magnitude might
provoke him into a more animated response. Given the misfortune of results
in the duration of his remaining tenure as England manager, an opportunity
for such a display never came. Our memory of Ramsey in victory is, therefore,
framed in that photo from a summer day in 1966. This chapter examines
Ramsey's seemingly dour public demeanour against the theme of masculinity
and modernity. His masculinity is considered in relation to his attitude on the
role of the England manager and, stemming from this, his commitment to
an English identity. As the chapter progresses, the interrelationship between

the masculinity of Ramsey and the masculinity of his World Cup players is addressed.

Viewed within a mythologised image of the mid-1960s Alf Ramsey (1920–99) cuts an anachronistic figure, and this rather explains his mockery over subsequent years. However, as Leo McKinstry contends in his biography of the manager, 'Alf Ramsey was far more representative of the British public than, say, John Lennon'.[4] Nevertheless, this is not how he is remembered and, even at the time, his stiff demeanour was ridiculed by some close to him. Cilla Black's version of the Bacharach and David song *Alfie* was released in January 1966, as a promotion for the film of the same name, which was eventually released in August of that year. It is reported that 'the tirelessly waggish Jimmy Greaves' took 'great delight' in singing the main line from the song, 'What's it all about, Alfie?', on the England team bus, as a means of teasing Ramsey in front of the other players.[5] Had the film been released at the time, the friendly joke might have been regarded as more of a barb than when made purely in relation to the song. The film *Alfie*, based on the play (turned novel) by Bill Naughton, stars Michael Caine in the title role as a 'cocky cockney Jack-the-lad strutt[ing] his stuff through a series of picaresque adventures'.[6] Alfie Elkins could not be more different to Alf Ramsey. Caine's character incorporates a rough working-class uncouthness into a modern London guise, as he flits between romantic dalliances with women. Elkins dismisses the devoted husband type – which Ramsey was – as merely a potential victim of his uncaring cuckoldry. He also ridicules the fraternity of conventional working-class masculinity, suggesting that while men share each other's company to discuss football, he shares the company of their wives.

An immediately noticeable difference between Alfie and Alf is in way of speech. Whereas Caine's Alfie accentuates a cockney brogue, Alf Ramsey was well-known for attempting to shed the linguistic evidence of his Essex origins. It is widely accepted that Ramsey undertook elocution lessons for this purpose, although, in the most thoroughly researched biography, McKinstry finds no evidence of Ramsey attending speech classes.[7] Whatever the case may be on that matter, Ramsey certainly aspired to social mobility. The related acceptance of the need to 'improve oneself', a tendency identified by Raymond Williams as prevalent since the mid-eighteenth century, is apparent in Ramsey's behaviour since the time he moved into football management.[8] In this regard, he bore similarity to other successful men of his generation such as the producer on the Beatles' records, George Martin (1926–2016). Martin was also reported to have received elocution lessons.[9] However, while Martin was able to wear the persona of the 'cultured gent' lightly and naturally, it hung on Ramsey like a rain-sodden overcoat, his discomfort and awkwardness often apparent in the

5　Sir Alf Ramsey and tape recorder. Evidence of the England manager's continuing distrust of the press beyond the 1966 World Cup.

media spotlight. Nevertheless, unforgiving parodies of Ramsey fail to acknowledge the difficulty of his position and the constant media pressure he was under as England manager. Michael Caine's celluloid Alfie adopted the unconventional technique of episodically addressing the camera directly. Looking the camera in the eye was a demand with which the real-life Alf Ramsey always struggled. While he was confident in the abilities of his players and in his own ability to coach them to success, his reluctance before the media reflected his uncertainty in presenting a public image of the England football team manager according to his understanding of the importance the role.

While Ramsey's development of a middle-class persona commenced before his appointment as manager of England, that appointment gave a different impetus to Ramsey's purpose. By becoming manager of the England football team Ramsey stepped into what he would have recognised as a role with status akin to holding senior public office, with an attendant obligation of 'service' (another term highlighted by Raymond Williams).[10] Primarily, this was to lead England to success in the 1966 World Cup. Ramsey's response to journalistic critics sometimes showed a frustration with what he perceived as their obstinacy to this goal. But beyond the primary instrumental ambition of winning the Cup, Ramsey seemed to want to dignify his position as England manager in a manner and to an extent he believed warranted. He followed in the role from the England manager he played under, Walter Winterbottom (1913–2002). Ramsey appears to have respected Winterbottom as a game tactician and as a leader, yet his own tenure as England manager was clearly going to be different from the outset.[11] Thus so largely because, unlike Winterbottom, Ramsey was to take full responsibility for team selection rather than have the team picked for him by a committee of the FA.[12] Ramsey believed that as manager, he had the necessary expertise to pick the best representative team for each match on behalf of the English public. He did not have similar faith in senior members of the FA and was happy for them to remain as arm's length as possible in their involvement with team-related matters.

This perceived disregard caused tension between Ramey and the FA hierarchy, especially Professor Harold Thompson, who, prior to becoming Chairman of the FA in 1976 is reported to have been the driving force behind Ramsey's dismissal as England manager in 1974.[13] Ramsey's dismissal was the culmination of animosity that had built up over the more than ten years he spent as England manager. Thompson, apparently, always resented the authority granted by the FA to Ramsey. In short, the problem for Thompson was that Ramsey came from what he regarded as a common background. Although the previous, long-serving manager, Winterbottom, was not of Oxbridge stock, he was a bursary recipient, educated and then employed as a lecturer in physical education at the respected Carnegie College in Leeds.[14] During the Second World War, he attained officer status in the Royal Air Force, reaching the rank of Wing Commander. By contrast, Alf Ramsey, born in Dagenham, Essex, in a then semi-rural setting, left school at fourteen to work for the Five Elms Co-operative store, with the aim of later starting his own grocery business. Football and the War halted these plans. In regard to the latter, Ramsey was conscripted into the army in 1940 and until VE day served on the home front, being stationed at Cornwall. During this time Ramsey was promoted to the non-commissioned officer rank of Quarter-Master Sergeant.[15] Had Ramsey been of a background more like that of Winterbottom, then the FA's agreement to cede him authority to select the England team might well have sat easier with the likes of Thompson. How Ramsey perceived himself in relation to the FA elite is unknown, other than in regard to football, in which domain he, unequivocally, held himself to be superior. His irritation with FA councillors was actually expressed in language and in a tone they might have used themselves. He snootily referred to them as 'those people' and saved the best for Thompson, referring to him as 'that bloody man Thompson'.[16]

The only subject Ramsey intellectualised on is football. He is not likely to have given any time to a sociological discussion of class. Yet that very quietness is indicative of him as a product of the British class system. Carolyn Steedman's words are pertinent here:

> delineation of emotional and psychological selfhood has been made by and through the testimony of people in a central relationship to the dominant culture, that is to say by and through people who are not working class.[17]

Relatedly, Ramsey was very much, to use Jonathan Rutherford's term, a 'son of imperialism'.[18] This is to be distinguished from the 'Imperial man', as such, a member of the social elite, public school educated and of officer class in the services. The likes of Ramsey came into the military to follow the orders of the self-assumedly higher breed and, in the case of those sent to war, to serve as cannon fodder as need be. Ramsey was spared from the latter fate during the Second World War and actually regarded his time in the army as an important formative episode in his life. Interestingly, he referred to the educative benefits of spending time with 'many older and more experienced men',[19] but whether he meant by this older enlisted men or those in the officer class above him is uncertain. Whatever the case, Ramsey accepted army hierarchy without complaint and, it would seem, the ideology of this particular army's defence of the realm. This background can be seen in his approach to managing England's football team. Although not dwelling on military and war analogies, Ramsey certainly emphasised a notion of duty in playing for England. He demanded officer-like respect from his players and assumed a measured degree of aloofness in his dealings with them. More significantly, Ramsey, quite justifiably, regarded the position of England manager as a senior appointment within the FA and expected to be treated accordingly by its board members. The personal difficulties with Thompson indicated the discomfiture Ramsey's attitude brought into the midst of the old imperial and elitist club that the FA still was during his tenure as team manager. Ramsey was no class rebel, but he did bring an elephant into the room at Lancaster Gate. His stiff public demeanour reflected the journey he had taken from Dagenham to the FA's upmarket Bayswater address. The change Ramsey effectively brought to the organisational role of England manager and the upsetting of class presumption this involved has not been regarded carefully enough by those preoccupied with his parodied image.

Alf Ramsey was not the Football Association's first choice to become England manager upon the departure of Walter Winterbottom. The appointment was initially offered to Jimmy Adamson, captain of Burnley who was coming close to the end of his playing career. Adamson had made a good impression during the 1962 World Cup when he worked as coaching assistant to Winterbottom. However, Adamson declined the offer and the FA decided to put the post out to advertisement.[20] This process failed to turn up any suitable candidates and, with the awareness that other experienced managers such as Bill Nicholson at Spurs and Stan Cullis at Wolves were not interested in the job, the FA then decided to approach Ipswich Town for permission to put an offer to Ramsey. Contrary to some interpretations that Ramsey kept the FA waiting one month for his decision, McKinstry's examination of the relevant communication indicates that Ramsey's acceptance was delivered in a little over one week.[21] He apparently took this time to consider two factors, which became conditional to his acceptance. Firstly, his loyalty and commitment to Ipswich Town made him unwilling to relinquish his existing managerial job until the 1962/3 League season had concluded. The second and most important of Ramsey's conditions was, as discussed above, the right to independently select the England team.

The appointment provided an increase in professional status for Ramsey, but not salary. Whereas he received a salary of £5,000 per year as manager of Ipswich Town, as England manager he was appointed on to a salary of £4,500 per year.[22] Had Ramsey's incentive been financial gain he might well have declined the England job and waited for another offer within the League to come his way. Having just steered lowly Ipswich Town to become champions of the First Division, Ramsey's prospects for a managerial appointment with one of the more prosperous English clubs must have been promising. That a number of other contenders snubbed the chance to become England manager suggests that the post was not widely regarded as superior to being manager at a leading club. Given that Ramsey has left no substantial autobiographical record of his managerial career, assessment of his intentions at the time remains speculative, but it is certainly reasonable to say that Ramsey took on the role as

England manager with a great sense of honour that went beyond a purely personal dimension of ego. This can remind us of Richard Sennett's book *The Fall of Public Man*, in which he distinguishes between those leaders who maintain an 'impersonal' relationship with their public from those who attempt to establish a 'personal' relationship.[23] Ramsey was of the former kind and, therefore, unwittingly lived up to the type of leadership Sennett lamented as having been in historical decline in the larger political sphere since the late 1800s. Especially problematic for Sennett was the resultant intrusion of the intimacy of the private sphere into the public domain. Modern statesmen began to favour style over substance and to prioritise the projection of their personal image to the public ahead of a focus on solid policy-making and related actions.

Football is, of course, a different matter to party and electoral politics. The imperative of immediate tangible results weigh on a football manager as in few other professions. However, this has not prevented the rise of high-profile managers within professional British football of a kind for which neither Richard Sennett nor Alf Ramsey would have fondness. A particularly idiosyncratic example of such a manager was Brian Clough (1935–2004).[24] A player with Sunderland when Alf Ramsey was appointed England manager, Clough had become a lower division manager by the time of the 1966 World Cup. During the 1970s he emerged as one of English football's most celebrated managers following successes at Derby County and Nottingham Forest that were reminiscent of Ramsey's own managerial success at Ipswich Town in the early 1960s. He also became a most controversial football pundit on television and in the press. During his time at Derby, Clough angered Ramsey immensely in April/May 1972, as England prepared for a home-leg quarter-final match of the European Championship competition against West Germany. Ramsey had selected Derby's Roy McFarland to play in the central defence, but Clough stymied the plan by declaring his player injured and thus not able to take part in the England game. This was adjudged a cynical move, as two days after the England match Clough fielded the player for Derby in the club's final match of the First Division season against Liverpool. A furious Ramsey responded:

> This man calls himself a patriot but he has never done anything to help England. All he does is criticize us in the newspapers and television.[25]

The player involved in the upset, Roy McFarland, claims had Ramsey been faced with the priority of Clough as a club manager, he would have acted in the exactly the same way.[26] However, this offers more of a defence of Clough than an understanding of Ramsey's sincerity on matters to do with the England football team and a genuine belief in national duty as discussed above. Ramsey's genuine expectation in this regard was exhibited in a near drama just ahead of the 1966 World Cup finals involving Bobby Moore. Prior to the opening match against Uruguay, on 11 July 1966, Ramsey was troubled by Moore's contractual uncertainty with West Ham, believing the unresolved matter of his club destiny might adversely affect his concentration when leading England on the field. In an emergency meeting at the England team lodgings in Hendon Hall, West Ham manager Ron Greenwood (1921–2006) acknowledged the imperative of Ramsey's concern by agreeing to immediately accept Moore's terms for a temporary contract that would have him settled until the World Cup concluded.[27] Despite underlying rivalry in regard to their reputations as innovative football managers, a mutual respect existed between Ramsey and Greenwood, the latter once nominating Ramsey as right full back for a best of all-time Great Britain football team.[28] When his age cohort peer successfully competed against Clough for the England manager job in 1977, Ramsey – although his opinion was not sought – no doubt welcomed the FA's decision in favour of Greenwood.

Given the slow emergence of England in international football, relative to other countries, Ramsey's call for the prioritising of the England team within 1960s' professional football was not an old-fashioned entreaty. Indeed, Richard Weight correctly recognises the modernising ambition of Ramsey's patriotism, driving him 'to revolutionize the management of the national team'.[29] The autonomy that he had grudgingly extracted from the FA enabled him to move ahead in this way. Ramsey was fully aware when he accepted the managerial appointment that the England team did not have the same type of standing within the national football culture as did other leading national teams in their countries. This bore most significance in the actual relationship between national league competitions and national representative teams. The example of West Germany illustrates the point. Ahead of the 1954 World Cup, national team manager Sepp Herberger, reportedly, was successful in requesting club managers to adopt a sweeper system to match his own plans for the West German team.[30] Ramsey could not have expected such a radical shift to occur within English football but, in an interview he gave prior to becoming England manager, he declared that the 'League will have to help' the national team towards success. This might involve, he suggested rather provocatively, a shortening of the playing season to give England players more time together in concentrated training episodes.[31] Such ambition remains hard enough to deliver today, let alone in the 1960s. Ramsey was probably aware of this and made the statement as somewhat of an ambit claim but, nevertheless, one that would press home his case about the England team being taken more seriously. The respective exchanges with Greenwood and Clough, over player issues, certainly indicated that he expected club managers to engage with the national team manager in a fully cooperative spirit.

The 'public man' Ramsey was not given to making idle boasts. However, this did not mean he lacked confidence. His most significant and well-known display of confidence as England manager occurred in June 1963, when, during a successful playing tour to Europe, he announced, 'England will win the World Cup'.[32] It seemed a fanciful claim and no doubt amazed the assembled journalists at the time, both in the outrageousness of the very prediction and in the daringness of Ramsey to say such a thing openly, even had he believed it to be true. Ramsey did not take up subsequent opportunities to mellow the claim, sticking doggedly to the line, not that England could win, but that they would win. A number of reasons can be proposed for Ramsey's obduracy. Perhaps he truly believed England would win the World Cup and stuck to the claim. Perhaps he made the prediction in a moment of overexcitement, but was too stubborn to admit this by way of tempering what he had said. And, perhaps, it was done quite deliberately as part of his managerial strategy. As suggested in Chapter 2, Ramsey may have had a view towards building public support for the England team well ahead of the World Cup finals tournament. Predicting in front of a room full of journalists that England would win was a certain way to ensure publicity, even at the risk of longer term embarrassment.

Reflecting upon the pre-World Cup period in his 1967 book *Forward for England*, Bobby Charlton states a number of reasons as to why he was confident by 1966 that England could win the trophy. One reason he cites is the 'support of English fans once they "throw off detachment"'.[33] Exactly how Charlton came to this view is not indicated, but it is likely to have developed within the team context in which Ramsey was highly influential. Ramsey's prediction of success was clearly not welcomed by all players. Veteran full back Ray Wilson initially believed that the prediction would merely place pressure on the team. Yet, in hindsight, he commented, 'Obviously, he knew something we didn't'.[34] Of course, Ramsey could not have known England would win the World Cup, but against the general perception of the odds, he did believe the team could win if he picked the right players, if the right strategy was in place, and if the players performed to the best of their ability. The prediction inevitably put pressure on the players, but they were operating in a high-pressure situation anyway, pressure that would only tighten the further England advanced in the competition. So Ramsey could be said to have prepared the players for the conditions of accumulating success. In so doing, as noted by Bowler, he placed more pressure on himself than on the players.[35] Had the England team fallen at any stage of the tournament, the 'England will win the World Cup' prediction would have come back to haunt Ramsey with him bearing the brunt of media criticism. Whatever the case may have been in regard to the initial utterance, there can be little doubt that Ramsey gave thought over time to its implications for the England team and chose to stand by it for a reason he deemed appropriate.

Another of Ramsey's well-known statements was made during a less publicly audible moment, but at a moment under maximum possible public glare.

This came in the break in play ahead of extra time in the World Cup Final, following West Germany's second equalising goal, just seconds away from regular full time with England leading 2–1 and in sight of victory. Bobby Moore is reported to have been extremely anxious as he saw Ramsey striding towards the crestfallen England players, waiting for him in ragtag assembly towards centre of field. Moore had half expected Ramsey to launch into a tirade against the players. His anger would have been understandable under these circumstances with a lead being surrendered in the last minute of play. However, to Moore's stated relief, Ramsey calmly let the players know he believed them to be the better team throughout the game and that they could prove this and win the match in extra time. By taking this approach, Moore claimed Ramsey restored the team's collective confidence and prepared them psychologically to regroup and get back into the game with gusto. He believed had Ramsey revealed his underlying displeasure at the conceded goal in an angry rant, the players would have totally lost their nerve, and the match along with it, during the added thirty minutes.[36] But what did Ramsey say? The words were said only to the gathered England players, so subsequent reports have relied on them as the source. Bobby Charlton retells what was probably an abbreviated version and words to this effect make up what tends to have become the popular memory: 'You have won the Cup once, now go out and do it again'.[37] Biographer Dave Bowler attained a similar recollection from Geoff Hurst, claiming Ramsey only needed a 'one liner' to rouse the players: 'We've won the World Cup once, now go out and do it again.'[38]

A lengthier version of Ramsey's address to the players was recalled by defender Jack Charlton in the first of his autobiographies. According to Charlton, Ramsey said: 'Forget it, forget what's just happened. Forget the last ninety minutes. You've been the better team; you're as fit as they are ... thirty minutes more, and you'll have done it. You still can do it you know'.[39] While there was no significant difference in the intent of the message, the version provided by Jack Charlton is slightly equivocal, 'you can still do it', rather than the emphatic 'go out and do it again', the latter sounding more decisive, even Churchillian. Charlton's version of his remark regarding fitness is also more tempered than the more popular understanding of what Ramsey said. Nobby Stiles offers a player's memory more in accordance with that version: 'You're tired, and so you should be. But look at them ... all laid out flat ... completely and utterly shattered!' At this prompt, Stiles claims the England players looked across and, in seeing the exhausted state of the West German players recovered their own spirits.[40] Semioticians could no doubt plunder the depths of meaning in these differing player recollections of Ramsey's words, but whichever version is closer to those actually spoken, it seems the message was most effectively communicated. Leo Mckinstry goes to the extent of claiming that Ramsey's address can be said to 'define the essence of his heroic stature'.[41] The position taken in this book, argued further below, is that Ramsey was not a hero, certainly not in a classical sense. Be this as it may, and while we might also want to take care to avoid overdoing statesmen analogies, there can be little argument with McKinstry that the rallying of his players, going into extra time of the 1966 World Cup Final, was the finest moment of leadership during Ramsey's tenure as England manager.

Contrastingly, remarks made by Ramsey following England's quarter-final win against Argentina are regarded by some as more of a career low point. The much discussed controversy pertains to remarks made by Ramsey during a television interview with the BBC commentator Kenneth Wolstenholme, in which he vented his anger over what he regarded as appalling sportsmanship from the Argentine players. The key incident of note within the game involved the sending off of Argentina's captain Antonio Rattin by the West German referee Rudolf Kreitlein for continuing verbal harassment. While a number of press reports claim that Kreitlein exacerbated tension by being overly officious in his dealing with Argentine players, the consensus among England players is that Rattin was visibly threatening towards Kreitlein, irrespective of any claimed misunderstanding over language. Beyond this particular incident England players claimed that a number of Argentine players resorted to foul tactics against them in back-play, such as pinching and raking studs on their legs.[42] It was this alleged conduct to which Ramsey took great offence and to which he was referring when he said:

> England played to win, and win we did, which was important. We are afraid of no one. We still have to produce our best football. It is not possible to until we meet the right type of opposition, a team which come out to play football, not as animals, as we have seen in the World Cup.[43]

Ramsey's remark caused great upset, not only to the Argentine football team, but to their country in general, once it had been reported there. Indeed, as discussed in Chapter 7, the Foreign Office feared that the anger in Argentina about the comment, accompanied by a belief that the match had been set up with Kreitlein's appointment as a biased referee, could develop into a fully blown diplomatic crisis. Academic opinion has judged harshly against Ramsey on this matter, while commentators within football have been more lenient. Kenneth Wolstenholme applied situational logic to his recalling of the event, i.e. it was heat of the moment with Ramsey coming into the interview room after the game without chance for his temper to subside. He also noted that Ramsey formally apologised for the remark, but that the apology went unaccepted in Argentina.[44] Senior writer with *The Observer* Hugh McIlvanney also emphasised the difficulty of the occasion, in that 'he [Ramsey] was obliged to speak under circumstances of considerable pressure'. He also noted that Ramsey did so 'without seeking to excuse himself' and that 'the Argentinians … showed hardly a sign of remorse' for the conduct that roused Ramsey to such an outburst.[45]

England players have remained uncritical of Ramsey's statement after the game, being inclined to indicate appreciation that he spoke in defence of them in so angrily criticising the conduct of the Argentine players. However, perhaps tempered by the passing of years, autobiographies, which have been written since the year 2000, note 'sadness' and 'regret' that such an important game of football ended up in an unruly spectacle.[46] Nevertheless, even if done more tentatively, the accusatory finger remains pointed at Argentina. On a further semantic note, Jimmy Greaves – a seemingly unlikely source of support for Ramsey – drew attention to the incorrectness of the popular allegation in regard to Ramsey's statement. In fact, if the statement is looked at closely, Ramsey did not actually refer to the Argentine players as animals.[47] In a courtroom situation this evidence might have been telling, but in the arena of international diplomacy, into which Ramsey had unwittingly stepped, intent of meaning and the actual words uttered counted as one and the same.

Argentine players were perhaps just as incensed by Ramsey's behaviour on the Wembley pitch after the match as they were by his performance in the infamous interview. Here, there was no doubt as to how he adjudged them personally. Another of the best-known photographs associated with the World Cup shows Ramsey interfering in the customary post-match player shirt swap, stepping in to prevent George Cohen from exchanging shirts with Alberto González of Argentina. Cohen recalls Ramsey's words at the moment as, 'George, you are not changing shirts with that animal.'[48] Accessible video footage of the incident shows González stepping away from the foiled attempt to swap shirts with Cohen and then, within a few steps, making an exchange with England's other full back Ray Wilson, without Ramsey becoming involved. Perhaps Ramsey merely failed to see this exchange occur, but, even if so, it suggests his vigilance was focussed on Cohen rather than other England players. Subconsciously or otherwise, Ramsey may have been concerned with defending the number 2 shirt of the right full back, the very same numbered shirt that Ramsey wore in his days as an England player. Outraged as he was by what he regarded as the dirty play of Argentina's players, he would have deemed them unworthy recipients of the England shirt to which he had a direct lineage.[49] This recognition might not alleviate the type of indictment made by author Johnny Rogan that Ramsey's denying of Cohen's right to exchange shirts was 'petulant' and a 'disgraceful act of bad sportsmanship'[50] but it helps to further understand Ramsey's possible motive for making such an extraordinary intervention.

When former England captain Terry Butcher learnt that a football shirt worn by Diego Maradona was to go on display in the National Football Museum, he

6 Alf Ramsey thwarts an exchange of shirts between George Cohen and
Argentine player Alberto González.

challenged its worthiness for such an honour by declaring he would not even
use the shirt to wash his car.[51] The shirt in question is that which was worn by
Maradona when he scored the so-called 'hand of God' goal against England
during the quarter-final match against Argentina at the 1986 World Cup in
Mexico. Butcher was one of the England players in that game left incensed
by the awarding of a goal to Argentina after Maradona punched the ball with
his left hand over the head of England goalkeeper Peter Shilton into the goalmouth. Butcher's outrage, generally shared by the English media at the time,
was against the rule contravention wilfully undertaken by Maradona, compounded by his playfully sacrilegious defence of the goal during a press conference as having been scored 'a little with the head of Maradona and a little with
the hand of God'.[52] The moral righteousness that came to bear on Maradona
implied he had gone beyond the pale of the still important Corinthian spirit
invested in football by its historical founders, the English. But, as noted by
a number of commentators, including Maradona's biographer Jimmy Burns,
obeying the rules of the game is not a universal ethic, and, indeed, successfully defying the rules can be regarded admirably within Argentina's football culture.[53] No Argentina player in 1966 tested the rulebook as brazenly as
did Maradona twenty years hence, but if we take the English players at their
word about the niggling antics in back-play then we might understand their

response, and especially that of Ramsey, to be indicative of the same type of cultural disparity between national football cultures to which Burns refers. Had an Argentine player artfully handled the ball into the goal, resulting in England being eliminated from the World Cup in 1966, he might not have been referred to as an animal, but there is a very good chance he would have been referred to as something much worse, and not just by the team manager.

Although the aftermath of the England/Argentina game caused alarm in diplomatic circles, it served to strengthen the bond within the England camp going into the semi-final stage of the World Cup competition. Ramsey had, yet again, shown a loyalty to the players that was appreciated and needed under the stressful circumstances of increasing public expectation, driven by heightened media attention. In the week prior to the match against Argentina, Ramsey had threatened to resign as manager if the FA pursued a request from FIFA for Nobby Stiles to be dropped from the England team following a reckless tackle that had injured French player Jacques Simon in the last match of the Group stage. The tackle had gone unpunished by the referee in the match, but FIFA followed up on the attention drawn to the incident by the French media. The English press exhibited annoyance with what was regarded as external interference, but in the view of some journalists Stiles's position had, nevertheless, become untenable because the great fuss about him risked seriously unsettling England's preparations if it was not resolved immediately.[54] But Ramsey ignored all of this, being interested only in Stiles's explanation of what had occurred. When Stiles told him the tackle was mistimed and that he had no intention of injuring Simon, Ramsey accepted this unquestioningly and stood his ground.[55] George Cohen notes that the unflinching support given to Stiles at this important moment validated all that Ramsey had impressed upon his players during training camp about loyalty.[56] It also provided the players with a most obvious example of their manager being quite prepared to defy the Football Association and thus tweak the nose of presumed authority.

From the outset, Ramsey's credibility as manager, from the perspective of players, was helped by his background as a leading professional player himself, both in club and international football. Ray Wilson regarded this to be an important advantage Ramsey held over the previous England manager Walter Winterbottom.[57] Winterbottom became the manager of England not only without the experience of having played football for his country, but also with a lack of professional playing experience compared to most England players under his leadership (his career at Manchester United in the 1930s had been cut short by a spinal problem).[58] Winterbottom was also regarded as a highly theoretical coach and his instructions to players were said to be peppered with terms, such as 'peripheral vision', which they did not comprehend. His 'impeccable accent' was also off-putting to the young men of working-class background under his charge.[59] Ramsey's accent, by comparison, was not challenging. Players seem to have recognised it as evidence of Ramsey wanting to better himself, but not of being a stranger in class terms. However, the degree of familiarity this allowed did not mean Ramsey was 'one of the lads' amongst his players. As indicated above, he worked hard at maintaining an appropriate distance and was adamant that the rules he set, especially during the pre-World Cup training period at Lilleshall in Shropshire, were abided.

The intensive training camp at Lilleshall, held between 6 and 18 June 1966, was a particularly important period of close contact between Ramsey and his players. A squad of twenty-eight players (reduced to twenty-seven due to Brian Labone of Everton withdrawing for personal reasons) from an initially bigger group of forty was selected for the Lilleshall camp. By the end of the camp, the final twenty-two player squad for the World Cup tournament in July had been determined by Ramsey. The knowledge that five players would be cut from those in training added a potentially ruthless competitive dimension to the player's relationships, but this was an atmosphere they were used to and accepted from professional club football. The camp has become renowned for the intensity of the physical training regime administered by Ramsey and steered by one of his two managing assistants, Leeds United training instructor, Les Cocker. One reason for such a focus on physical fitness would appear to be Ramsey's inclination that at some point a team advancing to the final stage games of the World Cup would have to deal with the demands of extra time. As much as the players might have disliked being pushed to their physical limits during June, come the afternoon of 30 July they realised the benefits.

However, there remains much predictable joking from players about the Lilleshall experience having been like boot camp, with related tales being rehearsed in their autobiographies. These anecdotes may be amusing, but they have possibly distracted players from providing a more serious discussion of the training regime at Lilleshall. One exception is the brief account provided by Bobby Charlton, in his post-World Cup biography *Forward for England*, of the daily agenda at Lilleshall.[60] As well discussing some of the arduous training methods, Charlton refers to instruction on bodily hygiene, foot care in particular. Players were taught by Ramsey's main assistant, Harold Sheperdson, how to cut their toenails in a way to avoid them becoming ingrown.[61] This was no small matter of importance to professional football players, but a type of instruction with which Charlton was unfamiliar and thus could regard as a particularly innovative aspect of Ramsey's approach to player management. Attention to bodily hygiene was part of the modernist personal development programmes developed in the earlier years of the twentieth century at such institutions as the Bauhaus in Germany.[62] Ramsey is unlikely to have had direct knowledge of this, but the bodily health ethos he instilled into his players matches to the modernism of his football strategy, which is the focus of discussion in the next chapter of this book.

In the concluding section of the present chapter, with a view to further drawing out the theme of masculinity, the relationship of Ramsey to his players is considered via a critical usage of a typology of football players constructed by the cultural studies academic Chas Critcher in the 1979 essay, 'Football Since the War'.[63] The typology is fourfold: 1) the *traditional/located* player who continues to draw upon the established value system of the 'respectable working class'; 2) the *transitional/mobile* player who benefits from the improving financial rewards of football to enjoy a middle-class lifestyle; 3) the *incorporated/embourgeoised* player who becomes a small scale entrepreneur; 4) the *superstar/dislocated* player who becomes a celebrity bigger than the sport of football.

The *traditional/located* player tends to be a player whose playing career was interrupted by the Second World War. The key characteristic is that the player saw himself as part of the local community, despite his relative fame, and as such, he stood as a representative of the working class. Such players were socially nurtured within an age of austerity to the extent that great economic reward from football was not part of their ambition. Their street dress was typical of the respectable working class and did not so much set them apart from other working men. Critcher names Stanley Matthews (1915–2000) as typical of the *traditional/located* player, but two other players he mentions in passing, Tom Finney (1922–2014) and Nat Lofthouse (1925–2011), are probably even better examples to fit with his model, as they played their entire careers for their hometown clubs, Preston and Bolton respectively. Although of this generation of England players, Ramsey is not well matched to this category. Indeed, Ramsey rather exposes the romance of the proposed type. He had no playing association with the major team closest to his locality, West Ham United, playing firstly with Portsmouth in the London War League and then professionally with Southampton from 1944–49. Ramsey's subsequent move to Tottenham Hotspur was a purely professional decision and gave no thought to the North London club's rivalry to West Ham. However, Ramsey's preference for Spurs over another offer from Sheffield Wednesday was partly based on his reluctance to leave the South for the North of England. Ramsey's particular middle-class aspirations make him hard to place within any category of footballer, yet his readiness to change clubs for a better arrangement was not atypical of his generation who tended to be 'representatives of the working class' by the circumstance of where they played rather than by conviction. A player in the 1966 England squad who matches the *traditional/located* player type, at least in terms of spending his entire playing career with his local club, is Jimmy Armfield (b. 1935) of Blackpool, who succeeded Ramsey as the mainstay right full back for England and was, in turn, succeeded by George Cohen (b. 1939).[64]

Critcher's second player type, *transitional/mobile*, is from the generation of players born before the Second World War, but whose playing careers commenced in the post-war period. These players came into professional football prior to the abolition of the maximum wage in 1961, but were young enough to benefit from its rewards. They are likely to have been signed by ambitious and leading clubs at a young age and hence drawn away from their local areas. An affiliation remains to the working class, but this player, according to Critcher, is more aspirational than the *traditional/located* player. Critcher draws upon Arthur Hopcraft's characterisation of Bobby Charlton (b. 1937) to identify him as a *transitional/mobile* player: 'he lives in a rich man's house in a rich man's neighbourhood. He is the classic working-class hero who has made it to glamour and Nob Hill.'[65] This is not to suggest that Charlton revelled in his fame. Even before 1966, Charlton offered cautious reflection upon the elevated status of the modern footballer:

> Over the course of the years I suppose millions of people pay a king's ransom to see me, and others like me, perform. We are big business, successful and often idolised to the point of embarrassment.[66]

The Charlton brothers' father Bob, like the majority of men from the Northumberland town Ashington, and surrounds, worked as a coalminer. They would normally have followed in his path, football being regarded for most men as little more than a recreational activity in their younger years. However, Bobby had been spotted as a star player within the local community from a very young age. His mother, Cisse Charlton (1912–96), played a key role in encouraging Bobby to focus on football as a professional career and oversaw his signing with Manchester United.[67] Mrs Charlton was from a family of successful football players, the most famous being Jackie Milburn (1924–88) of Newcastle United and England (a player of the *traditional/located* type), who, coincidentally, succeeded Alf Ramsey as manager of Ipswich Town. Bobby was deemed to have inherited the sporting pedigree and could thus declare, 'as far back as I can remember, there was never any doubt in my mind that one day I would become a professional footballer'.[68] This remark from his 1967 book *This Game of Soccer* gives some explanation as to why his reflections upon working-class life in the North East, in more recent autobiographical writing, give the impression of an outsider looking into a world through which they are merely passing, rather than being a part of. Sitting in the canteen near the pit face, young Bobby observed 'black-faced miners coming up out of the cage, singing and joking in the happiness that the shift is over'.[69] This was a kind of joviality he could understand, but it was not one he was destined to experience.

Brother Jack Charlton (b. 1935) considers himself fortunate to have avoided a working life down the pit. Having briefly trained as a miner at fifteen years of age, he decided to accept an apprenticeship with Leeds United, although initially regarding this more as a job than a step towards football stardom.[70] He knew from early on that he was not as talented at football as Bobby and claims, in totally good spirit, that his mother did not encourage him to think about football as a career.[71] Jack also recalls Alf Ramsey suggesting the limitations of his talent, by telling him that he was brought into the England team only because his physical robustness as a central defender complemented the more stylish and, at times, attack-oriented play of Bobby Moore.[72] Of all the England players from the 1996 squad, Jack Charlton assumed Ramsey did not like him and evinces an irritation with what he perceived as Ramsey's condescending manner. However, this interpretation comes in his autobiography *Jack Charlton*, published in 1996. The discussion of their interaction in the early autobiography *For Leeds and England*, published 1967, is somewhat different. In this book from the year immediately following the World Cup victory, Charlton refers respectfully to 'Mr. Ramsey' addressing the players during the warm-up for the Final and recalls that when he approached the stairs to go up to the Royal Box and receive his winner's medallion from the Queen, Ramsey clasped his hand and said, 'Great, big fella', which made Charlton 'glow with pride'.[73] Despite having a natural irreverent streak Charlton remained observant of what he considered to be appropriately respectful behaviour from professional football players. The criticism he makes of George Best in *Jack Charlton* in this regard is much more telling about his own identity than anything he says in reflection upon his relationship with Alf Ramsey.[74]

The oldest member of England's World Cup winning team was left full back Ray Wilson (b. 1934). His autobiography *My Life in Soccer* provides the most evocative account of a working-class background to be found in any of the books written by the cohort of players. In the opening chapter, titled the 'The Hard Way', Wilson waxes lyrical on the tough life of miners and railway yard workers from which he emerged: 'these men, fighters all, were the salt of Britain's earth … theirs was a romantic, devil-may-care existence of hard graft and fierce play'.[75] Of the two job options seemingly in wait, Wilson was set on the railway yard, as the thought of going down a mine shaft terrified him. Although sounding quite sanguine about the prospect of working life in the yards, a subsequent Sillitoe-esque reference to 'real Saturday night and Sunday morning people' suggests ambivalence, whereby the sense of attachment to place was matched by a desire for escape.[76] A combination of football and National Service ended Wilson's apprenticeship as a railwayman; his debut with the then declining Second Division club Huddersfield Town came in 1955, and in 1964, by that time an established England international, he moved to the First Division strength of Everton F.C. Wilson was one of the first players to be recognised by Ramsey, when incoming manager, as a likely candidate to maintain his position through to the 1966 World Cup finals. Wilson was not spared the manager's criticism at times, but referred to such episodes in the accepting terms of a generational masculinity, describing Ramsey as a man who would always look you in the eye and as a 'master of fairness and honesty at all times'.[77]

Wilson and ten others in the twenty-two player England squad for the 1966 World Cup finals were born prior to 1 October 1939, thus being of age for National Service. As well as Wilson and the Charlton brothers, Gordon Banks (b. 1937) and Roger Hunt (b. 1938) were players from this category to play in the Final. Alf Ramsey was conscripted into War Service unlike the peacetime obligation undertaken by this older cohort of his players. Nevertheless, the shared experience of involvement with the Armed Forces provided a certain link between Ramsey and his more senior players, in difference to those players born after the conscription date set by the National Service Act of 1948. Despite joking by players, Ramsey did not attempt to replicate military camp conditions at Lilleshall, yet, as indicated, he did invoke a disciplinary regime dependent on his authority going unquestioned. A stickler for time, Ramsey may well have benefited from the presence of the players with National Service backgrounds for obedience within the squad to such strictures as his 10.30 pm 'lights-out' rule. While Jack Charlton, for example, saw this demand as out of step with the laxer style of management of Don Revie at Leeds, he questioned neither Ramsey's authority nor rationale for the requirement.[78] Had the older players not been present then a greater off-field role within the squad would have been assumed by Bobby Moore (1941–93), who was inclined to buck Ramsey's authority on occasion. Rather, Bobby Charlton was regarded as the 'senior statesman' among the players and entrusted to deliver occasional entreaties from the squad to the often uncompromising manager.[79]

The term 'habitus', as used by the French sociologist Pierre Bourdieu, is useful to understanding the overall collective relationship.[80] The disciplinary regime of the armed services was a common life experience to both Ramsey and the older players in a way that hierarchical authority became habitually accepted. The younger players were from the first generation of British men in the post-war years not to undertake compulsory military service. In this important way, they did not have an aspect of habitus in common with Ramsey and the older players. Although outside the scope of the present study, the fading of this connection to players by the time of the 1974 World Cup campaign might partly explain Ramsey's declining fortunes as England manager.

The younger players within the 1966 England World Cup squad are placed by Critcher within the third category of his typology, the *incorporated/embourgeoised* player. Indeed, the youngest player in the squad, Alan Ball (1945–2007) is given by Critcher as the key example of this type of player.

Players within this category tend to have been born towards the latter years of the Second World War and to have become professionals just after the abolition of the maximum wage in 1961. Critcher is clearly critical of this category of player, who he identifies as conformist, business-minded and 'hardly laden with heroic qualities'. According to Critcher, this is an 'anonymous' type of player: 'a whole generation of such men played for England in the middle and late 1960s'.[81] This reference to the period when Ramsey was England manager is clearly intended as an indictment of him, his tactical approach to play and the type of football this cultivated, 'playing styles [became] more rigid: over-collective, remorseless and functional, the new demands were for the runner, the "worker" who could fit into a preconceived pattern'. The memory of Ball's tireless running in the World Cup Final makes him an obvious candidate to be located in this category. The second youngest player in the team, Martin Peters (b. 1943) might be similarly identified. Both players might be seen as suited to and styled by the so-called Ramsey method and playing 'system', which critics contend to have been contrary to the aesthetics of football and responsible for a collective decline in the playing style of British football immediately after the 1966 World Cup.

For the *incorporated/embourgeoised* player, Critcher suggests a homological fit between his style of play, purely functional and instrumental, and his off-field attitude and lifestyle. This, so-regarded, 'non-heroic' player is compliant with the dictates of football managers and clubs and focussed on his career as a profession rather than an as artistic calling. The *incorporated/embourgeoised* player is offered as a historical break from the prior player categories with the latter word of its dualism suggesting a complete conversion to middle-class orientation and severance from football's old working-class attachments. Problematically, this player-type appears to be sketched in dialogical opposition to the fourth category within Critcher's model, the *superstar/dislocated* player. This player supposedly emerges in rebellious response to the blandness of the *incorporated/embourgeoised* player, both in football playing style and in off-field appearance and conduct. George Best (1946–2005) is given by Critcher as the rather obvious example of the *superstar/dislocated* player and is suggested as a prototype for subsequent highly talented but rebellious, players who emerged in late 1960s' and early 1970s' English football, including Rodney Marsh, Charlie George and Alan Hudson.[82] Critcher suggests that supremely talented and highly individualistic players could not be constrained or systematised by Ramsey-type playing methods and became 'dislocated' from the sport – in the case of Best, dropping out of top flight football in what should have been his prime years.

However, a problem with Critcher's *superstar/dislocated* player type is that it accounts for players who are by far the exception rather than the rule. Even the 'maverick' players who followed Best, despite the wayward lifestyles of some, did not match his superstar status. This undoubtedly had something to do with Best being the first of a rare kind and with his football career neatly coinciding with the emergence of the so-called 'Swinging Sixties'. Martin Peters' take on George Best is interesting in this regard:

> In a way, he was a flag-bearer for youth, along with the Beatles, the Rolling Stones, Twiggy and Mary Quant, and he seemed to take that duty almost as seriously as his football commitments. This was the era of *Ready, Steady, Go*, miniskirts and Carnaby Street. The maximum wage for footballers had been lifted in 1961 and George was one of a growing number of famous young players who had money to spend and wanted to enjoy life. I was quite content to view the 'swinging sixties' from the back seats but George wanted to be in the thick of it.[83]

While going on to mention that some players, including Moore and Hurst, did enjoy the London nightlife of the time, Peters' mention of Best seems almost deliberately intended to disassociate the England World Cup players from the popular image of the 'Swinging Sixties' and its iconography. Indeed, he positions Best within that iconography in a way to suggest a dereliction of responsibility to football in favour of pure celebrity. This implied discrediting and Peters' insistence, within his autobiography, that he, unlike Best, was always focussed on football rather than the groovy youth scene of the 1960s may appear to validate Critcher's *incorporated/embourgeoised* player type and Peters' compliance with that category. However, while distancing himself from an involvement with youth culture in a way that would have adversely affected his football career, Peters, nevertheless, indicates an interest in the goings-on of the time, especially in regard to music. When left out of the West Ham 1964 FA Cup Final team by Ron Greenwood, Peters consoled himself against the ensuing disappointment across the summer by listening to the music played on Radio Caroline, the emergent offshore pirate radio operation.[84] Although hardly a radical activity, this turning-on and tuning-in exposed Peters to music coming from outside the cultural mainstream. As well as playing records from the Hit Parade, Radio Caroline DJs gave airtime to alternative and avant-garde offerings. The point of interest here is to advise against over-reading or assuming characteristics from the designation of Critcher's typology. While Peters' confession to hard work and ambition for his career may match to the traits identified by Critcher, this need not be taken to mean that he was totally conservative and unaware of ideas coming from 1960s' music that were socially challenging. That he shows no indication of having been connected to any youth subcultures, but mainly listened to music on the radio from home, makes him rather similar to a good number of other young people at the time.[85]

From the time Martin Peters joined West Ham as an amateur in May 1959 as a 15-year-old, he had become clear about football as a career choice. In the first of his autobiographies, written some ten years later, he notes how he had

7 A stylish Bobby Moore and Martin Peters take a stroll outside
England's Hendon Hall headquarters on the morning of the quarter-final
against Argentina.

heeded the warnings of senior footballers about the shortness of a career in
the sport and impending poverty if earnings were not treated frugally. A few
years hence he became engaged to his future wife Kathy and banked as much
of his earnings as possible and generally avoided 'conspicuous consumption'.[86]
He also secured agreement from the West Ham club to be guarantor for the
home he planned to purchase to coincide with his marriage in November 1964.
Having grown up in the early 1950s in Dagenham, by the time it had become an
industrialised suburb rather than the semi-rural village of Alf Ramsey's youth,
Peters bought a detached house further along the District Line in Hornchurch,
located in what he modestly describes as a 'pleasant, unpretentious Essex
Estate'.[87] This careful career-mindedness and matching life strategy evince the
conformism that Critcher sees typical of the *incorporated/embourgeoised* player.
But the only alternative offered by Critcher appears to be an unplanned career
and reckless lifestyle of excess that has become associated with his example of
the *superstar/dislocated* player, George Best.

Typologies in the social sciences are good to think with but usually end up
raising objections from those who put them to use. Such is the case here with
Critcher's post-war football player typology. The first two categories proposed

by Critcher are particularly useful when giving consideration to players whose careers were interrupted by the Second World War and to those born in the late 1930s whose careers commenced in the 1950s. Ramsey's is an interesting profile in relation to the model because his playing career trajectory is somewhere between the fixed and mobile points defined by Critcher. He does not need to be fitted in tightly; the model helps us make sense of his background and development as a player. The problem with the typology arises with the third category, which goes beyond the ambition of providing an analytical framework and into the tendentious territory of Critcher giving an explanation for the demise of heroic football in England. Every heroic tale needs a villain and a problem here is that Critcher fails to name the villain of the piece, Alfred Ernest Ramsey. The proto-type *incorporated/embourgeoised* player, Alan Ball, as identified by Critcher is clearly a product of Ramsey's making. But to spell this out would have exposed the sleight-of-hand at work in the construction of the latter stages of the typology. Ball needs to be held wholly responsible for his non-heroism for the heroic figure of post-war football, George Best, to be able to claim his accolade in contrast.

However, the heroic ideal proposed for Best by Critcher is of doubtful relevance in relation to football as a cultural domain. In heralding the 'death of the artist as hero' the anthropologist Bernard Smith highlighted three historical episodes in which artists rebelled against the social forces that imperilled their aesthetic identity.[88] The final such episode occurred with opposition to the dehumanising impact of the industrial revolution. Although George Best's football playing artistry might be acclaimed, he was no Blake or Wordsworth in relative heroic terms, nor could he have been. By the time football arrived as an organised sport, towards the end of the 1800s, it was inevitably marked by modernity and the vestiges of industrial organisation. True enough watching football provided relief for working-class men from the drudgery of factory life, but the romantic envelope should not be pushed too far. Ramsey realised this and challenged the mythology of the star player as artist. Accordingly, it became clear to the players he assembled to partake in the 1966 World Cup for England that while the media might continue to peddle 'personalities' he would not accept individuals being 'cast in the heroic mould of former days'.[89] For Ramsey, the team was an indivisible unit and aesthetic appreciation of football could not be made apart from the collective context. It is intriguing that Marxist-inspired scholars apply a bourgeois notion of individual artistry as the basis for an alternative perspective. Ramsey's understanding of heroism in football was distinctly modern. He would have smiled wryly, at least on the inside, had he heard reference to the young players he promoted as being non-heroic. Such a view for Ramsey would have been as redundant as the ways of the FA he so earnestly sought to bypass.

Notes

1 The photo, taken by Gerry Cranham, appears in Robinson et al., *1966 Uncovered*, p. 232. This volume contains a comprehensive detailing of photography during the World Cup tournament. See Robinson, '1966 Photography'.

2 Butler, *The Official History of the Football Association*, p. 155.

3 Goldblatt, *The Ball is Round*, p. 452.

4 McKinstry, *Sir Alf*, p. 292.

5 Rogan, *The Football Mangers*, p. 60.

6 Sargeant, *British Cinema*, p. 247, Naughton, *Alfie*. The motion picture *Alfie* was produced by Lewis Gilbert, released by Paramount Pictures, 1966. The DVD was released by Paramount Home Entertainment, 2002.

7 McKinstry, *Sir Alf*, p. 20–4.

8 Williams, *Keywords*, pp. 160–1. Prior to moving into football management, towards the end of his playing career in 1953, Ramsey became a Freemason. See Kidd and Scanlan, 'The Beautiful Game'. Becoming a Freemason was not an unusual commitment for a leading football player to make. Stanley Matthews and Nat Lofthouse were among those to do so before Ramsey and his successors as England manager, Joe Mercer and Don Revie did the same. Indeed, it seemed almost expected of football players seeking 'self-improvement' to join a Lodge.

9 Bowler, *Winning Isn't Everything*, p. 224; Gregory, *Who Could Ask For More?*, p. 35.

10 Williams, *The Long Revolution*, pp. 148–9; Bowler, *Winning Isn't Everything*, p. 154.

11 Ramsey, *Talking Football*, p. 36.

12 McKinstry, *Sir Alf*, pp. 199–200.

13 *Ibid.*, pp. 472–3.

14 Morse, *Sir Walter Winterbottom*, pp. 56–9.

15 McKinstry, *Sir Alf*, pp. 11 & 29.

16 *Ibid.*, pp. xxiv–xxv.

17 Steedman, *Landscape for a Good Woman*, p. 11.

18 Rutherford, *Forever England*, pp. 11–38.

19 McKinstry, *Sir Alf*, p. 29.

20 *Ibid.*, p. 197.

21 *Ibid.*, pp. 199–200.

22 *Ibid.*, p. 201.

23 Sennett, *The Fall of Public Man*.

24 Wilson, *Brian Clough*; Clough, *The Autobiography*.

25 McKinstry, *Sir Alf*, p. 444.

26 McFarland, *Roy Mac*, p. 130.

27 McKinstry, *Sir Alf*, p. 295.

28 Butler and Greenwood, *Soccer Choice*, p. 39.

29 Weight, *Patriots*, p. 459.

30 Bowler, *Winning Isn't Everything*, p. 148.

31 *Ibid.*, p. 152.

32 McKinstry, *Sir Alf*, p. 218.

33 Charlton, *Forward for England*, pp. 116–17.

34 Bowler, *Winning Isn't Everything*, p. 162.

35 *Ibid.*, p. 163.

36 Powell, *Bobby Moore*, p. 105.

37 Charlton, *Forward for England*, p. 161.

38 Bowler, *Winning Isn't Everything*, p. 220. A newspaper report from the following Monday has Ramsey simply saying, 'All right. You let it slip. Now start again.' See 'Ramsey proved right in World Cup: England surmount test of morale', *The Times*, 1 August, 1966, p. 5.

39 Charlton, *For Leeds and England*, p. 131.

40 Stiles, *Soccer My Battlefield*, p. 86.

41 McKinstry, *Sir Alf*, p. 399.

42 For example see Ball, *Playing Extra Time*, p. 49 and Cohen, *My Autobiography*, pp. 176–7; Against the England players' emphasis on the foul play of Argentina, some critics have pointed to the free kick count of 33 to Argentina, 19 to England. However, as Jonathan Wilson points out, this count is not a faithful indicator of the types of indiscretions that occurred in the game. Wilson, *The Anatomy of England*, p. 134, claims that 'certainly the bulk of the serious fouls were committed by Argentina', while offences by England players involved more minor pushing and blocking. To Wilson's observation it is pertinent to add that a number, perhaps majority, of the incidents remarked upon by England players occurred in the back-play, away from the referee's scrutiny and, thus, did not result in his intervention.

43 McKinstry, *Sir Alf*, pp. 311–12.

44 Wolstenholme, *They Think It's All Over...*, p. 102.

45 McIlvanney, 'England v. Argentina', p. 117.

46 For example, see Ball, *Playing Extra Time*, p. 50; Charlton, *My England Years*, p. 254; Hurst, *1966 And All That*, p. 101.

47 Greaves, *Greavsie*, p. 244.

48 Cohen, *My Autobiography*, p. 179.

49 For a related discussion of the football adage 'You're not fit to wear the shirt' see Hughson and Moore, 'Hand of God'.

50 Rogan, *The Football Managers*, p. 63.

51 Hughson and Moore, 'Hand of God', p. 220.

52 *Ibid.*, p. 224.

53 Burns, *The Hand of God*, p. 162.

54 See, for example, Brian James, 'FIFA warning hits England', *Daily Mail*, Friday 22 July, 1966, p. 14.

55 Stiles, *After the Ball*, pp. 170–1.

56 Cohen, *My Autobiography*, p. 170.

57 Bowler, *Winning Isn't Everything*, p. 151.

58 For a description of Winterbottom's chronic back problem, see Morse, *Sir Walter Winterbottom*, p. 74.

59 Pawson, *The Football Managers*, pp. 45–6.

60 Charlton, *Forward for England*, pp. 121–4.

61 Like many player autobiographies, Harold Shepherdson's *The Magic Sponge* is anecdote-laden without much on the business of football. As such, it does not pro-

vide a particularly useful source for further information on the training and related activities during the Lilleshall camp.

62 Wilk, 'The Healthy Body Culture'.

63 Critcher, 'Football Since the War'. An updating of this typology to account for more recent player types is sensibly proposed by Horne et al. in *Understanding Sport*, p. 162. For consideration of the England players from the 1966 World Cup, the original Critcher model is deemed most relevant to the exercise.

64 Armfield, *Right Back to the Beginning*.

65 Critcher, 'Football Since the War', p. 165; Hopcraft, *The Football Man*, p. 86.

66 Charlton, *My Soccer Life*, p. 20.

67 Charlton, *Cissie*, pp. 97–8; Charlton, *Forward for England*, p. 14.

68 Charlton, *This Game of Soccer*, p. 1.

69 Charlton, *My Manchester United Years*, p. 14.

70 Charlton, *Jack Charlton*, pp. 24–5.

71 *Ibid.*, p. 18.

72 *Ibid.*, pp. 73–4.

73 *Ibid.*, p. 134.

74 *Ibid.*, p. 69.

75 Wilson, *My Life in Soccer*, pp. 14–16.

76 For a discussion of the idea of escape in the fictional writing of Alan Sillitoe, see Hughson, 'Why He Must Run'.

77 Wilson, *My Life in Soccer*, pp. 114 & 97.

78 Charlton, *Jack Charlton*, p. 74.

79 Ball, *Playing Extra Time*, p. 67.

80 Inglis and Hughson, *Confronting Culture*, pp. 166–8.

81 Critcher, 'Football Since the War', p. 164. Critcher might have made more of Alan Ball's self-confessed support for the Conservative Party. In the 1978 autobiography, *It's all about a Ball*, pp. 143–4, Ball declares himself a Tory voter and states the view, 'once you enter a certain wage-earning bracket you are mad to vote Socialist'. Although, via an anecdote about his maternal grandfather, he expresses pride in his working-class background. A similar, and more detailed, expression of political view is offered by Nobby Stiles in *Soccer My Battlefield*, pp. 154–6. Despite coming from a Labour Party supporting background, Stiles states his politics changed upon becoming a professional footballer, from 'red' to 'blue'. He offers his opinion on a number of issues including foreign aid and recent immigrants to Britain receiving state benefits. He claims to be a representative voice of the 'working man', from whom he is separated merely because his ability to play football has placed him in a high income earning bracket. But this gives him an opportunity, denied to others, to publicly voice commonly held opinions of 'the ordinary bloke'. He also claims, 'most of the lads at Old Trafford have Tory leanings'. Although it is just one statement, it does prompt thought about how widespread Tory sympathies might have been amongst footballers at the time. If such sympathies were widely held this would challenge any suggestion arising from Critcher's model that conservative political views were especially relevant to the *incorporated/embourgeoised* player and not those in other categories of his typology.

82 *Ibid.*, p. 167.
83 Peters, *The Ghost of '66*, p. 137.
84 *Ibid.*, p. 41.
85 Hughson, 'Ten Years Ahead of His Time'.
86 Peters, *Goals From Nowhere*, pp. 71–2.
87 Peters, *The Ghost of '66*, p. 42.
88 Smith, 'The Death of the Artist as Hero'. For a discussion of Smith's essay in relation to sport, see Hughson, *The Making of Sporting Cultures*, p. 87–8.
89 Young, *A History of British Football*, p. 203.

5

Wingless wondering: modernism and the Ramsey 'system'

Soccer managers of today who think they are misunderstood by the media should refer back to the kind of press Ramsey used to get and think themselves blessed. The mutual antipathy was inevitable when you consider Alf's dislike of the spotlight and our inability to understand what he was doing. (Michael Parkinson)

On 23 October 1963 the Football Association celebrated its one hundredth anniversary year by staging a match at Wembley Stadium between England and a FIFA Rest of the World Select team. The occasion fell two days prior to the first anniversary of Alf Ramsey's appointment as England manager and, although the match had the status of a 'friendly', Ramsey greeted its significance as both a matter of honour and as an opportunity for his team to test its mettle against leading players from the international arena. Ten years earlier, in October 1953, Ramsey played in a corresponding game to mark the FA's ninetieth anniversary and scored the final goal from the penalty spot to earn England a 4–4 draw in an exciting contest. The 1963 match broke British football attendance records, a 100,000 plus crowd at Wembley amassing receipts of £90,000. Less high scoring than the match a decade earlier, the encounter was nevertheless engaging, its three goals occurring in the final twenty minutes of play, England prevailing 3–1. Despite England's victory, the spectacle of the match was largely attributed to the visitors, BBC commentator Kenneth Wolstenholme declaring, 'This Rest of the World side is like a theatrical exhibition of the arts and crafts of football'.[1] In contrast, the England team under Ramsey was rarely complimented for its artistry. At best it was regarded as industrious and, as such, inferior in playing style to more creative opponents from the Continent and South America. This chapter proposes a broadened understanding of the aesthetics of football, one which encourages comparison between Ramsey's football strategy and movements relevant to British modernism in the 1960s. Doing so challenges simplistic depictions of Ramsey's 1966 World Cup winning team as unattractive to watch and affords a reassessment of Ramsey as an artistic innovator within the history of football tactics.

Although generally regarded at the time as non-artistic, Alf Ramsey's tactical planning for the 1966 World Cup was not adjudged outmoded. Indeed, it was deemed analogous to Harold Wilson's plans for advancing the state of Britain. England's match against the Rest of World occurred in the same month – October 1963 – that Wilson first addressed the Labour Party Conference in Scarborough. His speech promoted the prospect of 'scientific revolution' as the means of 'invigorating the future'.[2] Wilson envisioned Britain in the latter part of the twentieth century 'being forged in the white heat of this revolution' and thus demanded a better nurturing and use of the country's scientific resources.[3] In this pronouncement he supported the view of the writer C.P. Snow who, in 1963, reiterated his earlier stated claim that Britain was divided between 'two cultures', 'the scientists' and 'literary intellectuals', in which the latter, who tend to be backward-looking, have traditionally exerted undue influence over official policy-making.[4] For Snow, it was those associated with the sciences, not the humanities, who have 'the future in their bones'.[5]

Some commentators have claimed Alf Ramsey's approach to football tactics was well matched to the emphasis on science and industry proposed by Wilson via Snow's ideas. According to biographer Dave Bowler, Ramsey's 'England [team] were modern, noisy and effective, the perfect machine for the age of the "white heat of technology"'.[6] Cultural studies academics John Clarke and Chas Critcher also explicitly identify Ramsey in terms of the misquoted phrase from Wilson and add:

> Ramsey himself personified the spirit of scientific management, rational, ordered and committed to making technological innovations in the footballing labour process. He saw the manager's task as the co-ordination of a team – a collective worker – which would be more than the sum of its individual parts ... His workers conscientiously subordinated themselves to the principles of teamwork, and reaped the benefits.[7]

Associated reference to Ramsey taking football into the 'space age' is more inclined to be sardonic than meant in praise. For example, Roger Hutchinson used the term 'Ramsey's Robots' to suggest the machine-like tedium which he observed in England's play during the 1966 World Cup, at least up until the semi-final match against Portugal.[8] This view connects with a familiar criticism made of Ramsey, which has been stretched to the point of blaming him for the decline rather than ascent of English football. The line between international and club football tends to become blurred in such criticism. In such cases, the blame is not so much placed on Ramsey, but on the trend his success in 1966 gave rise to. An example is Jimmy Greaves's claim that the tactics and team formation deployed by Ramsey in 1966 was 'aped' by managers and coaches in the English First Division in the latter part of the 1960s and into the 1970s. This resulted in 'dour battles conducted in midfield' and 'far fewer goals' being scored in matches.[9] In criticism focussed on the national team, blame is placed squarely on Ramsey's shoulders. A most strident example of such criticism was delivered by the author David Downing, who referred to England's 1966 World Cup success as 'the fatal victory'. From Downing's view, Ramsey's approach is regarded not so much as 'scientific management', and his team not even a well-oiled machine, but a re-jigging of tough masculinity formed into a unit and merely speeded up to suit the modern football occasion.[10]

Positions viewing Ramsey's approach to football management as being somewhere between scientific and industrous share a converse outlook of his approach as non-artistic. Some criticisms focussing specifically on this theme become preoccupied with Ramsey's presumed preference for hardworking, tireless players over those more naturally gifted with soccer's silky skills, but of a temperament not given to following tactical instruction or pitching in when the going gets tough. Rob Steen's book *The Mavericks* is dedicated to this topic. Steen makes the case for seven English football players – Rodney Marsh, Peter Osgood, Frank Worthington, Stan Bowles, Tony Currie, Charlie George and Alan Hudson – not receiving the national honours their ability as football-ers warranted. These stylish players, with wayward reputations, who came to prominence as professionals after the 1966 World Cup, were largely ignored by Ramsey during his reign as England manager and by those who followed him in the post during the remainder of the 1970s. Steen nominates the World Cup victory in 1966 as 'the worst thing ever to happen to our national game', because it set in train the trend to overlook 'maverick' players for the England team.[11] The watershed moment came when Ramsey overlooked Jimmy Greaves for re-inclusion in the team for the Final, despite Greaves being declared fit to play following his two-game layoff after the leg injury sustained in the last Group stage game against France. Ramsey's decision was vindicated to the extent that England won the match and, therefore, the World Cup, but for Steen the negative longer term impact was more significant. Leaving the proto-maverick Greaves out of the Final commenced a pattern of player selection for the England team that was pursued into the next decade.[12]

From Steen's perspective, the 'mavericks' are part 'performance artist', part showbiz personality, and in keeping with both characterisations, are individ-ualists disinclined to accept authority and related instruction about football play.[13] Much has been made of Ramsey's shunning of these players due to their extroversion, especially in Rodney Marsh's well-publicised dressing-room humour.[14] However, Ramsey was also known, over the years, to be fond of practical jokers in his teams, such as Ted Phillips at Ipswich Town, so his sup-posed antagonism to extroverted players might be overstated.[15] His refusal to countenance challenge to his authority is another matter, and the more likely basis for his reticence to select players of presumed artistic genius who refuse discipline. The youngest of Steen's named 'mavericks', Alan Hudson, titled his autobiography *The Working Man's Ballet*, suggesting he regards a professional football game as an artistic event performed before an appreciative audience.[16] To all reports, Ramsey was a player's player not known for reflecting upon the fan perspective, but this, of course, does not mean he did not possess an appreciative eye for the game. However, from a man bothered enough to declare 'I do not like "arty" shirts' we might not expect Ramsey to wax lyrical about the art of football. The closest reference of this kind came in response to his experience of playing against Italy in Florence in the May of 1952, from which Ramsey was enthused to describe his opponents as 'high-speed artistes'.[17] This comment prompts questioning of Ramsey's supposed lack of regard for the ability of foreign players and his indifference to visually attractive football.

In his book, *Inverting the Pyramid: The History of Football Tactics*, Jonathan Wilson, the journalist, concludes, 'Ramsey, certainly, was not a man blinded by beauty'.[18] Wilson's account of Ramsey's coaching career, focussed mainly on the 1966 World Cup success, observes him as a coldblooded rationalist, concerned with winning football matches and possessed with an analytical capacity geared to devising match plans purely intended to service such outcomes. Wilson works explicitly with a 'two cultures' divide, placing Ramsey unequivocally on the side of science, in opposition to art in the presumed dichotomy.[19] This claim has a particularly strong resonance given the globally known sobriquet of football as 'the beautiful game'. To be characterised as a football strategist more concerned with nullifying than creating beauty in the course of a football match is to be cast *culturally* adrift from the sport and, therefore, to be positioned at remove from those football managers deemed connoisseurs of the game. However, any suggestion of Ramsey being preoccupied with defence needs to be considered within the context of his overall career in football. When Ron Greenwood named his all-time great British team in 1979, as previously indicated, he placed Ramsey at right full back, indicating that the selection was based on Ramsey's innovation in attack from that position. In particular he praised the accuracy of Ramsey's 'centres' to players in the midfield or forward line.[20]

In *Talking Football* Ramsey emphasised 'accuracy' as the key to Tottenham Hotspur's playing style, according to which 'there is no such thing as an attacker, the whole … team are attackers'.[21] An advocate of the tactical approach of his Tottenham manager Arthur Rowe, Ramsey suggests that a focus on precision and efficiency need not equate to a preoccupation with results. He quotes Rowe as saying, 'Put good football before results. Do this and the results will come.'[22] Ramsey goes on to note that the so-called 'push-and-run' style developed at Spurs under Rowe, based on the idea of 'playing the way you are facing', whereby players run on to passes rather than wait for delivery of the ball to their feet, might not appeal to 'purists', but only because this approach challenges the traditional style of English football.[23] At the time that Ramsey was writing *Talking Football*, different aspects of modern design were featured within the Festival of Britain exhibits on London's South Bank and also in the related publicity. This included the well-known advertising poster for the event designed by Abram Games. Here it is relevant to recall Games's design credo, 'maximum effort, minimum means', in relation to Arthur Rowe's mantra for football as recited by Ramsey, 'make it quick, make it easy'.[24] Easy should not be confused here with easiness; Rowe's message was essentially similar to that of Games – like the designer, the football player should concentrate efforts on achieving outcomes by the simplest means. Both statements sound agreement with the better-known minimalist maxim, associated with the architect Ludwig Mies van der Rohe, 'less is more'.[25]

Alf Ramsey's time as a senior player at Tottenham Hotspur in the early 1950s seems to have provided him with something of an apprenticeship for his post-playing role of manager at Ipswich Town Football Club. During this period he was almost obsessively involved in the discussion of team tactics with Rowe; the move into management, therefore, represented more of a transition than a career change.[26] However, taking on a struggling team in Division Three (South) did not well place Ramsey to implement the type of tactical plan suited to a team of Tottenham's calibre. Nevertheless, he continued to think innovatively and came up with the masterstroke of playing journeyman Jimmy Leadbetter in an unfamiliar position of outside-left and in an unconventional manner by placing him in a deep ball-supplying position rather than up close to the forward line. The inability of opposing teams to close down Leadbetter was largely behind the extraordinary success Ramsey had at Ipswich, culminating in the winning of the First Division championship in the 1961–62 season.[27] The Ipswich victory in that season remains one of the greatest upsets in the history of English football. By then, Ramsey had five seasons at Ipswich to refine his strategic system. Ipswich came into the First Division with Tottenham Hotspur as reigning champions and also holders of the FA Cup (the first team to win 'The Double' in the twentieth century). A highlight of Ipswich's winning season was home (3–2) and away (1–3) victories against Spurs; then managed by Ramsey's former teammate Bill Nicholson. Nicholson was too shrewd a tactician himself not to adjust his team strategy for a third encounter. The 5–1 victory by Spurs over Ipswich in the 1962–63 opening Charity Shield match signalled a loss of potency in the Leadbetter deep-lying ploy.[28] Ramsey remained with Ipswich in a formal capacity for the season, but having accepted the appointment as England manager in October 1962 did not significantly invest time (or resources) into revising a team plan.[29] Regarded from the present, Ramsey's strategy at Ipswich Town appears rather elementary, and had other managers at the time had the advantage of video footage of matches it may well have been countered, at least by the time Ipswich moved into the First Division. Yet the proof of result indicates that the method was subtle enough to remain effective against the best players in England, at least for one season. Whether or not Ramsey would have eventually developed a successful plan B at Ipswich cannot be known, but, more important to the concerns of this book, elements of the strategy developed over the years at Portman Road were certainly kept in mind by Ramsey as he set about preparing his tactical blueprint for the England job.

As an international player Ramsey represented England during the era of the great wingers, Stanley Matthews and Tom Finney. Ramsey first played with Matthews in a Football League select team against the Irish League in 1948. Ramsey's performance in this match is mostly remembered for the presumptuousness of a positional instruction he gave as a rookie international to the star player Matthews – an incident Ramsey was bold enough to defend in *Talking Football*. Rather than suggesting arrogance, closely read, the account indicates that Matthews' intuitive positional play gave Ramsey the confidence to assume an attacking full back role from the time of this early representative match. Ramsey's further comment that Matthews 'played football as ... it should be played between a winger and full back' gave no indication of the so-called 'wingless wonders' formation he would come to favour for the World Cup winning team in 1966.[30] Indeed, care must be taken when portraying Ramsey as a tactical innovator not to overstate his removal of conventional wingers from the team as a prerequisite to his plan. The trialling of different wingers through the long lead-up period to the World Cup finals, as well as the use of wingers in the three first round matches in 1966, is ample evidence against such exaggeration. Journalist Frank McGhee contended, reasonably enough, had Ramsey had wingers of the calibre of Matthews and Finney at his disposal he would not have omitted them from the England team, but would have adjusted the team formation to accommodate them. 'For him [Ramsey] the system always has to be designed to fit the players, not vice-versa'.[31]

McGhee's view thus challenges depictions of Ramsey settling on a certain playing system and then selecting players according to their ability to slot into the system. Players' accounts have, perhaps, inadvertently led to this image of Ramsey. For example, according to Bobby Moore:

> Sir Alf's thinking was slowly evolving until, at last, he found what he wanted. From 1963 until 1965 ... he was probing, adjusting, experimenting. Then at last, he came upon the shape of things that might win England the World Cup and, as it happened, it came up trumps for him. It was the 4–3–3 system.[32]

Ramsey's own behaviour lent to this view of him as an alchemist in search of a secret formula. In an interview following the 2–0 victory against Spain in December 1965, when the wingless formation was first deployed in an international match, Ramsey spoke of 'the precious gem' taking shape and gestured as though his hands were around an imaginary football.[33] Ramsey first trialled the wingless formation in training against the England Youth team and then brought it forward for the 'friendly' match in Madrid, following three unconvincing performances by the England team in the latter months of 1965, including a 2–3 loss to Austria at Wembley in October. In more recent interviews, England players still speak of the confusion their tactics caused for Spain's defence, much in the way that the England team's inability to cope with the attacking play of Hungary at Wembley in November 1953 has been recounted in various reports.[34] It may also be the first match in reference to which players explicitly mention the Ramsey 'system'. For example, according to Ray Wilson, 'their full-backs didn't know who to mark, they were standing there, ball watching, and we ripped them to bits ... we absolutely toyed with them because of the system'.[35]

Ramsey's 4–3–3 formation in the game against Spain was made up of eight of the future World Cup winning team, as well as George Eastham and Joe Baker of Arsenal in the front three. When Baker was injured around the 25-minute mark he was replaced by Norman Hunter, who dropped back into a deep midfield position allowing Alan Ball and Bobby Charlton to become even more active in attack. Dave Bowler suggests it was at this point that Ramsey recognised the 'system' that could fulfil his prediction of winning the World Cup, although the playing personnel still required clarification. In particular, George Eastham did not impress in the 4–3–3 formation.[36] Although included in the twenty-two man World Cup squad, Eastham did not receive game time during the finals, playing his last game (and scoring) for England in a 2–0 'friendly' victory against Denmark (3 July 1966) eight days ahead of the World Cup's commencement. This game was part of a brief four-match tour to Scandinavia and Poland, involving the full squad, following the conclusion of the intense training period at Lilleshall in early to mid-June 1966. Ramsey was criticised in the press for taking the players on tour so close to the main tournament, but as well as a final opportunity for real match practice it gave him a chance to fully scrutinise the now whittled down squad from which his teams had to be chosen. An opportunity to play was afforded to all squad members and this facilitated experimentation with the use of wingers in particular. A 4–3–3 formation was used in each of the games (in order, against Finland, Norway, Denmark and Poland) but in varying patterns in regard to the wingers' role. In the one game in which two wingers were used, against Norway, Terry Paine of Southampton assumed the Jimmy Leadbetter deep-lying ball-supplier role, but he did not perform effectively in this capacity. The other two wingers in the squad, Ian Callaghan of Liverpool and John Connelly of Manchester United, took more forward playing roles on the tour, but neither performed to Ramsey's satisfaction. The deficiencies in performance by the wingers emboldened Ramsey to move to the fully wingless 4–3–3 formation for the final game of the tour against Poland in Katowice. The major personnel shift to this formation saw Martin Peters take his place in the team. Given his youth and inexperience as an England player (two earlier caps, the second gained against Finland on the present tour) relative to others, football journalists understandably regarded Peters as a fringe member of the World Cup squad.[37] That Ramsey assigned him the number 16 shirt within the squad of twenty-two further justified this expectation.

Yet Ramsey's teasing announcement at the press conference prior to the Katowice game, deliberately pausing before naming Peters as the eleventh man, suggests the West Ham utility player may have played a more prominent role in his thoughts up to that point than anyone had realised. In the years following the World Cup success, Peters claimed to have heard on the grapevine that Ramsey had once said he was not his 'cup of tea as a footballer'.[38] The assumption that Ramsey did say this prompts speculation as to when he changed his mind about Peters. Peters quickly earned a reputation for versatility at West Ham, playing in every position for the club, including goalkeeper.[39] This distinctive capacity was the basis for Ramsey's much better-known declaration in 1968 about Peters being 'ten years ahead of his time'.[40] It is likely that the closer Ramsey moved towards a wingless attacking system, the more Peters came into his view. Key to this was a shift to what might be referred to in present-day terminology as multitasking. According to the football historian Percy Young:

> A review of the conditions then obtaining led Ramsey, in the days of teambuilding, towards a new form of stylistic flexibility. In short, the player required a new kind of versatility, to be able to adapt himself to circumstance and occasion. In the end, after trying more than fifty players, Ramsey arrived at a team which understood the basic principles on which he worked.[41]

Going into the World Cup finals in July, player understanding of the 'uncompromising functionalism' of Ramsey's system applied especially to those occupying the right and left midfield positions, as these positions demanded the most all-purpose performances within the team.[42] From the quarter-final to the Final winning team these positions were filled by Martin Peters and Alan Ball, the youngest members of the squad and the only two to have made their senior professional debuts in the post maximum wage era. As discussed in the previous chapter, they were, for these and other reasons, players of a new generation in English football. Although this need not necessarily have predisposed them to Ramsey's methods, they, along with Nobby Stiles, seemed especially attuned to what Ramsey asked of them in their designated roles.[43]

Emerging players were perhaps always going to figure in Ramsey's team, the new 'system' demanding such inclusions. The need for freshness in receptive capacity, as well as youth, made it unlikely that a full quota of players from the period of Walter Winterbottom's management would make up Ramsey's preferred England team in the 1966 World Cup. Jack Charlton, a relatively senior player within the squad, may be considered in this regard. Charlton was one month shy of his thirtieth birthday when Ramsey awarded him his first England cap for a home international match against Scotland in April 1965. As previously mentioned, according to Charlton's own account, Ramsey chose him not in general admiration of his defensive skills, but because he believed Charlton had a way of playing that would well complement that of the more stylish Bobby Moore.[44] Again, in this case, Ramsey's observation was sharp and bore fruit. Had Brian Labone of Everton not withdrawn from the squad for personal reasons, he might have well have denied Charlton the number 5 shirt. But Charlton ably accepted the opportunity, applying himself most capably to Ramsey's requirements for the position.

The Jack Charlton as foil to Moore scenario further supports the idea that Ramsey developed his tactical system with the location of certain players (fitness and related factors allowing) inked into the blueprint, rather than devising the system first without any consideration given to personnel. Fate delivered Ramsey three players – Banks, Moore and Bobby Charlton – who, arguably, would have made any international team at the time, and who, most fortuitously, provided a spine running through the middle of the team. Banks's legend came to the fore at the 1970 World Cup in Mexico, due especially to his astonishing save against a downward header from Pele in the match against Brazil. Banks missed England's loss in the quarter-final to West Germany, being withdrawn at last minute due to a supposed episode of food poisoning.[45] On the evening following the match, a distraught and partially intoxicated Ramsey is claimed to have been overheard mumbling 'why did it have to be him?'; the subtext being that of all England's players, Banks was the one he could least do without. It is widely believed that had Banks been present, West Germany would not have scored the equalising goal conceded by his replacement for the match, Peter Bonetti of Chelsea.[46] Bonetti and Ron Springett of Sheffield Wednesday were the other goalkeepers in the 1966 World Cup squad, but Banks played in the position in all games during the final series.

Ahead of the first game of the Scandinavian tour, prior to the World Cup finals, Ramsey caused a stir by dropping Bobby Moore from the opening match against Finland. On the one hand, this helped fulfil the aim of giving all squad players a run. Norman Hunter of Leeds United replaced Moore. On the other hand, the dropping provided a personal signal to Moore not to become complacent about an assured position in the team.[47] However, it is doubtful that Ramsey had any intention other than Moore being at the heart of his defence and captaining the team through the final series. Moore's creative long-passing game from deep positions, his immaculate tackling, and overall sense of the flow of play throughout a game made him an ideal candidate to lead Ramsey's defensive line and the team at large.

The preferred defensive line-up was established by Ramsey fairly quickly: full backs Cohen and Wilson, if not players in Ramsey's own mould, offered attacking abilities to enhance their defensive competence. The primary attacking dimension of the team, from the middle to the front of field, was another matter, and although Ramsey characteristically went about his work without fuss, he no doubt spent hours wrestling with the options in playing personnel available to him, not only in regard to assessing on-field performances per se, but in deciding if players, even if playing well enough, would fit the mould of his perceived attacking system in complement to their teammates. However, it is reasonable to assume that the name of one attacking player predominated in Ramsey's thoughts from the time he took on the job as England manager. One of the clearest insights into Ramsey's view of the importance of Bobby Charlton to his World Cup ambitions is provided by Arthur Hopcraft in *The Football Man* from a personal interview he conducted with Ramsey at Lancaster Gate, following the 1966 World Cup.[48] Ramsey explained, 'I tried nine centre-forwards in three years; but I knew months, even years, before the World Cup that Bobby Charlton would have a number nine on his back.' As Hopcraft concludes, this remark challenges assumptions about 'Ramsey's reliance on controlled method', instead confirming that 'where the special talents were high enough they chose themselves'.

However, Hopcraft might have made more about Ramsey's particular point on his designation of the number 9 shirt to Charlton. Ramsey's dismissive remarks following Hungary's 6–3 thrashing of the England team at Wembley in November 1963, for which he played right full back, suggest he took no lessons away from the game. One of Hungary's main attacking players in that match, Nándor Hidegkuti, wore the number 9 shirt but struck from a deeper position than that of a traditional number 9. The role (now referred to as a 'False 9') was pioneered by Matthias Sindelar in Austria's *Wunderteam* of the 1930s, to England's detriment when they were defeated in Vienna in May 1936. Sindelar reportedly wreaked havoc on the England defence.[49] The 16-year-old Alf Ramsey may not have known much about that occasion, but his awareness of Hidegkuti's impact in 1953 was more intimate than he would have liked. Yet he may have benefited from the experience, which although never openly acknowledged, possibly influenced his future football strategising. Ramsey could easily enough have assigned Charlton another number – 7 or 8 – but to give him the number 9 shirt for the 1966 World Cup finals was to symbolise a particular importance for Charlton's role and a distinct break with the tradition – prior to Ramsey – of England teams being selected by the FA on the manager's behalf. Bobby Charlton sporting the number 9 was a flagging of

Ramsey's unwitting modernism, the unacknowledged lessons for which surely commenced in Ramsey's own playing days – the encounter with Hidegkuti of Hungary being the key example.[50]

The omission of Jimmy Greaves from the World Cup Final team has lent to the view that he was not a player fancied by Ramsey. Ramsey was believed to prefer harder working and more physically engaged forwards such as Geoff Hurst and Roger Hunt. This would seem true to an extent, but there is no evidence to suggest that Ramsey was planning to leave Greaves out of the team as England moved into the advanced stages of the competition. A Greaves / Hurst forward pairing was trialled on the Scandinavia tour against Denmark, a match won 2–0 by England, but in which Hurst was observed to hinder more than help his team's effort.[51] This rather marked his cards for the time being and it appears Ramsey became set on Greaves and Hunt as the preferred forward partnership. During the Group stage of the finals Hunt emerged as the more impressive player of the two. Scoring three goals across the three matches (two against France, one against Mexico) he was especially effective in off-the-ball running, making space that was exploited in attack by Bobby Charlton and Martin Peters.[52] Greaves struggled against close marking and did not make much of an impression during his appearances. Nevertheless, without sustaining an injury against France there is nothing to suggest Ramsey would have dropped him from the team going into the quarter-final stage.

However, Greaves's injury provided the opportunity for Geoff Hurst to come into the team for the match against Argentina, his selection rewarded with the winning and only goal towards the end of the controversial game. Hunt and Hurst capably filled the two forward positions, but they are rarely considered to have formed a playing partnership. Their most effective work in combination tended to be made with other players; Hunt again, especially in the semi-final match against Portugal, making space for Bobby Charlton, and Hurst proving an effective target player for long passes, his ability to be on the end of a teammate's delivery resulting in his four goals. Hurst's robust presence and direct mode of attack also opened space for Charlton to come forward on occasion free of markers. Together at the front, if working separately, Hunt and Hurst suited Ramsey's attacking system with Bobby Charlton as its fulcrum and Peters and Ball operating on either side of Charlton. These five players functioned as a dynamic unit, in a manner not so suited to an individualistic type of player such as Greaves. Sitting behind this attacking unit, in a primarily defensive role, was Bobby Charlton's Manchester United teammate Nobby Stiles. While Ball and Peters could be relied upon to track back in defence as much as required, Charlton was less dependable in this way. Although more than a stop-gap defender, second line coverage for Bobby Charlton was undoubtedly part of Stiles' role in the England team and the knowledge he had

of Charlton's play week-in-week-out in club football surely added to him being
of appeal to Ramsey.[53]

At the commencement of the BBC's live broadcast of the 1966 World Cup
Final, England's team formation was shown on screen according to the following 4–3–3 arrangement (see below).

4–3–3 formation

Banks

Cohen	Charlton J.	Moore	Wilson
Stiles	Charlton R.	Peters	
Ball	Hurst	Hunt	

However, the way in which Ramsey deployed Nobby Stiles actually involved
not a 4–3–3, but a 4–1–3–2 formation.[54] The respective player diagram would
appear as below.

4–1–3–2 formation

Banks

Cohen	Charlton J.	Moore	Wilson
	Stiles		
Ball	Charlton R.	Peters	
	Hurst	Hunt	

Given Bobby Charlton's prominence within the system it seems surprising
that on the day of the World Cup Final Ramsey's explicit instruction to him –
as recalled by Charlton – was to closely mark the formidable young attacking
midfielder for West Germany, Franz Beckenbauer.[55] Such a role seemed a more
likely assignment for the terrier-like Stiles who had expertly marked Eusebio
into a low-key performance in the semi-final against Portugal. It has since been
reported that the West Germany manager, Helmut Schoen, gave a similar
instruction to Beckenbauer, i.e. to man-mark Charlton throughout the game.
This has led to a facile popular view that Charlton and Beckenbauer cancelled
out each other's effectiveness. Ramsey could not have known of his opposing manager's instruction to Beckenbauer, but he could have assumed that
instructing Charlton to stick to the young West German player would prompt
a reciprocal tactic. To the extent that this strategy was a gamble, for the characteristically non-gambling Ramsey, it paid dividends. Rather than resulting
in mutual nullification, Charlton was able to free himself from Beckenbauer's

attention enough to lead a number of threatening attacks for England, particularly in the first half. On a number of these occasions Beckenbauer was clearly outmanoeuvred by Charlton, most embarrassingly a few minutes before half-time when he was 'nutmegged' by a Charlton pass to Peters whose subsequent shot on goal was blocked by Wolfgang Weber. More costly was a missed tackle, at around the 18-minute mark, which allowed Charlton to advance across field and pass to Bobby Moore. Moore was fouled and then quickly took a free kick directed to Hurst, which his West Ham teammate headed in for England's first and equalising goal. Charlton's superiority over his opponent was apparent enough for Hugh McIlvanney to refer in his match report in *The Observer* to Beckenbauer having 'a thankless first half'.[56]

The second half started during a spell of summer rain. The dampening of the pitch impacted on footing, and players on both sides slipped as they chased the football. This led to the game becoming, in the words of BBC television commentator Kenneth Wolstenholme, 'bogged down into a midfield stalemate'.[57] The heavy pitch also added to player fatigue, Bobby Charlton one player visibly affected. As Charlton's lateral running lessened, both Peters and Ball increased their already considerable involvement in attacking moves. It perhaps came as no surprise that the second England goal was scored by Peters with about thirteen minutes of play remaining, when he swooped on to the failed clearance of a shot by Hurst to poke the ball into the net. A few minutes later Peters released Bobby Charlton with a well-timed pass, but, appearing totally exhausted by this stage of the match, Charlton blasted his shot wide of the West German goal and then stumbled to the ground in an ungainly collapse. As the match moved into extra time, following the last-minute equaliser by Weber of West Germany, exhaustion seemed to overcome most players on both teams. Ramsey's pep-talk, appealing to what he assumed to be his players' superior fitness over that of their opponents, was given validity by the eventual outcome. However, had the seemingly tireless Ball, supplier of the cross for Hurst's controversial third England goal, not been present during the additional half hour, the match might have had a different outcome. Nevertheless, fitness beyond the usual level for English professional footballers at the time had been a key dimension of Ramsey's preparation. Renowned for his attention to detail Ramsey, as mentioned previously, would have been alert to the possibility of extra-time play occurring in any of the matches subsequent to the first round stage.[58] Even if most of the England players were close to the point of exhaustion by the 120th minute of the extended match, they were able to maintain a high enough skill level to gain victory. Indeed, the capacity of Bobby Moore to accurately deliver a long pass to an advancing Geoff Hurst for the final goal bears testimony to the importance of Ramsey's obsession with stamina within his game strategy.

When Ramsey's England team drew 0–0 in a friendly match against the Netherlands at Wembley in January 1970, they left the field to a chorus of spectators' boos. A similar Dutch team had beaten England 1–0 in Amsterdam the previous November, but Ramsey reportedly appeared unbothered by results against a team that had failed to qualify for the forthcoming World Cup finals in Mexico. For him, these matches provided occasion to experiment with his team formation ahead of the tournament, for which England automatically qualified as the reigning champions.[59] However, Ramsey's focus on his own priority could not have blinded him to the ability of some of the Dutch players on show, especially the 22-year-old midfielder from Ajax, Johan Cruyff. Along with two other members of the 1970 Netherlands' team – versatile defender Ruud Krol and the skilful, while rugged, midfielder Willem van Hanegem – Cruyff went on to glory, as unlucky runners-up, in the 1974 World Cup, for which England failed to qualify in Ramsey's last cycle as national manager. The Dutch team of 1974, under the managership of Rinus Michels and captaincy of Cruyff, has been credited with bringing 'total football' on to the international stage. Michels is said to have invented 'total football' during his first tenure as Ajax manager, which ran from the latter half of the 1960s through to mid-1971.

Despite the reasonableness of Michels gaining due credit, we are usefully reminded by Jonathan Wilson that seeds for 'total football' in Holland were sown some way back in time, initially by the 'founding father' of Dutch football, Manchester-born Jack Reynolds.[60] Reynolds was manager of Ajax in three different spells, commencing in 1915. As an Ajax player, Rinus Michels was tutored into an 'attack out of defence' brand of football when Reynolds returned as manager in 1945. A further step towards total football in Holland was taken when the former Tottenham Hotspur player Vic Buckingham came to manage Ajax in 1959, after a period in charge at West Bromwich Albion, when the Black Country club earned praise for playing attacking football. Buckingham retired as a Spurs player in 1949, overlapping briefly with the arrival of Alf Ramsey from Southampton. As a young player at Tottenham, Buckingham was a team-mate of Arthur Rowe and at this formative stage was exposed to the senior player's 'pass-and-move' philosophy, which formed the basis for Buckingham's own later obsession as a manager with ball retention and a short-passing game.[61] Buckingham's influence at Ajax was immediate, as his team won the Eredivisie in his first, the 1959–60, season. Although Buckingham's successful experience at Ajax was brief, he played an important role in developing a playing culture at the club for Rinus Michels to build upon when he became manager in 1965.

In partnership with the then teenage Cruyff, Michels advanced the possession game by focussing on the dominance of space, with an emphasis on player versatility in on-field positioning. As with the Netherlands team, when managed by Michels, Ajax 'aimed to make the pitch as large as possible' by having players turn up in unexpected positions to receive the ball.[62] The strategy was to confuse opponents and pull them out of their familiar defensive formations. Even more than previous playing patterns of this type, including that deployed by the Hungary team of the 1950s, this style required players to fill spaces left by teammates that might be exploited by the opposition should the ball be lost. According to Ruud Krol, the strategy involved a high level of player fitness, but also energy efficiency to minimise the amount of territory each player would be required to cover. The planning for this strategy was complicated enough for the author Dave Winner to regard it as being 'based on mathematical calculations'.[63] However, an emphasis on calculated precision has not prevented 'total football' from being appreciated in artistic terms. Indeed, Winner likens the special vision required to play total football to that of Dutch artists, from Jan van Eyk to Piet Mondian (thus spanning the first half of the 1400s to the first half of the 1900s). Across the generations these artists have understood the peculiarity of their country's landscape, its flatness and limited space, and this has impacted upon their art, particularly in regard to the meticulous preparatory procedures they undertook to correctly locate every object and item within the available space of their canvas. Quoting contemporary Dutch sculptor Jeroen Hennemann, Winner concludes that total football, like Dutch painting, exhibits a 'sense of beauty' derived from a collective and cultural understanding of space.[64]

Johan Cruyff was the star, among a number of outstanding players, in the Netherlands 1974 World Cup team. His name features highly in any polls taken on the greatest footballer of all time. Yet within 'total football', in which the integrity and functionality of the system remains paramount, recognition is not given to the star player. Here, the parallel with Alf Ramsey's system becomes apparent. When asked, following the match, to name the outstanding player in the 1966 World Cup Final Ramsey answered, 'You can start with Banks in goal and finish with Peters who was playing at outside left'.[65] At least Ramsey referred to his players by name. Rinus Michels reportedly identified his players merely as numbers within the system.[66] Relatedly, neither Ramsey nor Michels were interested in individual players being hailed for their artistic genius. If either of them thought of football as art, it was the playing system that would be so regarded. However, while Michels' Netherlands team from 1974 has been described as playing football beautifully, the same claim for Ramsey's England team from 1966 has yet to come to this researcher's attention. The remainder of the chapter will give consideration to how such a claim might indeed be made.

Firstly, how might the two teams or, more importantly, the playing systems in question be compared? It is worth recalling the description from Bowler – quoted earlier in this chapter – of Ramsey's 1966 team being 'modern, noisy and effective'. Similarly, Michels' Netherlands team can be regarded as modern and effective, but noisy may not be apposite. In conversation with Winner, Jeroen Henneman claims the quietness one feels when looking at the paintings of Vermeer or Mondrian also occurred when watching Holland or Ajax play football in the mid-1970s.[67] The contemplation of space, which is transferred from artist and footballer to the viewer of the painting and football match, explains the 'silence'. The 'noise' of Ramsey's team might be explained by the emphasis on movement rather than space. While Michels' players concerned themselves with enlarging the size of the pitch, Ramsey's attempted to reduce it by crowding space with frenetic movement. And, rather than slowing the game down, Ramsey's team speeded it up. In the 1974 World Cup Final, despite Holland generally being regarded as the more attractive team to watch, their West Germany opponents were able to get the measure of their game, deny the attacking thrusts, and go on to victory. In the 1966 Final, England's West German opponents appeared unsettled by the pace of the game and, despite the tied score at the end of regular time, England were more productive in attack throughout, which might further explain the West German players' exhaustion during extra time. Michels' team may rightfully be remembered as the originators of 'total football', but Ramsey's team at least deserve recognition for playing a proto-form of total football and, if this is so, Ramsey's 'system', like that of Michels', warrants consideration in relation to art – a consideration as yet to be afforded.

In likening 'total football' to abstract art within the Dutch tradition, Dave Winner refers to an international survey undertaken in 1995 into public attitudes about styles and genres of art, directed to the key question of what type of paintings people would like to have hanging on the walls of their own homes. Of the nationalities surveyed, only the Dutch favoured abstract artworks over those featuring romantic landscape imagery in representational form. Winner interprets this as a culturally ingrained readiness to find abstract renditions of space visually appealing. In a related way, both football players and watchers were culturally prepared to embrace total football.[68] To illustrate Winner's point, we may turn to Mondrian and his late painting *Broadway Boogie-Woogie* (1943) and, when doing so, imagine the players to be within a 'total football' formation, assembled on the field like the square markers on the painter's canvas. By this stage of his life, Mondrian was depicting the streets of New York rather than countryside in the Netherlands yet, in the manner of the Dutch landscape tradition, he still 'constructed a complete framework of inter-connecting parts' in his totally non-figurative matrix of primary colours intended to find harmony within the chaos of modern life.[69] Total football sought harmony by way of bringing an orderly, yet unpredictable, pattern of play into the chaos of a football game.

In the summer of 2014, Mondrian was the subject of two related exhibitions, in the galleries of Tate Liverpool and the Turner Contemporary, in Margate, respectively. What can be made of his general popularity in contemporary Britain may be reflected by the amount of visitors drawn to these exhibitions. Whatever these particular numbers may have been, the very holding of these exhibitions at two major galleries reflects a belated historical shift in Britain towards the institutional acknowledgement of abstract art. Around the time of the Second World War, Kenneth Clark, Director of the National Gallery and Surveyor of the King's Pictures, is reported to have shown a slide of one of Mondrian's paintings during a public lecture as 'an object of amusement'.[70] As a key patron of art Clark had a significant say in, and impact on, what became successful. In regard to English artists, Clark's treatment of Victor Pasmore was most telling. As a leading member of the Euston Road School, Pasmore was only able to become an artist on a full-time basis once he secured financial support from Clark in 1938.[71] In the latter 1940s, when Pasmore switched to a totally abstract style of artwork, Clark withdrew his patronage. Pasmore suffered not only from the immediate retraction of funds, but, also, a subsequent difficulty in being able to sell his works. Pasmore had not anticipated that the British public, as well as critics, would not be won over to his belief in the 'beauty of geometric forms'.[72] However, he pushed on regardless and in the 1950s led a movement which became known as the Constructionists, a second wave movement drawing some inspiration from an earlier 'constructivist' episode in which Mondrian was involved during his brief period of stay in England.[73]

At this point in time Alf Ramsey was a few seasons into his managerial career and had taken Ipswich Town into the Second Division of the Football League. There need be no suggestion that Ramsey had any awareness of developments going on in British art to propose the view that his innovations in playing formation bore some parallel to these developments. Ramsey's relationship to artists occurs within what Raymond Williams called the 'structure of feeling' of a given period, if we take this to mean an emergent commonality occurring across different cultural forms.[74] Furthermore, there is little point in trying to reproduce an argument for the connection between Ramsey's playing system and understandings of space within the history of English art in the way Winner does for 'total football' and Dutch art. Indeed, given the brief account in the paragraph above, the relevant connection for Ramsey is to artists who developed their art against the continuing pull of tradition in England, which opposed a presumed capitulation to 'modern' influences from Europe. In this regard, Pasmore's Constructionist associate Kenneth Martin warrants consideration. Martin put the idea of movement at the centre of his work, his spirally structured hanging mobiles being categorised as 'kinetic art'.[75] His painting was similarly inspired, and in 1960 he shared an exhibition with his wife Mary Martin (whose gallery works after 1950 consisted mainly of reliefs) entitled *Essays in Movement*.[76] The Martins were influential upon, and in some cases taught, a new generation of

British abstract artists (born in the 1930s) who 'began working in a constructive mode during the 60s, even though work of this kind was being ignored by the influential British art establishment'.[77] These artists, who included Anthony Hill, Jeffrey Steele, Gillian Wise and Peter Lowe, adopted a rationalist approach based in mathematical and geometrical formulations (of differing degrees of complexity) upon which the artwork was constructed. Unlike earlier examples of constructivist art, their works bore no Utopian promise; their preoccupation was solely in ensuring that the artistic object they created remained faithful to its own structural principles. A number of these artists went on to form, in 1969, what became known as the Systems Group. A brief comment by Peter Lowe gives view to the group's collective philosophy:

> In applying a system, first decisions are invariably arbitrary. From then on it's a dialogue between chaos and order. My works derive from preconceived rules, but although I know what the rules are, systems have the potential to generate configurations that I might never discover if I relied entirely on taste and ad hoc methods. I invent but also discover rules intrinsic to the number of elements, the material or the scale for example. My working methods allow me to modify a system without compromising its logical integrity and I can arrive at entirely unforeseen outcomes.[78]

An outcome that *was* foreseen by Alf Ramsey was England's winning of the World Cup in 1966. As intimated in the previous chapter, the assuredness in his prediction is likely to have been made for strategic reasons irrespective of how confident he actually was in victory coming to England. Yet, irrespective of any doubt that Ramsey may have kept to himself, he certainly believed that England could go on to win the trophy. He was able to do so because of the faith he had in his own footballing mind and his ability to develop a playing system most suited to defeating the opponents his team would encounter during the final stages of the tournament. Ramsey's intellectual commitment to the playing system, and the necessity of having the right 'blend' of players within that system, is similar to the artistic commitment expressed above by Peter Lowe. Again, there is no suggestion that Ramsey had any knowledge of the work of the artists who became known as the Systems Group, or of their forerunners in geometrical abstraction, Pasmore and Martin. But like these artists of his time, Ramsey departed from the established tradition within his cultural domain. His abstractly devised system of football play presented a radical break from what had gone before and, in so doing, upset those who retained a lingering romance for the individual wizardry of celebrated star players.

An advocate of the 'beautiful game', as conventionally understood, Ramsey may not have been, but need this mean there is no aesthetic quality in the style of play he introduced, as writers such as Jonathan Wilson have asserted? The Systems Group artists were criticised for being 'cool and clinical'. Behind the criticism was the assumption that their work lacked beauty. In a response to such criticism a retrospective of the artists' work held at the Southampton City Art Gallery in 2008 was titled 'A Rational Aesthetic'. Against romantic tradition, the title suggests there are not only different 'ways of seeing' art, but also different stylistic forms in which it can be made and appreciated.[79] Ramsey defended his method of football against criticism with a stonewall declaration: his task was to steer the team to victory in the World Cup and that was all. This merely encouraged further criticism rather than a more sympathetic hearing (or viewing). Had Ramsey been more interested in confronting criticism, he might well have argued a case for his focus on winning not involving the abandonment of a type of football worth watching for its own sake.[80] Ramsey was a rationalist, but this does not disqualify him from making an aesthetically rewarding contribution to football.[81] Fifty years on from England's victory in the 1966 World Cup his methods deserve re-evaluation, to at least open the possibility for a renewed appreciation not afforded by the weight of existing criticism.

Notes

1 McColl, *England: The Alf Ramsey Years*, p. 18.
2 Jones, *Remaking the Labour Party*, p. 85.
3 Edgerton, 'The "White Heat" Revisited', pp. 56–7.
4 Snow, *The Two Cultures*; Pimlott, *Harold Wilson*, p. 328.
5 Snow, *The Two Cultures*, p. 11.
6 Bowler, *Winning Isn't Everything*, p. 209.
7 Clarke and Critcher, '1966 and All That', p. 122.
8 Hutchinson, '... *It Is Now!*', p. 181.
9 Greaves, *The Heart of the Game*, p. 125.
10 Downing, *The Best of Enemies*, p. 118.
11 Steen, *The Mavericks*, p. 27.
12 *Ibid.*, p. 27.
13 *Ibid.*, p. 29.
14 Winner, *Those Feet*, p. 34.
15 McKinstry, *Sir Alf*, p. 179.
16 Hudson, *The Working Man's Ballet*.
17 Ramsey, *Talking Football*, pp. 61 & 55.
18 Wilson, *Inverting the Pyramid*, p. 39.
19 Such a dichotomous view of Ramsey's 'system' was expressed explicitly, and in criticism, by some football writers at the time of the 1966 World Cup. For example, Ralph Finn (*England World Champions 1966*, p. 13) commented: 'I only know I do not like Ramsey's pattern for success ... I do not go for over-systematised methods of play. Football, to me, is far more art than science'.
20 Butler and Greenwood, *Soccer Choice*, p. 39.

21 Ramsey, *Talking Football*, p. 54.
22 *Ibid.*, p. 52.
23 *Ibid.*, pp. 51 & 54.
24 Games, Moriarty and Rose, *Abram Games*; Ramsey, *Talking Football*, p. 51.
25 Schulze and Windhorst, *Mies van der Rohe*, pp. 364–81.
26 Finn, *England World Champions 1966*, p. 12.
27 Lodziak, *Understanding Soccer Tactics*, p. 38–9.
28 Bowler, *Winning Isn't Everything*, p. 140.
29 Jackie Milburn, who succeeded Ramsey as manager at Ipswich Town F.C. was surprised by the 'absence of infrastructure' at the club when he arrived, McKinstry, *Sir Alf*, p. 205.
30 Ramsey, *Talking Football*, p. 44.
31 McGhee, 'The Ramsey Era', p. 13.
32 Moore, *England!, England!*, p. 117.
33 Unnamed author, 'Architect of victory', *The Times*, 1 August 1966, p. 5.
34 For player comments, see the video *How England Won the World Cup* (Prism Leisure, 2006).
35 Bowler, *Winning Isn't Everything*, p. 186.
36 McKinstry, *Sir Alf*, p. 260.
37 *Ibid.*, pp. 268–9.
38 Peters, *Goals From Nowhere*, p. 27. This information possibly came to Peters from his West Ham club manager, Ron Greenwood. In his autobiography, *Yours Sincerely*, p. 217, Greenwood tells of a telephone conversation he had with Ramsey following an England under-23 match in which Peters had played. Ramsey said, according to Greenwood, 'this boy Peters cannot play'. Ramsey was unaware that Peters was carrying an injury during this match. Greenwood does not say whether or not he informed Ramsey of this circumstance, but it is possible that if he did so, it may have given Ramsey pause to reconsider his assessment of the player.
39 Irving, *West Ham United Football Book*, p. 120.
40 Tyler, *Boys of '66*, p. 124.
41 Young, *A History of British Football*, p. 203.
42 McIlvanney, 'Summary: Looking Forward', p. 170.
43 This claim is based mostly on the way these players discuss their involvement in Ramsey's system in their autobiographical writing.
44 Charlton, *Jack Charlton*, p. 73.
45 McColl, *England: The Alf Ramsey Years*, p. 63; Banks, *Banksy*, p. 182.
46 Dawson, *Back Home*, p. 271.
47 Bowler, *Winning Isn't Everything*, p. 195.
48 Hopcraft, *The Football Man*, p. 137.
49 Wilson, *Inverting the Pyramid*, p. 66.
50 Given that Ramsey was playing his club football with Spurs at the time of the 1953 England upset, and given the experience Arthur Rowe had coaching football in Hungary in the 1930s, it is likely Ramsey had more reflective conversations on the playing tactics of the Hungary team than he has publicly admitted.
51 McKinstry, *Sir Alf*, p. 287.

52 Charlton, *My England Years*, p. 214.

53 The England team Ramsey settled on thus benefited from two club combinations, West Ham (Moore, Peters and Hurst) and Manchester United (Stiles and Bobby Charlton), McKinstry *Sir Alf*, p. 311.

54 Recognition of the playing system involving a 4–1–3–2 formation is accredited to Nobby Stiles. See Wilson, *Inverting the Pyramid*, p. 150.

55 Charlton, *My England Years*, p. 268.

56 McIlvanney, 'England v. West Gemany', p. 158.

57 *The World Cup Final 1966: England V West Germany* (BBC Worldwide Ltd) was released on DVD in 2002.

58 Gordon Banks' comment, 'I have never known a manager so thorough in his preparation', typifies the opinion of England 1966 players on Ramsey. Banks, *Banks of England*, p. 30.

59 Bowler, *Winning Isn't Everything*, p. 239.

60 Wilson, *Inverting the Pyramid*, pp. 219–20.

61 *Ibid.*, pp. 220–1.

62 Winner, *Brilliant Orange*, p. 44.

63 *Ibid.*, p. 45.

64 *Ibid.*, p. 54.

65 *World Cup Winners 1966*, pp. 32–3.

66 Winner, *Brilliant Orange*, p. 44.

67 *Ibid.*, p. 54.

68 *Ibid.*

69 Busignani, *Mondrian*, pp. 10, 28, image p. 77.

70 Grieve, *Constructed Abstract Art in England*, p. 10.

71 Harrison, *English Art and Modernism*, p. 383.

72 Grieve, *Constructed Abstract Art in England*, p. 61.

73 Fowler, 'The Systems Group', p. 13.

74 '[The] *structure of feeling* is as firm and definite as "structure" suggests, yet it operates in the most delicate and least tangible parts of our activity … this structure of feeling is the culture of a period … And it is in this respect that the arts of a period, taking these to include characteristic approaches and tones in argument, are of major importance', Williams, *The Long Revolution*, p. 48.

75 Grieve, *Constructed Abstract Art in England*, pp. 135–50.

76 *Ibid.*, p. 150.

77 Fowler, 'The Systems Group', p. 15. Examples of artworks by most of the British artists discussed here can be found on Tate Britain's online collection. See www.tate.org.uk/about/our-work/collection. Accessed 24 May 2015.

78 Peter Lowe interviewed by Alan Fowler May 2005, www.peterllowe.plus.com/pages/page1.htm. Accessed 11 June 2014.

79 *A Rational Aesthetic*.

80 For an argument on the aesthetic defensibility of 'winning' in sport see Todd, 'Cover Driving Gracefully'.

81 An appreciation of Ramsey's aesthetic is revealed in the splendid poem 'World Cup' by Alan Ross.

6

'Out of time': the World Cup and 1960s' culture

a good living culture is various and changing ... the need for sport and entertainment is as real as the need for art ... (Raymond Williams)

An unexpected visitor to Wembley on 30 July 1966 was the world heavyweight boxing champion Muhammad Ali. Although Ali's presence in the stadium prior to kick off has been captured by photograph, he is reported not to have stayed to watch the World Cup Final.[1] The photograph shows Ali, at an elevated level within the stadium, with people below on Wembley Way, presumably gathering prior to gaining entry to the match. Ali, characteristically, looks at the camera while the assembled people look towards him. The following Saturday night Ali fought and defeated Brian London at the Earls Court Arena. His appearance at Wembley would seem connected to the promotion of that coming event, but it may well have been that Ali enjoyed taking in, and even being a part of, the spectacle of the overall occasion. The possibility of slightly upstaging the event may have appealed to Ali's cocky awareness of his international fame. Surely an occasion called the World Cup Final warranted the presence of the world's greatest sporting champion. And not staying to watch the game, in a way, exercised a sense of superiority. Stumbling upon the photo of Ali at Wembley is a reminder of the bigger cultural backdrop against which the 1966 World Cup took place. It prompts a consideration in this chapter about other, sometimes unexpected, connections between the World Cup and cultural life in the 1960s. Inevitably, the World Cup's coming to England put football into a different light, one that could not go unseen even by people not usually interested in football. What artistic representations and uses of art might this coming have encouraged? And, more directly, what about the creative work sponsored by the World Cup, particularly in regard to its publicity? To what extent did this and related activity make the World Cup a cultural event in more ways than the playing of football?

One of the most photographed figures of the 1960s, Muhammad Ali stepped well beyond the stage of sport and into other cultural domains, including film and art. His outspokenness and extreme extroversion, coupled with the controversy of his politics, played a part in the breadth of both Ali's appeal and notoriety, but his sheer visual beauty had as much to do with the seeming ubiquity of his presence within newspapers, magazines and on television. Andy Warhol was significantly enough drawn to Ali's stunning visage to make him the first subject in his series of artworks on great living athletes.[2] The colourful portraits of Ali now take their place alongside Warhol's other memorable silkscreen method representations of celebrities blessed with beautiful faces, including Marilyn Monroe, Elvis Presley and Elizabeth Taylor. The portraits of Ali were not done until the late 1970s, but earlier silkscreen portraits, such as the *Marilyn Diptych*, appeared in 1962, by which time Warhol had emerged as a key figure within Pop Art.[3] Pop Art, as a recognised movement, gathered momentum during the same year, driven by a symposium staged at New York's Museum of Modern Art in December. Over time, Pop Art has tended to be chiefly associated with American artists, such as Warhol, but the movement and term has British antecedents.

Indeed, coining of the term Pop Art is attributed to the English artist Richard Hamilton, who wrote in a letter dated 16 January 1957, 'Pop Art is: popular, transient, expendable, low-cost, mass-produced, young, witty, sexy, gimmicky, glamorous and Big Business'.[4] The definition followed Hamilton's involvement, the previous August, in the *This is Tomorrow* exhibition at London's Whitechapel Gallery. Hamilton's now familiar poster for the exhibition, which has taken the title *Just what is it that makes today's homes so different, so appealing?* provides illustration for some of the criteria subsequently set out in his Pop Art definition. But the collage of imagery, with a muscleman holding an oversized lollypop with the word Pop on its wrapper at centre, is inclined, in the present-day memory, to invoke the brightness and colour imagined more in connection with the mid-1960s than the mid-1950s. This is to suggest a time lag between the emergence of Pop Art in galleries and related subcultures and its transference into popular culture as such. The imagined 'Swinging London' rather matches to Hamilton's Pop Art definition, and Carnaby Street and Mod-related colourfulness fed back into subsequent Pop Art paintings and assemblages.[5] Where might the 1966 World Cup fit into this scene, reservations about overstated connections with a mythologised 'Swinging London' notwithstanding?

On the surface, there is not as much to be seen as one might expect. Despite the Pop Art fascination with a range of popular cultural forms, and the plundering of sport-related items and imagery by American Pop Artists, football has been relatively missing from British Pop Art. This includes an absence of work referencing the 1966 World Cup.[6] However, there are interesting connections to be considered, one of these being a now iconic image that appeared in the year subsequent to the World Cup, the cover of the Beatles' album, *Sgt. Pepper's Lonely Hearts Club Band*. The cover was designed by Peter Blake, a prominent figure within the Pop Art movement.[7] It famously features the Beatles in the foreground in Sgt. Pepper's (military-style) costume and then again as Madame Tussauds-like wax models in their superseded mop-topped and suited mode. Joining them in the cover's image are a host of famous figures from the arts, literature, philosophy, music, film and other areas of popular culture. Portrayals of three sportspeople are included among the seventy-odd characters assembled on the cover image: a black-and-white facial image of Johnny Weissmuller, the swimming champion and actor who played Tarzan; a full-length wax model of the boxer Sonny Liston, standing next to the wax models of the Beatles; and a colour facial image of the former football player Albert Stubbins.

Overall, it seems a rather random gathering, based on a selection of figures by the Beatles.[8] Little is concretely known about the whys and wherefores of the selections, so an attempted deep analysis in that regard is pointless. However, that need not deter some speculation about the choice of the three aforementioned characters by the reportedly non-sport-loving band members. Firstly, Johnny Weissmuller may well be there for his Tarzan rather than swimming fame. Sonny Liston is a particularly interesting choice. He famously snubbed the Beatles for a photo session during their 1964 trip to the US and an alternative photographic session was arranged with the challenger for his heavyweight title, Muhammad Ali (then, Cassius Clay).[9] The selection of Albert Stubbins is surely explained by his identity as a player with Liverpool, from 1946 until his retirement in 1953. Even if they were not football fans, or only remotely interested in the sport, Harrison, Lennon, McCartney and Starr would have heard of Stubbins when they were young boys growing up in Liverpool. Hunter Davies, who was in the company of the Beatles at the time, says that he suggested the presence of football players within the cover imagery and that John Lennon settled upon Stubbins because he found the player's name to be amusing.[10] More sympathetically, perhaps the name also seemed to fit well with the music hall balladry, which characterised some the album. Whatever the case, when football met Pop Art and pop music in 1967, it did so via the ambassadorship of a face from its Brylcreem-haired past rather than its blow-dried present. The most obvious choice from contemporary football stardom would have been George Best, but to have him on the album cover might have meant, for the Beatles, taking the popular reference to 'the fifth Beatle' from a point beyond parody to self-mockery.

Had the Beatles been football fans, then Roger Hunt and Ray Wilson might well have offered them interesting faces from the present, both members of England's 1966 World Cup winning team, yet neither attempting anything like the affectation of rock star style. Both groomed and carried themselves in a way that would not have them look out of place in a team photo from Albert Stubbins' playing days. Including Hunt (Liverpool F.C.) and Wilson (Everton F.C.) on an album cover would also have heightened the ambiguity and speculation about whether or not members of the band supported either of Liverpool's two famous clubs. Even though, or perhaps because, the Beatles were uninterested in football, they seemed to take some pleasure in stirring the discomfiture of those wanting answers. George Harrison is quoted as saying, 'There are three teams in Liverpool, and I support the other one'.[11]

However, the 1966 World Cup had to settle for a more obscure reference from the Beatles, this occurring in a version of the song 'Glass Onion'. The song appeared originally on the Beatles' eponymously titled double-album (popularly known as *The White Album* because of its all-white cover, designed by Richard Hamilton), which was released in 1968. An alternative version is featured on *Anthology 3*, the final edition of Apple Records' *The Beatles Anthology* series, released in 1996. This version of the song contains part of Kenneth Wolstenholme's famous BBC commentary of the World Cup Final. Towards the end of the 2-minute 8-second track, just above the sound of break-ing glass, the cheering crowd and Wolstenholme's cry (repeated seven times) of "It's a goal!" can be heard, until the track fades out. The ending of the song on *The White Album* version is entirely different. John Lennon's singing and the accompanying tune stop abruptly, to be immediately followed by the drone of a slightly distorted violin sound – no smashing glass, no Kenneth Wolstenholme.

Of most interest here is the decision to opt for one version over the other for the original release. The songs for *The White Album* are reported to have been mostly written in the early part of 1968, when the band was in India undertak-ing transcendental meditation, and recorded in May of that year ahead of the album's release in late November.[12] Most of the songs on the album, including 'Glass Onion', although customarily attributed to Lennon and McCartney, are believed to have been written by Lennon. A first assumption, then, is that Lennon came up with the idea of including the Wolstenholme commentary on the track, a second, that it may have been a suggestion from one of the other band members in contribution to the collective creative process. Either way, it shows that the recent memory of the World Cup had registered enough with the band to have them consider incorporating part of the well-known commentary on the Final into their music. *The White Album* is, arguably, the Beatles' most obscure and non-commercial recording project, conceived when away from Britain, and the songs prepared in a way to reveal, rather than conceal, the cre-ative influence of drug taking. As such, the football commentary may have been regarded as somewhat at odds with the spirit of the project. The preference for a distorted violin sound at the end of 'Glass Onion' may have been based on the decision that it was more in keeping with the psychedelic audio effects used on the album. Kenneth Wolstenholme might have found his way more or less comfortably on to one of the tracks on *Sgt. Pepper's Lonely Hearts Club Band*, but, by the time of the third album released by the Beatles since the World Cup, 1967's 'summer of love' had left the summer of 1966 feeling somewhat further back in time than just one year before, and, another year on, Kenneth Wolstenholme sounded like a voice from the distant past. Interestingly, however, the discarded ending of 'Glass Onion' came to light on *Anthology 3*, thirty years after the World Cup and in the year that England hosted the European championships to a chorus of musical and other references to former glory. This may be taken as coincidence rather any kind of attempt to belatedly cash in on a 1966 World Cup related soundbite. A few fading seconds of Kenneth Wolstenholme do not amount to that much, and *Anthology 3*, containing rare and alternative tracks by the Beatles, was always going to achieve its market potential without his help.

The choice of a violin over Kenneth Wolstenholme at the football also indicates a preference for the sound of a high culture, rather than popular culture, form. The Beatles were not averse to making reference to popular culture but, for the psychedelia of 'Glass Onion', classical music trumped sport. The Beatles' influential producer George Martin seems to have made the intervention in favour of the violin.[13] Martin's production and arrangement, and knowledge and subtle use and blending of classical instrumentation, is credited, almost as much as the contributions of the band, for establishing the enduring artistic regard enjoyed by the music of the Beatles. Football is, of course, a very different type of cultural activity to music. It cannot connect with another genre or related cultural form in the way that popular music can with classical music. This was recognised by the musicologist Hans Keller, who, although writing about the aesthetics of football as well as classical music within the one book, did so in discrete chapters and in avoidance of any temptation to draw on musical metaphors to describe either football play or players.[14] But this does not mean that football is unsuited to reference in other art forms, music or poetry for example, or to depiction within the visual arts, such as painting and sculpture. Indeed, football has been of considerable interest to visual artists, from those working within more traditional figurative styles to those favouring modernist representations and even total abstraction. The 1966 World Cup offered a rare chance for football in art to be brought to public attention.

A dedicated exhibition, titled *Football in the Picture*, was held at the Manchester Art Gallery to coincide with the World Cup finals.[15] The art and sport nexus, at what we now refer to as mega-events, commenced with the Olympic Games, initially as Arts competitions at the behest of Baron Pierre de Coubertin, founder of the modern Olympic movement.[16] The contests were replaced by an Arts Festival by the time of the Melbourne Olympic Games in 1956, and since the Games of the 1990s, this has been absorbed into a grander scale Cultural Olympiad. As the Arts competitions were dispensed with ahead of the 1952 Helsinki Olympics, the last Arts competition coincided with the London Olympic Games of 1948. On the Organising Committee for those Games sat Stanley Rous, in his capacity as Chairman of the Central Council of Recreative Physical Training, a post he held as well as being Secretary of the FA. Rous makes no mention of his involvement with organising the Olympic Games going beyond sport, but it is possible that awareness of the Arts competition opened his mind to related possibilities for football.[17] As part of the celebration of the Football Association's 90th anniversary year in 1953, the *Football and the Fine Arts* competition was held in conjunction with an exhibition in London that then toured to a number of regional locations. Rous proclaimed the exhibition to be aimed at breaking down the 'barrier between football and art'.[18] However, the art critics remained snooty, regarding most of the paintings in the exhibition as being of dubious painterly quality. This seems largely to do with the paintings being mostly conventional romantic depictions of men playing football.[19] Had the artworks been more like those of the modernist European painters who had dealt with football as subject matter, the reception might have been somewhat different.

The art exhibition held in conjunction with the 1966 World Cup offered more in this regard. It impressed Michael McNay, art critic for *The Guardian*, enough to declare 'football painting' worthy of being a genre. He singles out a few works for praise including 'Shoot', a Pop Art silkscreen montage, by Alan Whitehead, featuring the Manchester United attacking triumvirate, Charlton, Best and Law and a 'silvery picture of a woman swooning at the brown legs of a star player'. Describing the work as 'at once masculine, glamorous and erotic', McNay tends to evoke Warhol as a stylistic influence, rather than Richard Hamilton whose images involving swooning women suggested criticism of chauvinistic masculine assumptions within 1950s' and 1960s' advertising and popular culture.[20] However, although unrecognised by McNay, perhaps Whitehead's work was bringing this type of criticism to football via an interest in Hamilton as a leading figure in British Pop Art.[21] And McNay might have referred to a genre of 'football art' rather than just painting, to include works of sculpture, given his particular praise for Geoffrey Clarke's modern sculpture of a number of 'aluminium maquettes … symbolising incidents in a game'. Significantly, for McNay the sculpture reminds us of what is 'too often forgotten' about football, that it is primarily about fun. Here, McNay inadvertently sounds agreement with the claim by the Dutch cultural historian Johan Huizinga about the essence of sport as play and that 'play is the direct opposite of seriousness'.[22]

One of the best-known English artists on exhibition in 1966 was C.R.W.

Nevinson, with his painting *Any Wintry Afternoon in England* (dated 1930). McNay's appreciation of this painting was qualified by the opinion that it is 'successful the more it keeps clear of vorticist theory, and the nearer it comes to evoking the feel of footer under industrial smoke on a rain-sodden muck heap'.[23] However, McNay's assessment is made without proper consideration to Nevinson's biography. This is not an artwork concerned with seeing football as fun, and it is via its Futurist (rather than Vorticist) stylistic invocation that the painting offers a critique of football within modern life. Nevinson is best known for his images from the Front in the First World War, in which he inverted the Futurist love of the machine and dynamism to express the catastrophe of war, which he had personally witnessed.[24] First exhibited in 1934 *Any Wintry Afternoon in England*, not one of his better-known works, reverted to his earlier Futurist style of faceted figures to depict the movement of football players, much in the way that he had depicted soldiers marching towards battle in his 1915 painting *Returning to the Trenches*. Negative comments about football in Nevinson's autobiography, considered in light of his general pessimism about the likelihood of a second world conflict occurring in the 1930s, indicate that he regarded the sport as an unfortunate diversion to which people devoted attention in ignorant bliss of the state of international politics that was leading them back into a proverbial hell. *Any Wintry Afternoon in England* may have even been deliberately intended by Nevinson as a companion painting to *Returning to the Trenches*, as the young men playing football, like the soldiers before them, are pawns in a game, being marched off to a calamitous destiny.

Nevinson's ambition for the painting when it was created is one matter; how it is interpreted and appreciated by audiences over time is another. In the context of the *Football in the Picture* exhibition in 1966 the painting provided an art historical link between conventional figurative representation and abstraction of the kind offered by Clarke's sculpture. Indeed, the distorted figures in Nevinson's painting, who are obviously enough playing football, may have helped viewers make sense of the figures in Clarke's work in which the subject matter is lost to abstraction. For someone who claimed to know nothing at all about football, Nevinson, perhaps more than any other painter, including L.S. Lowry, captured the essentially modern aesthetic of the sport. With the game becoming strictly codified and professionalised, and its participants coming predominantly from the working class, football play bore some relation to the mechanised rhythm of the factory floor. Indeed, as indicated in McNay's review, the scene in *Any Wintry Afternoon in England* is closer to the factory floor than it is to the greenery of a football field. The football match is played on the street with terraced housing behind the players and industrial chimney stacks in the background. In L.S. Lowry's *Going to the Match*, his award-winning painting from the 1953 *Football and the Fine Arts* exhibition (which was also displayed at the *Football in the Picture* exhibition in 1966), a sense of demarcation between work and football as a domain of leisure is created by the inclusion of a stadium within the industrial landscape. But Nevinson makes no such concession: football, housing and the workplace are claustrophobically inseparable in *Any Wintry Afternoon in England*.

If the chimney stacks were swapped for ship cranes, the mucky street in Nevinson's painting might be just like that on which a teenage Albert Stubbins played his football in Wallsend on Tyneside. Interpreted in this way, *Any Wintry Afternoon in England* is an image which must have been familiar to the experience of a number of the 40-something-year-old men who attended the *Football in the Picture* exhibition in 1966. Whether or not it had only a perceived historical relevance to them, or something more, we can only speculate. Perhaps more contemporary minded viewers made a connection between the robotic-like movements of Nevinson's football players and the journalistic criticism, which referred to the England team as 'Ramsey's robots'. Nevinson claimed to have more faith in the artistic appreciation of the average person than in those with high culture pretension, so he would have been happy for football-going, rather than exclusively gallery-going, people to make their own interpretations of the painting in good faith. A self-confessed 'blueblood' in politics, Nevinson, who died in 1946, may nevertheless have agreed with directions in cultural policy as set out in 1965 by Jenny Lee, Minister for the Arts in the Wilson Government. Lee was especially concerned with upturning the tendency for art galleries and museums to be the preserve of a privileged few. She maintained that these institutions needed to be less 'gloomy and 'solemn' in the pursuit of a 'more appreciative public for the arts'. Overall, Lee claimed, 'a new social as well as artistic climate is essential'.[25] The *Football in the Picture* exhibition fitted nicely to the new direction for the arts, seeking an audience that may have not been regular gallery goers, but presenting them with artworks that dealt with a cultural theme to which they could relate.

A key aspect of Lee's policy approach was concerned with arts provision being better developed in the regions. In keeping with the point made above, *Football in the Picture* matches this ambition, although an elitist response to the extension of culture debate would be to say the point is to take Titian, not football, to the people living outside the Home Counties; the latter they already have. But while Lee's policy was certainly intended to bring great masters to as many people as possible, it was surely also intended to encourage greater breadth in respect to what is deemed *as* culture. As such it was a forerunner to the cultural policy approach developed by Chris Smith in the Labour Government of the late 1990s, which put the arts and sport into direct conversation.[26] The Football Association's working relationship with the Arts Council for the *Football and the Fine Arts* competition and exhibition in 1953, and then with the Manchester Art Gallery in 1966 for *Football in the Picture*, were early examples of the institutional partnerships needed for this conversation to be meaningfully enacted. The 1953 touring exhibition might not have broken down the 'barrier between football and art' as Sir Stanley Rous had wanted, but it, and then *Football in the Picture* to accompany the 1966 World Cup, made a laudable step in that direction.

Another direct means of connecting artwork with football has come via the advertising posters prepared for major tournaments such as the World Cup. Again, the initial inspiration comes from the Olympic Games, for which art-based posters commenced with the Stockholm Olympic Games in 1912.[27] The poster for those Games, featuring a naked athlete in classical pose, with genitalia covered by streamers to maintain modesty, caused controversy when presented before the public. Naked bodies in the art gallery were acceptable, but, when displayed in public spaces, such as railway stations and cafes, not so, according to civic authorities.[28] Greater historical controversy surrounds the posters for the 1936 Winter Olympics held in Bavaria and the Olympic Games held in Berlin in August of that year. The art posters, created respectively by Ludwig Hohlwein and Franz Würbel, are regarded by some critics as endorsements of the Aryan physical superiority promoted by Hitler's Nazi regime.[29] The poster for the 1934 World Cup perhaps gave inspiration to these designs. Representative of Mussolini's Italy, the imagery was bound to be robustly indicative of the regime. Designed by the Futurist ideologue Filippo Marinetti, the poster features an oversized national team player in action, poised to kick a football. The poster's figure is as bold and imposing as any representation of athleticism in the history of Olympic posters.[30] Adorned with the insignia of the National Fascist Party it is also more blatantly ideological than the posters for the 1936 Winter and Summer Olympic Games.[31]

Football posters can be traced back to the 1912 Stockholm Olympics. A poster advertising the football competition for those Games places a black-and-white photograph of a football match within a colour painted image of a brown building and surrounding greenery.[32] Both the photomontage technique and subject matter are in keeping with developments in modern poster design of the period. Subsequent World Cup posters continued to reflect awareness of current trends. They appealed to the mood of international modernism in which intentional political sloganeering played no part. The 1934 poster exemplified a rare case of politics being connected to the World Cup in the most overt way. Nothing of this kind was apparent in 1966. Ahead of the World Cup coming to England, three official posters were designed by Carvosso and produced by McCorquodale and Company. This industrial design firm was engaged by the Football Association to deal with both the advertising posters and programmes for the World Cup.[33] The simplicity of the three posters, with coloured images of freestanding objects against a white background is, to an extent, reminiscent of earlier minimalist posters, for example, Man Ray's *Keeps London Going* (1938) (double) poster for London Transport, and Richard Beck's poster for the 1956 Melbourne Olympic Games. However, the surrealist effect of these posters, Man Ray's featuring the London Transport roundel as a revolving planet, and Beck's featuring an invitation card appearing to float on an all-blue, ocean-like background, is not apparent in the 1966 World Cup posters. The objects, including a football and a world globe appear to be fixed, rather than in movement. The block san serif typeface is typical of the period, as is the minimal amount of text used. Even the third poster, containing the names of regional host cities, and Wembley and White City as London's hosting stadiums, keeps text to a minimum.

Each of the three posters contained the image of the official World Cup insignia, designed by the commercial artist Arthur Bew. The insignia met with the requirement of displaying the Jules Rimet trophy, by incorporating it into a central circular image with a football surrounded by key wording announcing the tournament. Observable behind the circular image, and filling the backdrop of the rectangular frame, is the outer reaches of the Union Jack.[34] Joining this insignia in the bottom left of one of the posters is a cartoon of a furry little creature that became the best-known symbol of the 1966 World Cup finals – World Cup Willie. The rationale for World Cup Willie's creation, as given by Harold Mayes in the FA's official World Cup report, is worth quoting:

> Such a dignified emblem [Bew's design] did not lend itself … to commercial application on a wide scale, and so the quest began for a symbol which could be employed on a much broader basis, both for commercial use and the expansion of publicity operations. That is how World Cup Willie was conceived.[35]

Two pages earlier in the report, Mayes indicated that the FA's ambition was to achieve as much publicity as possible via a minimal financial outlay. The enlistment of World Cup Willie seems to have matched this ambition. Mayes does not explain just what he meant by 'commercial application on a wide scale', but it would appear to extend to publicity aimed to attract international visitors to the World Cup in England, to achieve as broad a possible demographic of support for the World Cup in England, including women, children and men not normally highly interested in football, and to maximise the potential of World Cup symbols within merchandising.

World Cup Willie, who appeared in July 1965, was designed by Reginald Hoye, a graphic artist in the employ of Walter Tuckwell and Associates, the company appointed to produce and negotiate licenses relevant to World Cup insignia. He seems to agreeably service each of the targets surmised above. The more formal insignia by Bew might have given symbolic dignity to the World Cup's promotion, but World Cup Willie injected an element of fun, obvious enough to people both abroad and at home. However, cute though he may

8 The official insignia for the 1966 World Cup, designed by Arthur Bew.

be, Willie is not an entirely naive character, decked out as he is in his Union Jack shirt. Some academics criticize this clothing choice for Willie, suggesting, given the World Cup was to be hosted by England, that Willie might have more appropriately sported a shirt adorned by the red cross of St George.[36] Given that Willie appears to be a football player, there is something to this criticism; perhaps not that he would have worn the St George cross as such, but that he might have worn the same shirt as players on the England team, in either its red or white variant. But apart from the particularity of playing shirt recognition, it is hardly surprising that a Union Jack was chosen in 1966 for the dressing of Willie, any more than it was a surprise to have it appear in backdrop to the more formal World Cup emblem designed by Bew. The Union Jack flew from the towers of Wembley Stadium during the 1966 World Cup finals, just as it had flown from those same towers during the London Olympic Games of 1948. On each occasion, barely a thought would have been given to the cross of St George flying in its place, and in 1966 the thought of alternative regalia appearing within official World Cup insignia would not have arisen.

It could hardly be claimed that general public resistance to the display of the Union Jack was evident in 1966. Although the 'Swinging Sixties' may be

9 A World Cup Organisation employee displays World Cup related products featuring World Cup Willie. One of the official World Cup posters is displayed in the background.

over-imagined, the Union Jack was nevertheless a popular icon of a period when London, indisputably, became a fashionable and desirable destination. The Union Jack found its way into the commercialised variant of Mod culture and distantly related fashion and design items and paraphernalia. World Cup merchandising benefited from this popularity, especially when the Union Jack mingled with 'souvenirs of the England team's triumph'.[37] World Cup Willie remained the predominant image within World Cup knick-knackery, and, in his fluffy material form, laid claim to being the 'first mascot for a major global sporting event'.[38] Willie was thus a pioneer followed by other mascots, those of the Olympic Games becoming best known. Like him, Olympic mascots have played a 'strategic role as marketing agents', but they also, as Magdalinski points out, perform a 'political function' by serving as 'goodwill' ambassadors for the Games and the host nation.[39] World Cup Willie did his job in this regard, his innocuous cuddly appearance detracting from the overbearing signification of Empire in the Union Jack. Only over-zealous academics could miss the irony of his 'square-shouldered' strut and in po-faced seriousness contend that World Cup Willie was ideologically insidious.

Another graphic design project associated with the 1966 World Cup was the issue by Royal Mail of three stamps in 4*d*., 6*d*. and 1*s*.3*d*. denominations. The proposal for a World Cup Stamp Series was put by the FA to the General Post Office (GPO) in April 1964. Although enthusiastic from the outset, the announcement of the GPO's agreement to a special stamp issue to mark the World Cup was not made until October 1965. Following an involved process, with detailed instructions being given to tendering artists, thirty-nine designs were submitted. Despite an overall view that submissions were not of 'outstanding merit', three designs were adopted for stamps, from David Gentlemen (4*d*.), William Kempster (6*d*.) and David Caplan (1*s*.3*d*).[40] Prior to issue controversy arose when the original 'flag' design by Caplan for the 1*s*.3*d*. stamp was deemed unacceptable by the Foreign Office. Caplan's design had featured a football encircled by the flags of the sixteen nations competing in the tournament.[41] Objection arose due to the design containing the flag of North Korea; having done its best to thwart that country's participation in the tournament, the Foreign Office did not welcome the display of its iconography on a Royal Mail Stamp. Although tiny and ephemeral in immediate purpose, stamps are significant objects of national symbolism and monitored closely by relevant gatekeeping agencies of the state.[42] In this case the stamp's designer, Caplan, was critical of the vetoing and spoke publicly in this regard. The revised version of the stamp, which Caplan regarded as inferior to the original design, necessarily shifted to safer subject matter, football action. It features a goalkeeper's attempt to clear the ball, impeded by a teammate and an opponent jostling in front of him. The solid figured players bear some similarity to the toiling construction workers in paintings by Fernand Leger. As such they might be said to show the influence of the 'purist' modernism, associated with Leger.

Another goalmouth scene was featured in the design for the 6*d*. stamp by

William Kempster. Kempster was a talented muralist whose large-scale depictions of modern life reflected the stylistic influence of medieval murals, with which he became familiar under the tuition of the art historian Ernest Tristram at the Royal College of Art. His paintings exhibited a diversity of genre influence, from late Cubism to Pop Art; his design for the World Cup stamp a figurative representation of football players rendered in, nevertheless, modern technique. The competing teams remain unclear. If meant to be national teams, perhaps we are seeing a red-shirted England against Brazil in their former white-shirted attire (although the green shorts worn by the Brazilian players militates against such a literal interpretation).

The 4*d*. stamp was designed by the versatile illustrator David Gentleman. Gentleman is well known for his work in a range of media, including postage stamps. In 1962 he designed three stamps in commemoration of National Productivity Year, featuring arrows in a modernist design reminiscent of some of the poster work of his former teacher Abram Games (Games joined a first sitting of the GPO's Stamp Advisory Committee to consider designs for 1966 World Cup stamps, but not the later meeting from which the recommendations for adoption were made). A further opportunity came to Gentleman in 1965, by which time Harold Wilson was Prime Minister and Tony Benn Postmaster General in Wilson's Government. Benn, who took to his appointment with zeal, wanted postage stamps to have broader public appeal. He declared that the symbolic purpose of stamps should be to:

> Celebrate events of national or international importance, to commemorate appropriate anniversaries and occasions, to reflect Britain's unique contribution to the arts and world affairs, to extend public patronage of the arts by promoting philately, and to raise public revenue.[43]

Gentleman answered this call by proposing a number of relevant themes for stamp illustration, including a series on regional landscapes. This idea was accepted, although the commission went to Leonard Rosoman for what was named the Landscape Pictorial series, issued in May 1966. Nevertheless, Gentleman had a significant input to the design for this series via another proposal he put to Tony Benn. This was for the large portrait of the Queen on postage stamps to be replaced, either by a cameo image of the Queen or by the removal of her countenance altogether. Although Benn actually favoured the latter suggestion, this was a step too far, rejected by the Queen herself. However, the cameo proposal was accepted and Rosomon's Landscape stamps were the first to carry the Queen's face in silhouette.[44] The precedent established, the Royal Mail stamps for the World Cup finals, issued on 1 June 1966, carried the Queen's image in cameo, somewhat imposingly on the right-hand sides of the 6*d*. and 1*s*.3*d*. stamps, by taking up approximately 20 per cent and 25 per cent, respectively, of the overall surface space (the same spatial apportionments had been used for the Landscape Pictorial stamps). However, on the Gentleman-designed 4*d.* stamp the Queen's cameo is reduced to a size enabling it to fit within the right-hand corner, thus denying it a dedicated framed dimension within the stamp's surface space. It seems appropriate that the person who proposed the alteration of the Queen's image on a postage stamp was the first to design a stamp with that image to appear in such a radical rendition. It is, therefore, an interesting, if largely unremarked upon, part of 1966 World Cup history that it became the first event of 'international importance' to be honoured by a stamp series following the announcement of Benn's criteria, and that one of the stamps in that series has a very particular significance within British philatelic history.

David Gentleman's design for the 4*d.* stamp apparently caused controversy, not so much because of its dealing with the Queen's image, but because of its depiction of football players. Mayes reports, 'it was the unusual attitudes portrayed [by the players] … neither of whom was a professional … which caused considerable comment'.[45] Given that the predominant imagery of footballers in popular circulation, as seen in cigarette cards and postcards throughout the 1900s, involved known players in either action or still-portrait pose, this response is not so surprising.[46] It is likely that public expectation was for a stamp featuring then current England players, and the balletic type movement of the two players featured in the illustration might have prompted a view that the artist responsible did not really know his football. The poses of the players in the image were decided upon from a series of photographs of men rehearsing football-like action. The young photographer employed by Gentlemen, Peter Boyce, was told not to involve professional footballers, so he simply used two of his friends as models for the shots. It was Boyce's disclosure to journalists from the *Daily Mirror* about this seemingly haphazard approach to the photographic project that sparked questioning in regard to the integrity of the final image as shown on the stamp.[47]

David Gentleman's insistence on not using professional footballers as models for the image makes it rather clear that he wanted to avoid any type of romantic depiction of star players or to be faithfully representing football play at the professional level. Having Boyce take in excess of 300 rapid-shot photographs suggests that he was more interested in capturing a sense of the dynamism of movement involved in football by whomever it is played. In this regard, the concept for his image again bears some relation to Abram Games. Games designed one of the postage stamps to coincide with the London Olympic Games of 1948 (as well as a travel poster for the BEA airline company). His semi-surrealist image features the profile of an athlete in movement emerging out of a revolving globe of the world. It was described by the Royal Post Office as symbolising, 'the athletic striving of all the nations taking part … the athlete and the lines running from him express the movement and vitality of the

[Olympic] Games'.[48] The image gains in significance when considered against the popular memory of the 1948 Olympics as the 'Austerity Games'. Abram Games' stamp design defied this association, presenting Britain as a confident and forward-looking nation, rather than one wallowing in post-war misery.[49]

There is further interesting parallel here with the stamp David Gentleman designed for the 1966 World Cup. Although 1966 was a rather different time to 1948, a time supposedly marked by 'affluence' rather than 'austerity', as already indicated, it coincided with a Labour Government finding its way in office and wanting to project an image of Britain as modern and technologically advanced. Although there is no suggestion to be made that Gentleman deferred to this particular cause, his design of graceful, yet dynamic, football players was well-suited to Labour's desired image of modernity. A stamp featuring well-known football players in more portraiture-like form would have been fine enough, but would have been nothing new. The Gentleman stamp stepped away from the conservative representation of footballers as great men and was, therefore, in keeping with the non-traditional direction in which Tony Benn wished to steer stamp design as Postmaster General. When the England team victory in the World Cup Final prompted a hasty issue of a commemorative stamp – there was no time for a new design to be sought – Gentleman's 4d. stamp provided a ready choice. The decision was taken to reissue the existing design with the words 'England Winners' added towards the centre top of the stamp, between the signification of the 4d. denomination and the cameo of Queen Elizabeth.[50] A front page headline on the day of issue, 18 August 1966, reported that the rush for 'England Winners' stamps resulted in two people being injured as a crowd of more than 1,000 people surged into the Trafalgar Square post office to secure a first batch purchase.[51] The report goes on to say that the complete allocation of 102,000 stamps (of a total 12,500,000) at Trafalgar Square was sold out in under half an hour. It seems that as well as answering Tony Benn's ambition that stamps should mark major international occasions, the 1966 World Cup stamps also serviced his plan for stamps to be raisers of public revenue.

Another commemorative project borrowed for the World Cup from the example set by the Olympic Games was the 'official' film. The film to mark the 1966 World Cup was titled *Goal!* World Cup films commenced with *German Giants*, a documentary account of the 1954 World Cup in Switzerland, won by West Germany. FIFA holds a controlling hand in the commissioning of these films, in the manner of the IOC in regard to the commissioning of Olympic Games films.[52] Like Olympic films, World Cup films are usefully considered according to categories developed by Ian McDonald, which he has adapted from pre-existing categorisations of more general documentary films.[53] Of particular relevance to films of the Olympic Games (and so too may we say films of World

Cup finals tournaments) McDonald refers to the categories of: 1) *poetic* documentaries, 'which evoke particular moods and stimulate ways of thinking rather than presenting evidence to support a particular argument'; 2) *expository* documentaries, which 'address the viewer directly, with titles or voices that advance an argument about the historical world', often through use of a narrator to steer the audience to a particular way of understanding the visuals; and 3) *observational* documentaries, which avoid didacticism by allowing the film-maker 'to go out into the field and shoot in a relatively unobtrusive manner' – the camera operates merely as a recording device, the film intended to 'present real life as close to reality as … possible'.

Given their primarily documentary recording (and non-editorial) purpose, we might expect Olympic Games and World Cup films to match most closely to the observational category, the very reference to the camera going 'out into the field' prompting such categorisation. Most are greatly concerned to capture the sporting action in an objective way, again matching to the observational category. Yet even those sport documentaries directed and produced according to objective ambitions are likely to contain some elements of poetic and expositional, as well as purely observational film-making.[54] Atypically, some films might be primarily categorised as poetic documentaries; McDonald names Leni Riefensthal's *Olympia* (the film of the 1936 Berlin Olympic Games) and Kon Ichikawa's *Tokyo Olympiad* (the film of the 1964 Olympic Games) in this regard.[55] Both films are concerned more with 'aesthetic expression' than in capturing the reality of the sporting contest and the aesthetic ambition is delivered by film-making techniques not best suited to matter-of-fact representation. Despite the political controversy surrounding *Olympia* and its historical connection to Nazi propaganda, it is still regarded by many film buffs as a documentary of significant, if scarred, beauty.[56] *Tokyo Olympiad* tends to be read as a response to *Olympia*, fascist sympathies dispensed with and replaced by the humanist ideal intended for the modern Olympic Games by their founder Baron de Coubertin. However, in another paper, McDonald contends that such a comparative reading denies an appreciation of *Tokyo Olympiad* – a film of intimate and emotional beauty in its depiction of both athletes and audiences – in its own terms.[57]

McDonald's cautionary words are worth bearing in mind as consideration turns to an assessment of *Goal!*, as the inclination to view the 1966 World Cup film against *Tokyo Olympiad* is hard to resist. Many of the cinematographic techniques of Ichikawa are seemingly followed in *Goal!* and, given that it was filmed in the year subsequent to the release of *Tokyo Olympiad* (1965), influence is easily imagined. The rights for making the official documentary on the 1966 World Cup were awarded by FIFA, via tender, to Chilean film producer Octavio Señoret.[58] For the making of *Goal!* Señoret appointed a directorial duo, the South African Ross Devenish, who went on to further success as a film and television director, and Abidin Dino, a Turkish artist, best known as a painter of modern still-lifes and portraits, who worked across a range of media, including photography and cinematography. The commentary for the film was written by the football journalist and author Brian Glanville, its narration delivered by the actor Nigel Patrick. *Goal!* was filmed in Technicolor on 35mm film gauge. Two examples of reviews, published respectively in the *British Film Institute Monthly Film Bulletin* and the magazine *Variety* give indication of a mixed critical reception for the film.

The *BFIMFB* review suggests that *Goal!* will be confusing to those people who view the film in expectation of it providing a documentary account of the football action that took place during the World Cup tournament.[59] While acknowledging that highlights of soccer action are shown in the film, the review claims:

> the emphasis throughout is on pinpointing the football as a dramatic rather than sporting event. This is, in fact, something of an art film on the essence of football, rather on the lines of *Tokyo Olympiad* but nowhere near as successful. The result is often an irritating mélange, with crucial moments in the matches missed as the cameras probe an incident or an expression at the expense of the action on the field.

An example given of related frustration is the filmic focus on Antonio Rattin's long walk to leave the arena after being sent off against England in the quarter-final, without any 'recording of the incident' that led to his dismissal by referee Kreitlein. The use of Glanville's commentary is also criticised for its attempted arty effect. The announcement of goals before they are scored is regarded in the review as an atmospheric failure because it merely blunts a sense of excitement for the game.

The review in *Variety* magazine takes a rather different position to that of the *BFIMFB* review, due mainly to an underpinning assumption that *Goal!* will be watched by people who have been exposed already to the football action of the 1966 World Cup. Upon this understanding, the 'close-up' filming of players and 'slow-motion' portrayal of football play is regarded as adding a 'new dimension' to the viewing experience. Glanville's commentary and its delivery is complimented as 'smooth ... not over laden with technicalities' and 'neatly blended with sound effects and John Hawkesworth's [jazz flavoured] lively score'. Rather than finding excitement denied by the filming techniques used in the making and production of *Goal!*, this review finds the film as not only 'exciting', but 'alert' and 'witty'. A 'technical' comparison is made with *Tokyo Olympiad*, but even this positive review finds Ichikawa's film to be superior in capturing the 'rhythm and poetry' of the sporting occasion. Fairly, though, it notes the limitations faced by *Goal!*, given the necessary focus on only one sport.

Both the reviews discussed above would locate *Goal!* within the poetic category of sport documentaries. The *BFIMFB* review deems the film to be unsuccessful because it fails to achieve the aesthetic standards of *Tokyo Olympiad* and it does not provide enough footage of football action to be regarded as an observational documentary. Contrastingly, the *Variety* review declares *Goal!* an aesthetic achievement, and unburdens it from the more routine demands that accompany the observational documentary. A telling point in the favourable *Variety* review is the reference to the close-up and concentrated view on certain players in *Goal!*: Nobby Stiles, Antonio Rattin, Eusebio and Pele are named. This recognition directly counters the suggestion in the *BFIMFB* review that the lengthy camera focus on Rattin leaving the field of play is laboured with little aesthetic benefit. These assessments are ultimately subjective, but to this author the camera's concentration on players during moments of anguish – Rattin's self-righteous consternation in the belief that he had been treated unfairly by referee Kreitlein, mixed with the genuine concern that his removal from the game left his team with only a slim chance of winning; the physical pain of Pele, a literally fallen hero from the numerous kicks by Portugal players to his legs, then attempting to play on despite being unable to run; Eusebio's dissolving, within seconds, from graceful dignity in defeat to inconsolable tearfulness, following Portugal's loss to England in the semi-final at Wembley – brings a very poignant effect to *Goal!*

These vignettes lend insight into, not so much the heroic ideal, but, the heroic ordeal. In each case, if for different football related reasons, each of these players, reasonably enough, imagined their team winning the World Cup in 1966. The moments of focus in *Goal!* on Rattin, Pele and Eusebio give view to the hero's (or anti-hero's) realisation that triumph is slipping, or has slipped, from their grasp. The slow-motion close-up on Nobby Stiles, to which the *Variety* review refers, comes at the beginning of the film, when the England team forms a defensive wall, in an unsuccessful attempt to prevent what became West Germany's second and equalising goal in the Final. The anguish and urgency in Stiles's grimace was a portent to the near-desperation felt by the England players when they surrendered what should have been a winning lead just ahead of the whistle to sound regular full time. At the end of the film, the emotional relief in eventual victory is captured by the camera in the respective responses of the Charlton brothers: Jack dropping to his haunches, face in his hands in prayer-like position; Bobby openly crying as he moves into an embrace with George Cohen. But joy is finally revealed in a slow-motion focus on the smiling face of the young Martin Peters, as he takes the equally jubilant Roger Hunt and Alan Ball under each of his long arms.

Goal! won the 1966 Robert Flaherty Award from BAFTA, for the best documentary film of the year (*Tokyo Olympiad* won the same award in 1965). How much this can be put down to the film's capturing of the raw emotional expressions of players at key moments is a matter of speculation, but surely this recurring aesthetic was influential upon the judgement. The inclusion of Abidin Dino in the directorial team was clearly aimed at bringing a dimension of this kind to the film, and, as with some of Dino's paintings, a Picasso-like sensitivity to portraiture is evident in the particular focus on player's faces in *Goal!*

Though it might be a primarily poetic documentary, *Goal!* nevertheless bears aspects of both the observational and expository documentary. In the former regard the film, to an extent, does present a reliable documentary record of the 1966 World Cup. The related criticism made of the lack of football action does not recognise the director's limited ambition to present detailed match-by-match highlights. The extent to which *Goal!* is an expository documentary, comes, unsurprisingly, via tendentious remarks in Brian Glanville's commentary. Examples include an image of Jimmy Greaves in action against Uruguay being accompanied by the remark, 'a world class forward, but allergic to World Cups'; a skilful piece of play by Uruguay prompting, 'Once Uruguay was known for such virtuosity, but this is 1966, the year of negativity'; as the England versus Uruguay match ends, 'the World Cup starts with the epitome of the modern game, a goalless draw'. These negative remarks on the state of football, evident in the opening game, serve the somewhat redemptive narrative that accompanies the Final between England and Germany. As the teams leave the pitch at half-time, the commentary offers assurance, 'Those who feared a tedious defensive game have been happily surprised'. Similar points could have, perhaps, been made with less journalistic assertiveness and in a way not seeming to implicitly regard England as the victims of negative play and the restorers of positive football. This inserts a sense of bias that does not match well to the film's more encompassing humanistic ambition.

Goal! is also let down by Glanville's commentary in regard to an error made in mention of the World Cup Final's unexpected celebrity visitor. Accompanying filmic imagery of Muhammad Ali's presence we hear the narrator remark; 'Cassius Clay, here to defend his world title, but, today he is just another fan'. There is no reason to believe the commentary is intentionally provocative, but, given that Ali changed his name in 1965, it appears a careless and disrespectful mistake to have made; a mistake, it should be said, not attributable to Glanville alone once *Goal!* was put into final production. Referring to Ali as Cassius Clay also plays to the perception of the 1966 World Cup being a bit out of step with its time, not quite up to the pace of the desired external image of England swinging 'like a pendulum do'. The error in name is compounded by the probable misassumption that Ali was in attendance of the Final like 'just another fan' to watch the game. Whether or not he stayed long enough for kick off we might not actually know, but the description of him as 'just another fan' will seem ridiculous even to those reluctant to wholly buy into Ali's self-promoting accolade as 'The Greatest'.

The mistaken name and inappropriate reference to Ali poorly serves an otherwise mostly intriguing documentary about the 1966 World Cup – an event bearing cultural significations and material by-products warranting more thoroughgoing attention than has thus far been afforded. The 1966 World Cup occurred after the time that Pop Art had magically met Carnaby Street, and football seemed to be playing catch up. The Technicolor images of *Goal!* are easily imagined in monochrome, and some aspects of the film even appear to wryly anticipate such incongruity. The sight of caretaker Mr McElroy climbing the steps to open a rather shabby old side door to enter Wembley Stadium is hardly the stuff of Technicolor. From the footage shown it is not even a place in which one can imagine an event called the World Cup Final taking place; at that moment appearing more like the outside of a lower-league ground than that of the nation's main football stadium. But this visual ploy, understood as such, can serve as a reminder that there was more going on, in and around the tournament, than readily meets the eye. It is a ploy that invites us to look beyond the bright colours of mid-1960s' cultural exaggeration to indeed see England's World Cup as an event of its time.

Notes

1 Robinson et al., *1966 Uncovered*, p. 223.
2 Bockris, 'Fifteen Minutes of Fame', p. 23.
3 Moorhouse, *POPARTPORTRAITS*, p. 114.
4 Shanes, *Pop Art*, p. 18.
5 cf. Sandbrook, 'The Age of Boom', p. 15.
6 An exception is 'Shoot' by Alan Whitehead discussed further on in the chapter.
7 Vaizey, *Peter Blake*, pp. 11–12.
8 Davies, *The Beatles*, p. 65.
9 Lipsyte, 'Winner by a Decision'.
10 Davies, *The Beatles*, p. 65. In a related point of football interest, the cover artwork for John Lennon's fifth solo studio album, *Wall and Bridges*, released in 1974, features a painting done by Lennon when eleven years old (this assuming the ascription is not apocryphal). The image, which is signed and dated June 1952, appears to feature players in Arsenal and Newcastle United strips. That Arsenal and Newcastle played in the FA Cup Final the previous month suggests Lennon's artistic inspiration was that match. From this, we may also conclude that Lennon, even if not a football fan, was influenced by the sport's cultural popularity.
11 www.theguardian.com/football/2003/dec/11/theknowledge.sport. Accessed 12 March 2015.
12 MacDonald, *Revolution in the Head*, p. 311.

13 *Ibid.*, p. 314, n. 3. *The Beatles* has been regarded as a 'postmodern album' in an academic study by Whitley, due to its uses of 'fragmentation and genre mixing', as well as other devices favoured by artists generally regarded as postmodernists. Whitley, 'The Postmodern White Album', p. 105.

14 Keller, *Music, Closed Societies and Football*.

15 *Football in the Picture* was held at the Manchester Art Gallery Athenaeum Annexe between 12 July and 7 August, 1966. The possibility of a 'World Cup painting' was considered and rejected at a meeting of the FA's World Cup Organising Committee, 9 March 1965.

16 O'Mahony, *Olympic Visions*, pp. 24–5.

17 Rous, *Football Worlds*, pp. 121–4.

18 Physick, 'Football and the Fine Arts', p. 45.

19 cf. *Ibid.*, p. 53–4. Physick uses the term 'realist' to describe football paintings arguably better described as 'romantic'.

20 M.G. McNay, 'Football in the picture', *The Guardian*, 12 July 1966, p. 7.

21 The author has been unable to locate this painting and is thus reliant on the description of it provided by McNay, as per the citation immediately above.

22 Huizinga, *Homo Ludens*, p. 5.

23 McNay, 'Football in the picture', p. 7.

24 Hughson, 'Not Just Any Wintry Afternoon'.

25 Lee, 'A Policy for the Arts'.

26 Smith, *Creative Britain*.

27 Hughson, 'The Cultural Legacy of Olympic Posters'.

28 *Ibid.*, p. 750.

29 *Ibid.*, pp. 751–2.

30 Marinetti was best known as the ideologue of the Futurist movement two decades earlier. In those years, Nevinson was his main supporter in England. However, with the experience of the First World War, Nevison changed his mind, and although the footballers in *Any Wintry Afternoon in England* are painted in keeping with the Futurist technique, the former ideological adherence is removed.

31 Benito Mussolini was so obsessed with using the World Cup in Italy for political grandstanding that he commissioned a trophy honouring his leadership to be presented along with the official World Cup trophy to the winning team. Goldblatt, *The Ball is Round*, p. 255.

32 Goldblatt and Williams, *A History of the World Cup in 24 Objects*.

33 See FA minutes, World Cup Organising Committee, meeting 23 January (11 March minutes) 1963, pp. 54–5.

34 Approved 30 June, 1963; Mayes, *World Cup Report*, p. 43.

35 *Ibid.*

36 Crolley and Hand, *Football, Europe and the Press*, p. 28; McGuinness, 'Some Reflections on Representations of the England Football Team Through Ephemera'.

37 Harris et al., *1966 and All That*, p. 43.

38 McGuinness, 'Some Reflections ...', p. 7. He was also featured in song: 'World Cup Willie' by Lonnie Donegan became the first, if unofficial, England World Cup anthem in 1966.

39 Magdalinski, 'Cute, Loveable Creatures', p. 75.
40 Bates, '1966 World Cup Football Competition'. The stamps, printed by Harrison & Sons, were reportedly sold out on the first day of issue, 1 June 1966, and, in doing so, outsold 'Churchill Crowns', coins originally issued in 1965, but reissued on the same day as the World Cup Stamps in 1966. *Daily Mail* 'Big Rush for Soccer Stamps', 2 June 1966, p. 13. The stamp project was handled by the Grants and Loans Sub-committee of the FA's World Cup Organising Committee. Relevant meeting minutes reveal that the Sub-committee shifted quickly from a position of acknowledging that 'there should be a measure of cooperation with the GPO' in selecting stamp designs (September 1965), to recognising that the 'final authority' for the designs rested with the Postmaster General (January 1966).
    The issue warranted an official first day cover, which was designed by John Denison-Hunt. It featured a simple design, reasonably described as modernist, with a football centred within a block green background. The wording, 'World Cup 1966' sits below the football in sans-serif type. The retail cost of the cover was five shillings. An official postmark was not produced for the World Cup; however, postmarks were used in post offices in both Liverpool and Sheffield, featuring the wording 'WORLD CUP CITY'. See Bates, '1966 World Cup Football Competition'.
    Images of the designs adopted for the 1966 World Cup Stamps, as well as those of rejected designs, can be viewed online at the British Postal Museum & Archive: www.postalheritage.org.uk/collections/search/?s=1966+World+Cup&cbpt=2&cb_sort=title. Accessed 11 July 2015.
41 Bates, '1966 World Cup Football Competition'; Watson, 'World Cup Football Competition, 1966'.
42 Osmond and Phillips, 'Enveloping the Past', p. 1138.
43 West, *First Class*, p. 146.
44 *Ibid*. p. 147.
45 Mayes, *World Cup Report*, p. 80.
46 Davies, *Postcards From the Edge of Football*.
47 Patient, D. 'Peter Boyce from Snaresbrook photographed two of his friends for England's 1966 World Cup stamp', www.guardianseries.co.uk/news/local history/11341319.Photographer_reveals_story_of_World_Cup_stamp/. Accessed 15 March 2015.
48 Hughson, 'Modern Design for Modern Events'.
49 Martin Polley makes a similar point in regard to the 1948 Olympic Games related poster designed by Abram Games for BEA. Polley, *The British Olympics*, p. 132.
50 Watson, 'World Cup Football Competition, 1966'.
51 T. Daly, 'Buyers hurt in Cup stamp crush', *Daily Mail*, 18 August 1966, p. 1.
52 The FA's World Cup Organising Committee minutes for 9 March 1965 refer to a meeting of the FIFA Executive in Zurich (26–27 February 1965) at which provisional acceptance of a tender for the World Cup film was discussed.
53 McDonald, 'Situating the Sport Documentary'.
54 See the author's study of the 'official' film of the 1956 Melbourne Olympic Games in this regard; Hughson, 'The Friendly Games'.
55 McDonald, 'Situating the Sport Documentary', p. 211.

56 Hughson, 'Cultural Legacy of Olympic Posters', p. 751.
57 McDonald, 'Critiquing the Olympic Documentary'
58 'Goal! World Cup 1966', Variety (magazine review), Wednesday 19 October, 1966, p. 20.
59 'Goal! World Cup 1966', British Film Institute (BFI) Film Bulletin (review), 1 January, 1966 (erroneous), p. 384. (British Library Periodical Archive, online, p. 173).

7

'Tomorrow never knows': the mythology of England's World Cup victory

England is perhaps the only great country whose intellectuals are ashamed of their own nationality. In left-wing circles it is always felt that there is something slightly disgraceful in being an Englishman and that it is a duty to snigger at every English institution, from horse racing to suet puddings. (George Orwell)

Alf Ramsey is known to have favoured group cinema visits as a social bonding exercise for his players. Most often this was to see the latest Hollywood Western, but Ramsey was also known to enjoy British comedy and to select films within this genre for squad evening outings. It seems likely that one movie on the itinerary, in the years subsequent to 1966, was the film version of the British television comedy *Till Death Us Do Part.*[1] For those players involved in the 1966 World Cup Final this would have been a novel cinema-going experience, as footage from the match is featured in that film. The commencement of the television series of the same name was almost coincidental with the 1966 World Cup tournament, the first episode being broadcast on 6 June 1966 on BBC1.[2] Focussing on the daily life of bigoted, working-class East End resident Alf Garnett (played by Warren Mitchell), the programme gained popularity quickly, its humour appealing to those who recognised Garnett as a figure of ridicule and, as its creator Johnny Speight reluctantly admitted, to a minority of viewers who positively identified with Garnett's prejudiced rants.[3] Following the conclusion of its first successful television run in February 1968, the film version of *Till Death Us Do Part* was commissioned and released in 1969.[4] It provides a more extended biographical sketch of Garnett's adult years – from the Blitz to 1968 – in complement to the episodic foci on his life in the television show. Towards the end of the film, Garnet's ongoing frustration with life's circumstances culminates in his refusal to relocate to high-rise council accommodation in Essex, following the 'slum clearance' of his old neighbourhood in Wapping. The *Till Death Us Do Part* film and its leading protagonist are used in backdrop throughout the present chapter. Alf Garnett's experience of the 1966 World Cup Final, and England's victory, is read against the critical writings of academics. Humour and parody, such as that provided in this film, help us to see that in some cases – despite the undoubted importance of critical scholarship – criticism has been made for the sake of being critical rather than with the aim of providing a fair assessment of the cultural significance of the 1966 World Cup.

A rare occasion of happiness for Alf Garnett occurs when he attends the 1966 World Cup Final in the company of his usually loathed son-in-law Mike. Their support for the England football team – although Alf seems incapable of symbolically distinguishing between club and country; he wears his West Ham United scarf and rosette to the match – displaces, for the day, their usual heated clashes across axes of politics, religion, age, sexual mores and cultural attitudes.[5] To see the two get along is quite a statement on how much the film buys into the unifying potential of football. An interlude though their friendly union may be, through football camaraderie we see the possibilities of seemingly entrenched hostilities being forgotten when a shared ambition is realised. The point is reinforced by Alf's readiness to embrace, and kiss on the cheek, a black male supporter of England standing next to him as the referee blows the whistle to effectively sound *their* country's winning of the World Cup. However, Alf's sheepish expression immediately following the kiss signifies its aberrance and gives clue to a return to form once the heady occasion of the World Cup and England's glory has passed. Indeed, by the second run of *Till Death Us Do Part* on television, in the early 1970s, a key target of its protagonist's racist vilification is Clyde Best, a Bermuda international footballer who played in the English First Division for Alf's own beloved West Ham. With the return to daily routine, Mike once again became the son-in-law Alf did not want and Clyde Best the manifestation of the black neighbour he feared coming to live in his East End street.

Alf Garnett's World Cup Final bonhomie was extended, within the spirit of the occasion, to all those at Wembley in support of England. Indeed, the uncharacteristic generosity in mood that allowed Mike and the black England team supporter to be his friends for the day was balanced by Alf's heightened aversion to the particular 'other' for the occasion, 'the Germans'. On the way to Wembley, Alf and Mike stop for a 'quick pint' at the local pub. In response to the publican's comment along the lines of West Germany having a strong team with a good prospect of beating England in the Final, Alf exclaims, 'Gawd blimey, we've beat them twice already haven't we, two bleedin' wars mate!' While watching the match, Alf has a number of exchanges with a supporter of West Germany standing on the terrace just behind him. When Helmut Haller scores the first goal, Alf interrupts the man's celebration to remind him, 'you ain't won yet … same in the bloody War … started off well, didn't ya? Got well clobbered in the end though …' When Peters scores England's second goal for the lead, Alf jostles the deflated West Germany fan and taunts him, 'look at that ... Blitzkrieg eh!'

While expressions of wartime rivalry no doubt came to the surface at some points during the World Cup Final, Alf Garnett is offered as a fictional exaggeration of a working–class 'little Englander', rather than as a real life characterisation of the England fan at Wembley. After all, we are being invited to laugh *at* Alf, rather than *with* him. Christopher Young suggests that 'much of the "humour" around Anglo–German football relations' can be read 'through the prism of pantomime'.[6] The World Cup scene in *Till Death Us Do Part* anticipates this possibility, and Alf's goading of the West Germany supporter initiated the type of dialogue that developed within the discursive framework to which Young alludes. As hostile as this language may seem, its articulation, in the manner of Alf Garnett, is pseudo–confrontational, egotistically performative, but not genuinely targeted to offend. However, with the World Cup won, the later adoption by England football fans of the chant 'Two world wars and one World Cup, doo dah, doo dah', has coincided, as Paul Gilroy indicates, with the emergence of an ugly and visceral sporting nationalism – one collectively flaunted especially when the England team is playing abroad.[7] While Orwell's often repeated maxim on sport being 'war minus the shooting' was made with particular reference to his concerns about international football reflecting Cold War tensions in the immediate aftermath of the Second World War, there is little doubt that, had he lived long enough, he would have been prepared to regard the above inflammatory chant as further vindication of the truth of his claim.[8]

It is no coincidence that the ramping up of aggressive nationalistic support for the England team, from the 1980s to 2000s, coincided with an overt shift to jingoistic reporting on football in tabloid journalism. Indeed, that some newspapers simultaneously encouraged football-related belligerence, while condemning the 'hooligans' who acted upon their thinly veiled promptings, remains an especially disgraceful episode in England's media history.[9] Thankfully, both journalistic professionalism and editorial responsibility, as it was in 1966, militated against the type of bellicose headline and accompanying imagery with which the *Daily Mirror* greeted the England versus Germany semi-final in the Euro 96 tournament played at Wembley in June of that year.[10] The relative closeness in time of the 1966 World Cup Final to the Second World War also made it unlikely that crass and direct association between football contest and wartime enmity would be suitable in newspaper headlines; the emotional scars of those not so distant years were still too raw for such media angles to be contemplated in 1966. But were the seeds for the later explicit newspaper discourses on football and national animosity sown in England's World Cup year? Although related academic accounts tend to accept the view that the newspapers in 1966 'remained largely free of militaristic rhetoric',[11] there is still an inclination for them to seek out examples contrary to the norm.

Enter the *Daily Mail*, the tabloid newspaper recalled for its sympathies to European and British fascism in the 1930s, and subsequently known for lending editorial support to the Conservative Party. Hardly a newspaper to find favour with politically left-sympathetic academics it is not so surprising to see it held responsible, in critical studies, for running a particularly provocative line on World Cup Final day. Repeated in a number of academic works, is the attributed phrase: 'If Germany beat us at Wembley this afternoon at our national sport, we can always point out to them that we have recently beaten them twice at theirs'.[12] These words, incorrectly quoted, are from an editorial piece titled 'How I got mixed up with these cow kickers', by Vincent Mulchrone, that appeared on p. 6 of the *Daily Mail* on 30 July 1966. To avoid further confusion, it is best to quote Mulchrone at length:

> If the Germans beat us at our national game today, we can always console our-selves with the fact that we have twice beaten them at theirs. And how's that for narrow nationalistic hedging from one who has never in his life paid as much as half a dollar to watch 22 men disputing possession of the hide of a cow? ... You may have hated the World Cup, as I think I did, but you couldn't ignore it. It has encroached more deeply into the inward looking British temperament than any international event since the one we now know as World War II. Indeed, it has *been* war. And a very valuable little war, too. If only because it showed us how nationalism can raise its idiot cry over a cowhide ... Our children, who were being brought up as woolly minded internationalists, now whip out nasty little pistols at the mention of Argentina ... Win or lose, tomorrow's papers are going to be sheer hell. The shame of a defeat will only be exceeded by the horrors attendant on a victory. The deductions that will be drawn about the future of the British nation are already terrifying. And what bothers me is – how the hell did I get mixed up in it?

Regarded within its fuller context, the quote attributed by academics to the *Daily Mail* is hardly jingoistic, but a lead into a playful mockery of the World Cup as a forum for aggrandising nationalism and, more generally, of football as a socially useless activity. Mulchrone's article offers a sardonic retelling of Orwell's 'The Sporting Spirit', for circumstances twenty-one years on. Rather than tub-thumping the World Cup Final 'as a rerun of two world wars'[13] the article warns precisely, if wryly, against such associations. Additionally, an unambiguously light-hearted take on the World Cup Final was presented on the front page of the *Daily Mail* on 30 July 1966, in a small cartoon showing an arm extending above the parapet of the Royal box at Wembley to twirl a football supporter's rattle. The cartoon playfully suggests that the Queen, although aware of the impartiality required of her role at the Final, is nevertheless unable to completely hide her favouritism for England.

This cartoon is embedded within the framing of an article clearly suggesting criticism of World Cup related festivities. The article, 'England wives left out of party', by John Spicer, reports that the wives and partners of the England squad members were not invited to attend the formal post-Final function to be held that evening at the Royal Garden Hotel in Kensington. Responsibility for the non-invitation is clearly placed with the Football Association, as a spokesperson for the Government's Hospitality Department is quoted as indicating that blank invitations were offered to the FA in the expectation that wives would be asked to accompany players to the event. Additional information is given in the article to emphasise the extent of the insult to the wives and partners. This being, that while the official function was to be held in the hotel's Palace Suite, the female partners of the England players would have 'a separate dinner in a restaurant above known as the Chophouse'. While sexism is imputed to the FA because of the snub, the *Daily Mail* article is not free of chauvinism in its representation of players' female partners. The article is accompanied by a full-length photo of Tina Moore (married to Bobby Moore 1962, separated 1984) emerging from a West End boutique carrying a parcel containing 'a special outfit', which is described in some detail.[14] The concluding impression may be that the subject matter of the dinner snub provided the *Daily Mail* with an opportunity to stir tabloid controversy rather than exhibit a genuine concern about sexism in football administration. Nevertheless, the running of this story on its front page suggests a rather different take by the *Daily Mail* on the World Cup Final than that attributed to it via erroneous references to the Mulchrone article.

Hugh McIlvanney's article in *The Observer* on 31 July 1966, titled 'Deserving of Kipling', appears to be taken at face value by one academic critic as a further example of nationalistic journalism within the English press, this time in a broadsheet rather than tabloid newspaper.[15] However, such imputation ignores the article's intended irony. McIlvanney does not actually suggest that England's World Cup victory was worthy of Kipling's pen. His reference was made in criticism of the journalistic flourishes that had occurred earlier in the week following the semi-final between England and Portugal. Enthusiasm was expressed, in some reports, for the way this game was played, as much as it was for England's victory. This followed the upset and discomfiture over the quarter-final match between England and Argentina. For example, J.L. Manning of the *Daily Mail* (27 July 1966, p. 11) wrote, 'this was not only a night for Ramsey and his team, it was a night when football came sailing home too'. McIlvanney's article also reports on the response by West German media commentators in the wake of the World Cup Final loss. Dusseldorf-based journalist Ulrich Kaiser's view of supposed claims within the English media, about their team beating 'the world', as being 'dangerous', was shared by television commentator Werner Schneider. Schneider went further in claiming what he saw as an English media obsession with winning the Cup as evidence of a militaristic national character. These rather excessive interpretations prompted McIlvanney to point out that football-related references from the West German side were not necessarily free of wartime connotation. In particular, he notes the remark by former and legendary national team manager, Sepp Herberger, that in the endeavour to beat England in the World Cup Final, West Germany 'will have at least two strikers running parallel, with powerful units backing up from behind', as being reminiscent of the words of Rommel. The naming of a particular German Second World War general might have been overdoing the point, but Herberger's words do, even if unintentionally so, make football strategy sound analogous to that of the battlefield. Whatever conclusion might be drawn about McIlvanney's reference, again, it needs to be read within the context of the overall article, and, when done so, irrespective of how one deliberates on the piece, it can hardly be regarded as pro-England jingoism.

The World Cup victory was certainly reported as an achievement that brought euphoria to the 'nation', mostly regarded uncomplicatedly in the English press, without need to distinguish between England and other constituent countries of the UK. The 'smouldering sulk' of Scottish journalists in the Wembley press room after the match, to which Hugh McIlvanney (himself a Scot) refers, gave indication to the limitations of revelry over England's triumph within the fuller British context.[16] Nevertheless, it was the appearance of mass celebration that made the newspaper headlines. Peter Wilson of the *Daily Mirror* remarked, 'I cannot recall a sporting occasion in which emotion so effervesced in, and then over-brimmed, human confines'.[17] *The Observer* welcomed the morning after victory with the front page exclamation, 'Britain erupted with joy last night after England had won football's World Cup Final at Wembley'.[18] Yet while celebration was assumed to be nationwide, the article's focus was on London, centred on the major squares in proximity to the West End. The scenes at Leicester, Trafalgar and Parliament Squares, and Piccadilly Circus, were reported as displaying 'patriotic fervour, unequalled since VE Day'. This type of remark has not gone unmissed in subsequent academic discussions of the celebratory significance of England's World Cup win. For example, Clarke and Critcher take reports comparing the post-match celebrations in London to those of VE Day as 'evidence of a nationalism which incidentally happened upon football'.[19]

The suggestion of these authors is that the English public were sweating on another opportunity for collective public celebration of the kind that occurred on VE Day, and the 1966 World Cup win just happened to provide it. Yet, even if this should be the case, how reasonably is it described as nationalistic if not meant to involve antipathy towards people of another nation. The film *Till Death Us Do Part* includes an evocative scene of a VE Day celebration party being held in Alf Garnett's street. Between the bunting suspended from one side of the terraced houses to the other, two banners are clearly visible, one saying 'Victory', the other 'End of War'. It seems reasonable to assume that a good number of people who participated in celebrations much like the one in this filmic representation were festively inspired by the war being over rather than by thoughts of glory in the vanquishing of a rival. Even the readily belligerent Alf, rather than summoning up one of his familiar anti-German out-bursts, attempts to regale his inattentive partying neighbours with, 'It's all over now innit, all over now!' The similarity to Kenneth Wolstenholme's famous words in commentary as Geoff Hurst scores the final goal is obvious enough, but whether or not intended as a World Cup reference is uncertain.

Alf's celebrations after the World Cup win are confined in the *Till Death Us Do Part* film to the post-full time embraces discussed earlier in the chapter. Descending upon central London was perhaps more for younger people, as would seem to be the case from brief footage of the frolics in and in front of the fountain in Trafalgar Square, shown towards the end of the documentary *Goal!* The young people caught on camera appear to be teenagers and thus not even born at the time of VE Day. It is hard to believe they have any thoughts about the Second World War in mind as we see them kicking around joyously in the water. And perhaps these young people were not even football fans at all; perhaps, in keeping with Clarke and Critcher's suggestion about many people who celebrated England's World Cup victory, football was incidental to their joyous expression. Too young to know the War, not interested in football, what kind of nationalists might these young revellers have been? The display of the Union Jack in their midst prompts thoughts of Billig's term 'banal nationalism', but the World Cup was hardly an everyday occasion and some of the uses of the Union Jack symbol within banners, jackets and other material items was too imaginative to be dismissed as 'ordinary'. Perhaps the symbolism of nation was itself incidental to a deeper, more innate, desire for collective celebration; an understanding that can be lost in academic accounts that draw upon and interpret public episodes in the expression of 'national' identity according to a pre-intended 'critical' exercise.

An alternative way of understanding the celebrations in Trafalgar Square and other sites, on the evening of the World Cup Final, is by seeing such collective behaviour as an expression of what the sociologist Georg Simmel referred to as 'sociability'. Simmel believed that humans had a natural propen-sity towards association with others in situations that provide an opportunity for a pure type of sociality, involving the suspension of individual concerns for a mutual feeling of togetherness. Such situations tend to occur outside of work

10 Revellers in Trafalgar Square on the evening of 30 July 1966.

life and other social arenas strongly governed by rational conduct. Accordingly, Simmel referred to sociability as the 'play-form of association ... [with] no ulterior end, no content and no result outside itself'.[20] Mellor and Shilling proffer the term 'sensual solidarity' as a means of updating Simmel's 'sociability'.[21] 'Sensual solidarity' speaks to a heightened desire in contemporary societies for sociability as an ethos of individualism becomes more culturally predominant. With greater affluence and disposable incomes, even for the young, sociality becomes more consumption- than production-oriented. Although situations of 'sensual solidarity' cannot be contrived, people are drawn to experiences from which a collective emotional 'effervescence' can be attained in large gatherings. While some experiences of 'sensual solidarity' may occur almost entirely spontaneously, these are likely to involve small-scale happenings. Larger experiences of 'sensual solidarity', those that come to general public attention, are likely to involve a significant degree of organisation, with spontaneity coming into effect subsequently. The Woodstock rock festival that occurred in upstate New York in August 1969 might be regarded in this way. In this case, there was a significant degree of organisation, but the spontaneous and unexpected response by in excess of 400,000 young people to attend the gathering has etched Woodstock into the cultural history of the 1960s. The 1966 World Cup was a rather different occasion, organisationally and in its sense of common appeal, but, at this point, as we discuss the celebration that followed England's win – in England – we are right to regard that response, which could not have been predicted prior to the tournament (meaning here, the popular response to England's win, not England winning) as a semi-spontaneous experience of 'sensuous solidarity'.

Functional sociological explanations for the public response to England's victory tend to be overlooked in academic accounts preoccupied with identifying the 1966 World Cup Final as a recurring symbolic device, advantageously deployed by power elites to keep the public interested in an illusory notion of national identity and thus to distract them from the sort of protest in which they might otherwise engage if the inequalities of social life are not mollified by something to look forward to, or, indeed, back to. A 'myth of 1966' has thus been identified within academic accounts – the term has been used explicitly by Critcher[22] – as a construction by elements within the media and other politically motivated interlocutors for this ideological purpose. The 'myth of 1966', according to Critcher, is pitched to a general preconception of Englishness and English values. Victory in the World Cup, he suggests, has been cast as an outcome of the England team playing the game to the heartbeat of national character:

> We played it our way, to our traditional strengths: pride, determination, organisation. We did not, so we like to believe, resort to the underhand tactics of lesser

nations; even our brutality was honest. The very ordinariness of the English
team itself became a kind of virtue; it could have been any one of us, had we been
blessed with the talent.[23]

But, without so much as a sleight-of-hand, Critcher shifts from reference to the
discursive construction of myth to presumptive suggestion about a receptive
audience in waiting:

> The English pride themselves that they flourish in adversity, declining to ask
> how they got into such a situation in the first place. They also prefer, given the
> option, to stand alone and face the enemy, then wonder why they have so few
> allies. They are suspicious of fancy ideas and prefer the established home truths,
> surprised to find the rest of the world has moved on.[24]

Critcher might as well be describing Alf Garnett and, by doing so, has the
'myth of 1966' being pitched to a mythical audience of people like Alf. Yet this
does not prevent him going on to propose real political consequences for the
'myth of 1966'. He links it to post-Thatcher conservatism and related entreaties
that England (Britain) needed to recapture its fighting spirit to overcome the
political and economic problems, which, according to the discourse, beset the
nation at that time. Without reference to any plea in particular, Critcher suggests that the Conservative Party's sloganeering evoked the 1966 World Cup
success within the image of a desired, but lost, past.[25] England's failure to qualify for the 1994 World Cup, he suggests, further evoked the longing for 1966,
and, we might also assume, prodded unwelcome memories of a similar failure
some twenty years earlier when Ramsey's last England team failed to qualify for
the Finals in 1974.

By ultimately using the 'myth of 1966' to service a critical reflection upon
the ideological workings of Conservative politics around the time of writing, Critcher's 'myth', as Young argues, 'is one for its time, and probably
too coloured by it'.[26] And might not the same be said of other invocations
of the 'myth of 1966' that have arisen in subsequent academic work? Most
recently, Silk and colleagues examine what they refer to as the 'mythopoeia
of 1966' in regard to its currency within discourses on the 'corporate nation'
intended to service certain powerful interests, especially and ultimately those
of media moguls and their related commercial enterprises and to the benefit
of the state (whichever UK political party may happen to be in government),
given its inextricable connection within late capitalism to mega-corporations
in an increasingly monopolised private sector.[27] According to these authors,
the 'mythopoeia of 1966' offers a 'politics of nostalgia', which becomes bound
up with the 'dictates of corporate capital'. The events of 1966, they contend,
are lifted out of their historical context and reshaped according to 'corporate

relevancies' of the present. This process relies upon not only a public remembering, but also forgetting. A 'collective amnesia' is effected by the dissemination of an 'authorized' past that is formed within the commemorative discourse churned out by mass media operatives.

A key example provided by Silk et al. is the song *Three Lions*, the official anthem of the England football team for UEFA's Euro 96 tournament held in England. The song, performed and written by Ian Broudie (music) of the band *The Lightning Seeds*, and the comedians Frank Skinner and David Baddiel (lyrics), with vocal accompaniment on the chorus provided by the England players, has been rehashed in variant forms for the subsequent major tournaments in which the England team has competed. A number of 1966 World Cup references, both explicit and implicit occur in the original song. The chorus, 'It's coming home, it's coming home, it's coming, football's coming home', refers to the tournament coming to the country credited with inventing the modern game of football, but also implies the return of success on home soil, Euro 96 being the first major tournament to be held in England since the hosting and winning of the World Cup in 1966. More explicitly referencing the 1966 victory is the lyric 'Thirty years of hurt, never stopped me dreaming'. Two other explicit references to England players from 1966 are made, 'Bobby belting the ball' (presumably to Bobby Charlton's long-range goal against Mexico in England's second match of the tournament), and 'Nobby dancing' (obviously meaning the brief skip by Nobby Stiles – often referred to as a jig – as he paraded the trophy on the pitch at Wembley after England's win).

Silk et al. regard the *Three Lions* song as a piece of nostalgic trickery:

> Collapsing distinct temporal moments, and disrupting the linear chronology of the past, the song harks back to the 'halcyon' date in which England lifted the Jules Rimet trophy and the hurt that has since ensued – the song [is] part of a colonial and ethnocentric nostalgic/political discourse, an attempt to reconstruct an imperial Britain that posits that England lost its way and its world position and that now, after '30 years of hurt', football is returning to its 'rightful' place (the national psyche of England).[28]

They go on to criticise the song's accompanying video, which reconstructs highlights of football play and celebration by England players over the years, starting with key moments from the 1966 tournament. The convenient remembering of popular moments from 1966 is used, Silk and colleagues suggest, to forget or overlook the cultural homogeneity of that period in English football culture, even to the point of reinserting that homogeneity into the present by not including non-white participants in the video's re-enacted football scenes.[29] However, this reading suffers from a far too literal interpretation of the text, without allowance for its engagement with humour. As Young suggests, considerations of the *Three Lions* song and its video in particular, need to regard the connection with Skinner and Baddiel's television programme from the time, *Fantasy Football League*, which also featured football-related reconstructions.[30] These playful re-enactments introduced postmodern irony to the representation of football on television, in a way that did not merely glorify the moment in recollection, but offered the viewer multiple possibilities in reading. Such interpretative possibilities cannot be denied to the *Three Lions* video. Even given its 'official' promotional purpose of the England team at Euro 96, the *Three Lions* is invested with layers of meaning that potentially cut across its most apparent celebratory grain.

There is no argument to be had with Silk et al. that the memory of England's victory at the 1966 World Cup was seemingly ever present during media reporting on Euro 96. Reading issues of the *News of the World* from the time reveals especially crass comparisons, particularly when the name and image of Bobby Moore, who had died a little over three years earlier, is invoked.[31] But Silk and colleagues' focus on the example of the *Three Lions* song and video shows a surprising indiscrimination between media offerings, carrying the suggestion that the media operates as a monolithic block in the interests of capital, whereby events such as Euro 96, and the representation of the 1966 World Cup in relation to that event, are inevitably depicted and reported in keeping with other discourses on the 'corporate nation'. The messages given out, it seems, are irresistibly seductive. Silk and Francombe contend, in a related chapter, that:

> Popular cultural discourses act as very normalizing public pedagogies, educating us about belonging, being, other, us, them; the remnants and rampant mythologizing of 1966 in our present is a powerful *cultural pedagogy* that can shape, mould and educate citizens in our present conjectural moment.[32]

Underneath the complexity of jargon this account returns to a fairly basic political media production model, focussed entirely on message making and dissemination, without adequately considering what happens to media messages upon reception by an audience. A problem with such an approach is that it risks reducing media users to cultural dopes who are easily manipulated by the propagandistic material served up to them. A good deal of work within academic cultural studies has sought to address the balance by focussing on how audiences interpret, rather than just passively receive media messages.[33] Although some of this work has been criticised, in turn, for investing too much interpretative power in the audience, it at least gives important regard to people as active agents within mass communication processes. In regard to sport, John Fiske has argued that many fans have an 'expert knowledge' and thus engage critically with related media, making judicious decisions as they engage with sport broadcasts, match analyses and editorials.[34] Popular interpretations of sports history can be the subject of such 'expert knowledge', and, for example, people who have acquired knowledge about the history of English football are likely not to simply accept facile re-callings in the media of past events, such as the 1966 World Cup Final. Furthermore, people who are particularly interested in that match may happen to regard it as a great moment within the history of English football, while not buying into subsequent comparisons with British military victories. The 'rampant mythologizing of 1966' is unlikely to make much of an impression on the minds of such people.

However, this is not to suggest that 'expert knowledge' about the 1966 World Cup is required to avoid manipulation by the 'cultural pedagogy' to which Silk and Francombe refer. Even at the other end of the scale of football interest, people who know little more about the event, other than that England won their one and only World Cup, might accept that Bobby Moore deserves to be honoured as the captain of the winning team. This need not be taken to mean that such people are prepared to accept the tying of Moore into a glorious past along with Montgomery, Nelson and Richard I. Ahead of the 2010 World Cup, people may have purchased a Bobby Moore T-shirt or one of the other 1966 themed items to which Silk et al. refer[35] without being complicit in a nationalistic project beyond supporting the England team during that particular World Cup tournament. And even then, such supporting need not have involved a considerable emotional investment in either team or country. We come back again to the notion of 'sensual solidarity' and the need for awareness that an event like the World Cup offers an occasion for such expression. It seems a fairly simple point to make that a bit of singing and camaraderie with work friends at the pub watching England play football in a World Cup might best be primarily regarded as a matter of sociability. But sometimes the seemingly obvious is worth stating in the face of academic wisdom that suggests otherwise.

The criticism of academic work is not to deny that the media has constructed a 'mythology' of England's 1966 World Cup victory, which is trotted out when major football tournaments come along. The selective narrative offered by sound and image bites from 1966, entangled with highpoints from subsequent England games, is, to paraphrase Young, 'the hallmark of myth-making'.[36] The criticism, thus far, has been intended, mainly, to challenge the assumptions of some academics about the effectiveness of a 'myth of 1966' to impact upon a perceived popular or collective imagination. The criticism may also be extended to the academic interpretations of events from the 1966 World Cup being made in rather selective ways, aimed to service the particular intellectual positions that are advanced. Indeed, it is possible that academic accounts present their own 'myth(s) of 1966', towards such ends. In the attempt to critically reread the 1966 World Cup to counter what they regard as the popular glorification of England's victory, there is a tendency for this victory to be recast as tarnished, by suggesting that the Cup was unfairly won by England, and by challenging the honourableness of England as hosts and champions.

Accordingly, Silk et al. refer to accusations, in regard to the England/ Argentina quarter-final, of a conspiracy by FIFA 'to keep the home team in the tournament'.[37] In doing so they refer to this as one of the events associated with the 'real' World Cup (as opposed to those associated with the 'mythopoeia of 1966'), in a way suggesting the flimsy allegation of conspiracy to be factual.[38] By this interpretation, referee Kreitlein was a stooge, intent upon seeing England through to victory and, thus, the semi-finals. His dismissal of the Argentine captain Rattin, in the first half of the match without a goal then being scored, rather put England on to this course. The alleged cheating in this accusation is compounded by the bad sportsmanship and chauvinism attributed to Alf Ramsey for firstly attempting to prevent his players swapping shirts with their opponents, and then his infamous 'animals' remark, seemingly directed at Argentine players. Critcher claims that Ramsey's post-match comment 'ignored the foul count' of 19 against Argentina to 33 against England.[39] The fact of the foul count is not in dispute, but more telling is its ready acceptance as an indicator of the England team playing 'dirtier' than the Argentine team.[40]

England's unworthiness as victors is most readily challenged via reference to the disputed second goal scored by Geoff Hurst in the first half of extra time during the World Cup Final. On this incident, Critcher comments, not unreasonably, 'the ball hit the bar and came down in an ambiguous relationship to the goal line'.[41] Tony Mason reports, in characteristically good humour, on a Wembley Stadium tour in the 1990s, which featured a video of the controversial moment, 'showing the ball bouncing down on or over the goal line'. Visitors were asked to vote, via a computer device, on whether it was a goal or not. According to Mason, most claimed the ball had not crossed the line.[42] Dil Porter embellishes a story told by Hurst himself, as an indicator of ongoing disputation over the goal's legitimacy. According to this retelling Hurst is periodically reminded by Scottish people that the ball 'never went in', in the manner required for a goal to be properly registered.[43] In a subsequent paper Porter removes any doubt by stating, 'the third "goal" did not cross the line'. Similarly, Richard Weight avers, 'the shot bounced off the crossbar on to the goal line'.[44] 'Scientific' evidence can be called upon – and no doubt will be – to affirm opinion of this kind. Using a process known as 'goal-directed video metrology', engineering science researchers at the University of Oxford claim to be able to show beyond doubt – based on their examination of stills taken by photographers from *The Sunday Times* – that the ball did bounce down on to a part of the goal-line rather than come down clearly behind it.[45]

Yet, whatever proof may be offered by subsequent scientific investigation, a question is raised as to why scholars, in academic fields (history, sociology, cultural studies) renowned for taking issue with ultimate truths, would be interested in a correct verdict finally being handed down on a goal that could not be determined with assurance by the camera technology of the time – let alone by the naked eye of the referee or that of his linesman. Gordon Banks has queried why so much discussion has focussed on challenging the Hurst goal and claims he cannot imagine this happening in a country other than England.[46] His particular querying of the intention of computer-based studies might well apply to the writing of social science and humanities academics; and a related deeper questioning of the personal relationships to Englishness that motivate scholars towards a negative disposition on England's 1966 World Cup success could, indeed, be revealing. Alf Garnett's view on the Hurst second goal was, contrastingly, predictable. His celebration of Hurst's apparent score is interrupted by son-in-law Mike telling him the referee has not awarded a goal and that 'he is going over to see the linesman'. Only momentarily disconcerted, Alf responds, 'eh, we're alright, he's a bloody Russian linesman in' he', and then yells in the direction of the pitch, 'remember Stalingrad!' Alf's assumption that a Russian should somehow be thankful to the English for Russia's victory over Germany in the Battle of Stalingrad is matched by his mistakenness about the nationality of the linesman in question. The linesman, whose verdict seemed to sway referee Dienst towards awarding a goal, was Tofic Bahramov from Azerbaijan (then part of the Soviet Union). Yet Alf was hardly alone in making this error: reference to Bahramov being a Russian has been well rehearsed in journalism and even repeated in some academic accounts.[47]

Even if Hurst's second goal was to be removed from the ledger, the final score would still have been 3–2 to England. However, those wanting to deny England a World Cup victory in 1966 are able to grasp a final straw of complaint by pointing to the people on the pitch at the time of Hurst's third goal, as referred to in Kenneth Wolstenholme's famous line of match commentary. Thus, Porter affirms, 'the fourth goal should have been disallowed because spectators were on the pitch'.[48] Young goes into a fuller explanation, referring to a photograph from a 'German publication', which shows that 'three English supporters were bearing down on the 18-yard box and would certainly have interfered with the German goalkeeper's concentration'.[49] To the very letter of the law the game might have been stopped by the referee had he glimpsed interlopers encroaching upon the playing area, but Young's very mention of the photograph indicates that in a circumstance of this kind, with the match about to end, if the intruding parties did not threaten interference then halting play would not have been necessary. This was likely the view taken by the referee at the time, and the presentation of one photograph in evidence to the contrary need not, irrespective of Young's genuine enough claim, offer a repudiation of the official judgement. After all, photographic angles can be very deceptive and a shot taken from another position at the ground, at the very same moment as the photograph to which Young refers, might well give the impression that the spectators offered no problem to the goalkeeper as Hurst approached to make his shot on goal.

Some England players have disputed West Germany's second goal in the belief that, from an initial shot by Emmerich, Schellinger made contact with the ball with his arm before it ricocheted into the path of Weber, who then drove it into the goal to equalise the score just seconds ahead of the referee's whistle sounding full time.[50] Alf Garnett was not so perturbed. When son-in-law Mike complains, during the brief break prior to extra time, that England had the match won but 'chucked it away', Alf confidently assures him, 'stan-ima [*sic*] that's what our lads have got, stanima'. Thus, at the moment when Alf Ramsey rallies his players on the Wembley pitch to tell them that the exhausted West German team cannot keep pace with them during extra time, his namesake delivers something of a similar message from the terrace. Yet this deliberate filmic coincidence is not intended to draw a parallel between the two Alfs, so much as to mock the simplistic stereotyping of England football players, according to a perceived trait of English manhood's seemingly natural propensity for physical fitness and related staying power. While Alf Garnett's hope for England was based in such belief, Alf Ramsey's was based in the confidence that the hours of training his players had put in prior to the World Cup tournament would now come back to provide them with a decisive advantage at its conclusion. But whatever their difference in orientation to reasoning on the match's outcome, both Alfs turned out to be right.

Alf Garnett was seemingly correct in not claiming 'handball' against the second West German goal by Schellinger. Video footage indicates the ball hitting the player in the lower back, rather than on the arm. However, Alf does protest at the particular free kick awarded to West Germany, a key refereeing decision, which provided that team with the opportunity to equalise the score. As the free kick is awarded by referee Dienst, against Jack Charlton, while making a clearing header, for seemingly holding or impeding Uwe Seeler, Alf yells: 'What's up with ya? That wasn't a bleedin' foul. He jumped on his blee-din' back there. You're blind ref, you're bloody blind mate.' Characteristically, Alf would have been unconcerned about offering a muddled interpretation of the incident, as long as it fitted the ambition of his argument. Seeler could not have jumped on Charlton's back as he was positioned in front of the England player. Indeed, if any jumping was involved in foul play, it was the jump made by Charlton. Yet Jack Charlton has claimed that the only possibility of illegal contact being made in the exchange involved a West Germany player backing into him.[51] Amongst other reporters, Hugh McIlvanney challenged the decision, referring to Charlton being 'doubtfully penalized'.[52] The BBC television coverage of the World Cup Final provides a rather clear view of the incident, to this viewer's eye, showing a clean, if rather high, jump by Charlton to head the ball away from Seeler. No bodily contact that might be deemed illegal, in football terms, appears to be made by either player. Thus, irrespective of how their particular appeals may have been presented, both Jack Charlton and Alf Garnett appear to have a case against the referee's determination in this instance. The free kick awarded to West Germany against Charlton was at least as decisive in respect to the outcome of the World Cup Final as referee Dienst's acceptance of the opinion of linesman Bahramov in regard to Hurst's shot clearing the line for England's third goal and as dubious in merit. Yet, while written accounts seemingly intent on challenging the legitimacy of England's win have been loud enough in mention of the latter incident, they have not, as convenience may have it, had much to say on the former.

In 1966 England became the third country to host the FIFA World Cup finals tournament and have its team emerge as trophy winners. The feat was accomplished previously in the first and second World Cup tournaments, hosted and won respectively by Uruguay in 1930 and Italy in 1934. In the intervening five tournaments, the host nations fared no worse than to make the quarter-finals. During this period, the only host country to experience great disappointment with its team's final placing was Brazil in 1950. In a tournament not involving a final, the highly fancied Brazil team needed only a draw in its final game against Uruguay to win the tournament, but Uruguay won the game and in doing so leapfrogged Brazil into first place and World Cup winning position. Nevertheless, despite this upset, holding the tournament had clearly proven advantageous to the prospects of success for hosting nations. In the case of England in 1966, no-one apart from manager Alf Ramsey (and perhaps Alf Garnett) gave the England team much chance of lifting the Jules Rimet trophy on Cup Final day. So perhaps Ramsey, in particular, was alert to the ways in which playing at home might be helpful in taking his team towards what he saw as its winning destiny.

Given his southern–centrism, Ramsey was no doubt pleased to have his team based in London and their Group 1 matches scheduled for Wembley Stadium. Hendon Hall Hotel was chosen as home base for the England team during the tournament, mainly due to its proximity to Wembley for match days. Criticism has been made of 'home' advantage being overplayed in favour of England and listed as another mark against the Football Association's discourtesy as a hosting organisation. The criticism is sharpest in regard to the semi-final played against Portugal on 26 July 1966. Critics who suggest that unreasonable administrative intervention was made on behalf of England point to a switch in the planned semi-final programme, whereby the game featuring England was moved from

Goodison Park to Wembley, with the other semi-final between West Germany and the Soviet Union being relocated from Wembley to Liverpool.[53] The problem with this criticism, as indicated in Chapter 3, is that the arrangement for the semi-finals was not actually predetermined, as the accusation of a switch or swapping of matches implies. FIFA wanted to keep options open to account for the contingencies presented by the participating teams and ultimately made the decision on where the semi-finals would be played based on an assessment of which grounds would best serve the respective crowd sizes. Any suggestion given in advance that a semi-final involving England would be played in Liverpool was, at most, clumsy public relations by the FA. As England could almost be guaranteed to draw the biggest crowd in a semi-final, FIFA unsurprisingly, allocated the England/Portugal game to Wembley Stadium. Ahead of making the decision, a FIFA official indicated awareness that whichever way it went, upset was bound to ensue.[54]

There is no evidence to suggest that the allocation of semi-finals was made by FIFA with a view to favouring England. It can certainly be believed that Alf Ramsey would have greatly preferred a semi-final at Wembley to Liverpool. His team had become used to playing on the notoriously difficult pitch, whereas the Portugal team was yet to experience it, having played two of its Group 2 games at Old Trafford, the other at Goodison Park, and the quarter-final against North Korea also at Goodison Park. The England squad was well settled into accommodation at Hendon Hall, near to Wembley Stadium, meaning a short bus ride on the day of the semi-final, rather than relocation to lodgings in Liverpool, and the journey involved, ahead the match. But there is no evidence to indicate that the England manager's preference had any bearing on the decision. Had there been a prevailing view within FIFA that the West Germany/USSR game would have attracted a larger crowd, Ramsey and team would most likely have been on their way to Liverpool. England perhaps did gain some advantage from playing all of its games at Wembley, but this does not constitute cheating on behalf of FIFA or the FA. The fairest decision all round might have been for the England/Portugal match to be played in Liverpool, but financial imperatives prevailed over any other considerations. Ongoing criticism is best addressed in these terms rather than in suggestion of a pro-England conspiracy.

The year 1974 was not a good one for either of the Alfs discussed in this chapter. Alf Garnett's longsuffering wife, Else, left him to go and live in Australia, and Alf Ramsey was dismissed as England manager following his team's failure to qualify for the World Cup tournament in West Germany. It was a rather better year for the politician that Alf Garnett loved to hate, Harold Wilson, who returned as Prime Minister after spending close to four years as Leader of the

Opposition. Upon losing the election in 1970, legend has Wilson blaming his loss on England's failure to retain the World Cup in Mexico in the summer of that year.[55] Alf Ramsey survived the disappointment of Mexico, but, by his own reckoning, Wilson did not. Yet when Wilson reclaimed office on 4 March 1974, Ramsey lost his only a little over a month later, effectively leaving Lancaster Gate on 19 April.[56] Alf Garnett blamed Harold Wilson, almost singlehandedly, for what he regarded as the economic collapse of Britain, even referring to him as a 'scourge' and 'pestilence', sent by God to punish Britons for being lazy and complacent during the preceding years when they had 'never had it so good'.[57] Ramsey may not have been referred to as a pestilence, but the criticisms made of him suggest that for some he has been a scourge to English football. The subsequent failures of England teams under Ramsey's management in World Cup campaigns have been paralleled to socio-cultural debates about 'decline' in the 'condition of England'.[58] Within the 'decline' paradigm, Ramsey is doubly and contradictorily condemned for bringing a stylistic nadir to English football with his tactics in the 1966 World Cup, while simultaneously taking the England team to its zenith of international achievement by winning that tournament, only to then oversee its subsequent failures, especially elimination at the qualifying stage of the World Cup in 1974.

Clarke and Critcher credit Ramsey with introducing a 'modern game' to English football. But they do so backhandedly by contending this was done in a way that obscured 'deeper conditions of decline', which started to resurface after the World Cup success.[59] Yet what if Ramsey's fortunes had been a little different? What if England had won the World Cup in 1970 (not a preposterous imagining) and qualified and done well at the finals in 1974? Where would this leave the 'myth of 1966'? This would probably depend on what happened after that. If we rewrite history only for those first two World Cups of the 1970s then we may talk of a Ramsey golden age and collapse following from then. However, it may well be that this would not have been enough to satisfy critics. There remains, after all, the playing tactics that Ramsey deployed, blamed as they may well have been for a decline in the 'condition of football'. Even had he won more trophies with England, this accusation would probably continue to haunt him. In this case he would still be blamed for ruining the culture of football play, not just in regard to the England team but for the dullness of matches in professional club football caused, as critics have it, by coaches following his style. If they are correct in this latter regard, had Ramsey won more trophies with England, his tactical methods would probably have been copied all the more.

Under the critics' spotlight Ramsey is a modernist like few others. He modernised English football, but in a way that draws upon the assumed qualities of English tradition – hard physical work and endless toil. Without rehearsing the argument from Chapter 5 here, this misunderstands Ramsey's modernism, its basis in the 'less is more' minimalist philosophy and Ramsey's ability to put that philosophy into practice in football tactics. International modernism was about adapting modern trends to the national environment and Ramsey did this superbly in 1966. That others failed in their attempts to copy his achievement is hardly his responsibility. Ramsey's failures after 1966 are another matter, rightfully criticised in their own terms, but not when written back on to the so-called 'myth of 1966'. In terms of a cultural event or item, there is no myth of 1966 – England won the football World Cup. Of course, the intellectual desire to rehash the 'myth of 1966' goes beyond an interest in football. Ramsey and team become necessarily drawn into another game, one in which they are collaterally damaged on the academic shooting range. Had Ramsey been successful after 1966, critics would be denied the 'thirty years of pain' trope, which has so usefully served discussions about the way in which the public has been duped into longing for a return to that one mythologised moment of glory. But subsequent victories could be readily tarnished by a sieving through the evidence to find controversies indicating either luck on the football field or English complicity in favourable treatment by authorities. In one form or another demythologising of England football victories would go on, as long as scholars feel the need to dovetail criticism of football play and strictly associated matters with criticism of the socio-political circumstances of the time. This is not meant to deny sociologists or cultural studies theorists their place. Their work has made a purposeful contribution to warning against simplistic celebration of the 1966 World Cup victory and attempts by certain interest groups to manipulate related benefits. The point of this chapter has been to, in turn, offer scrutiny of the criticism in a way that might give pause to further reflect upon the cultural meanings of the event so many years on.

Notes

1 Ramsey's interest in this particular film is suggested by Jonathan Wilson in *Inverting the Pyramid*, p. 143.

2 Indeed, television critic Peter Black complained, albeit in good humour, about the temporary suspension of *Till Death Us Do Part* from BBC1's programming schedule to make way for broadcasts of World Cup matches, *Daily Mail*, 12 July 1966, p. 3.

3 Speight, *It Stands to Reason*, p. 232.

4 *Till Death Us Do Part*, produced by J. Pennington, distributed by British Lion, 1969. Available on DVD, 2006.

5 Alf Garnett was unable entirely to resist bringing politics to the World Cup, or at least in expressing his belief that Harold Wilson had done so. When the England team came into the Wembley arena wearing red shirts, Alf complains that they should be sporting the customary white and concludes that the wearing of red was Wilson's idea, connected to a plan to symbolically associate an England victory with

the Labour Party. Son-in-law Mike, who is inclined to take Alf up on such far-fetched outbursts, lets the matter pass on this occasion.

6 Young, 'Two World Wars and One World Cup', p. 12.
7 Gilroy, *After Empire*, p. 117.
8 Orwell, 'The Sporting Spirit'.
9 Poulton, 'English Media Representation of Football-related Disorder'.
10 The *Daily Mirror*, 24 June 1996, featured a full front-page image of England players Stuart Pearce and Paul Gascoigne with First World War style helmets transposed on to their heads. The image is accompanied by the headline, 'Achtung! Surrender: For you Fritz, ze Euro '96 Championship is over'.
11 Young, 'Two World Wars and One World Cup', p. 8.
12 This particular wording is used by Weight, *Patriots*, p. 459 and Young, 'Two World Wars and One World Cup', p. 21, n. 30; The same phrase with the word 'game' substituted for 'sport' is used by Taylor, *The Association Game*, p. 288, n. 84; Another incorrect wording, 'if the Germans win we can "take comfort that twice we have beaten them at theirs"' is taken out of its ironic context and described as a 'xenophobic and militarist' referent by Silk, Francombe-Webb and Andrews, 'The Corporate Constitution of National Culture', p. 723.
13 Weight, *Patriots*, p. 459.
14 In her book, *Bobby Moore*, Tina Moore (p. 8) claims that she was not surprised by the World Cup Final evening banquet being 'stag', as this was customary practice at the time. She also suggests that Alf Ramsey was responsible for the 'no wives' decree. Alan Ball (*It's All About a Ball*, p. 61) describes the omission of players' partners from the reception at the Royal Gardens Hotel as 'the only sour note of the World Cup'. He suggests his teammates believed the same, but puts no blame on Ramsey for the decision. He rests blame with officials of the FA, accusing them of wanting to 'bask in the glory'.

  The official record is not especially helpful in clarifying the matter. Minutes from a meeting of the Football Association's International Committee, of which Ramsey was a member, held on 27 July 1966, recommended to the Finances and General Purposes Committee that the wives of all players in the World Cup party be guests at the match, at a luncheon before the match and a dinner on the evening, and that they be accommodated on both Friday and Saturday evenings. The 'dinner on the evening,' referred to in this record, may have been intended to mean a dinner with the players, or as turned out to be the case, a separate dinner.
15 Weight, *Patriots*, p. 459.
16 H. McIlvanney, 'Deserving of Kipling', *The Observer*, 31 July 1966, p. 14.
17 P. Wilson, 'Heroes with a Gold Cup', *Daily Mirror*, 1 August, 1966, p. 23.
18 'London goes wild for Cup Victors', 31 August 1966, *The Observer*, p. 1.
19 Clarke and Critcher, '1966 and All That', p. 121.
20 Simmel, 'The Sociology of Sociability', p. 255.
21 Mellor and Shilling, *Re-forming the Body*, p. 174.
22 Critcher, 'England and the World Cup'.
23 *Ibid.*, p. 87. This is not to suggest that Ramsey was unaffected by long-standing stereotypes of Englishness and 'otherness'. Following the World Cup Final he

declared, 'I don't think there was a faster or stronger team than England in the Cup, but we still lack some of the techniques of the South American and Latin sides. I don't suppose we can hope to beat them at this ... our players are not built the same.' Quoted in B. James, 'What follows glory', *Daily Mail*, 1 August, 1966, p. 12. However, and importantly, Ramsey did not take the old-fashioned view of English stamina and toughness for granted or as being enough to win England the World Cup, as some criticism might imply, hence his focus on physical training and his obsession with the development of a playing 'system'. Care also needs to be taken today when reading such phrases as 'our players are not built the same'. When said by an English person of his generation the inference is as likely to be cultural as much as racial. 'Race' tended to be used as an encompassing term for populations from other countries to account for race, ethnicity and/or culture. Given Ramsey's fixation with football, it is not unreasonable to accept he was thinking in cultural terms relevant to the sport, and that his intention was, for example, to propose that English players cannot be expected to play in the manner of Brazilian players because they have been nurtured, as players, within a different (football) cultural context.

24 Critcher, 'England and the World Cup', p. 87.
25 *Ibid.*
26 Young, 'Two World Wars and One World Cup', p. 15.
27 Silk, Francombe-Webb and Andrews, 'The Corporate Constitution of National Culture'.
28 *Ibid.*, p. 724.
29 *Ibid.* The song prepared as an anthem for England's World Cup campaign in 1990, 'World in Motion', performed by New Order and written by members of the band, featured black England player John Barnes on accompanying rap style vocals. The song commences with a rehearsing of Kenneth Wolstenholme's words at the conclusion of the Final, although not in the original form. Wolstenholme rerecorded the commentary especially for the production.
30 Young, 'Two World Wars and One World Cup', p. 16.
31 R. Ryan, 'The picture all England fans hope to see one Moore time', *News of the World*, 2 June 1996, p. 39; 'Pick our no. 1', *News of the World*, 23 June 1996, p. 82.
32 Silk and Francombe, 'All these Years of Hurt', p. 267 (italics in original).
33 Hughson et al., *The Uses of Sport*, pp. 86–8.
34 Fiske, *Power Plays*, pp. 84–6.
35 Silk et al., 'The Corporate Constitution of National Culture', p. 724.
36 Young, 'Two World Wars and One World Cup', p. 15.
37 Silk et al., 'The Corporate Constitution of National Culture', p. 723.
38 The familiar version of the conspiracy accuses England and West Germany of colluding to have their teams advance to the semi-finals, by having an English referee appointed to the quarter-final match between West Germany and Uruguay and a German referee to the match between England and Argentina. In the aforementioned match, referee Jim Finney sent off two Uruguayan players, which, to some eyes, looked suspicious in light of Kreitlein's dismissal of Rattin in the parallel game. FIFA is roped into the conspiracy conjecture due to Sir Stanley Rous being

its President at the time. A letter sent from the Foreign Office in London to a number of their representatives in South American countries, as well as consuls in Lisbon, Madrid and Rome, indicates a diplomatic awareness of the upset over the refereeing issue, especially in Argentina, and that 'a good deal of odium' had been expressed towards 'Britain as a whole' over the matter and not just FIFA. However, the letter indicates that the accusations against Rous and FIFA were regarded by the Foreign Office as fatuous, arising from an 'emotional' rather than evidence-based response; Foreign Office/Commonwealth Office, confidential correspondence 12 August 1966 (IPG 2/546/2).

Contrary to the idea of a pro-England conspiracy, FIFA interventions, on two occasions during the World Cup finals, worked directly against the interests of the England team. Firstly, a tackle by Nobby Stiles, which injured Jacques Simon, during England's game against France, raised protest within the French press, as it was not penalised by the match referee. FIFA took up the complaint and pressured the FA to suspend Stiles from the forthcoming quarter-final against Argentina. The initiative failed, reportedly, only because Ramsey stood firm, insisting that if Stiles was suspended, he would resign as England manager; B. James, 'FIFA warning hits England', *Daily Mail*, 22 July 1966, p. 14. See the related discussion of this latter incident in Chapter 4.

In an even more telling intervention, FIFA is reported to have registered as 'unconfirmed' a foul against Franz Beckenbauer, issued by the referee in West Germany's semi-final match with the Soviet Union. Had the foul been allowed to stand on the official record, then Beckenbauer, widely regarded as West Germany's emerging star and most influential player, would have been ineligible to play in the World Cup Final. His absence from the game would have been enormously advantageous to England. The FIFA action is strongly indicative against any suggestion that England was being helped to victory in any way possible by the governing body, and the lack of protest against the action by the FA, while perhaps indicating organisational toothlessness, may indicate some graciousness on behalf of the host nation; B. James, 'No ban on top German', *Daily Mail*, 28 July 1966, p. 12.

39 Critcher, 'England and the World Cup', p. 81.
40 For a discussion of the 'fouls' issue in this match, see n. 42 for Chapter 4.
41 Critcher, 'England and the World Cup', p. 81.
42 Mason, 'England 1966', p. 94.
43 Porter, 'Your Boys Took One Hell of a Beating!', pp. 47–8.
44 Porter, 'Eggs and Chips with the Connellys', p. 534; Weight, *Patriots*, p. 460.
45 Reid and Zisserman 'Goal-directed Video Metrology'.
46 Banks, *Banksy*, p. 138.
47 For example, according to Silk and Francombe ('All these Years of Hurt', p. 264) 'England won the final against West Germany, courtesy perhaps of a generous Russian official'.
48 Porter 'Eggs and Chips with the Connellys', p. 534.
49 Young, 'Two World Wars and One World Cup', p. 15.
50 For example, see Banks, *Banksy*, p. 137.
51 Charlton, *Jackie Charlton*, p. 130. The erroneousness of the 'foul' against Charlton

was also noted by Sport Minister Denis Howell, a formally qualified football referee. See Howell, *Soccer Refereeing*, p. 100.

52 H. McIlvanney, 'Worthy champions of the World: Hurst hat-trick clinches it for England', *The Observer*, 31 July 1966, p. 16.

53 Young, 'Two World Wars and One World Cup', p. 14.

54 H. Miller, 'If we win, it may be "goodbye" to Wembley', *Daily Mirror*, 22 July 1966, p. 23.

55 Wilson's supposed view on the link between his election loss and England's elimination from the 1970 World Cup is discussed towards the conclusion of Chapter 3.

56 McKinstry, *Sir Alf*, p. 473.

57 Excerpt from *Till Death Us Do Part* television series (unreferenced and undated) www.youtube.com/watch?v=8o2icJ8–R2A accessed, 4 May 2015.

58 Porter, 'Your Boys Took One Hell of a Beating!'

59 Clarke and Critcher, '1966 and All That', pp. 125–6.

8

'An unforgettable day': memories of England's World Cup victory

> Memory alone cannot resurrect past time, because it is memory itself that shapes it, long after historical time has passed. (Carolyn Steedman)

No sooner had celebrations quietened in England after the World Cup victory than news came through from the United States of a tragedy in Texas. A student, former US Marine Charles Whitman, had killed and wounded a number of people at the University of Texas, Austin, most from a sniper's vantage point on the observation deck of the University's landmark clock tower building.[1] The near coincidence of date does not in itself warrant mention of this occurrence in relation to the 1966 World Cup Final, but a study conducted into the public's remembrance of the Texas tragedy is pertinent to the consideration of how England's World Cup victory has been, and still is, remembered. Rosa A. Eberly examines the difficulty of tallying individual memories of what occurred in Texas with the more formal public discourse, or non-discourse as it may be in this particular case.[2] This is especially so because preparedness by the University of Texas and civic authority in Austin to leave the episode in the past has resulted in an 'institutional forgetting', which has, in turn, led to the individual memories of those who choose not to forget being expressed in forums that remain open to such articulation, principally local talkback radio on anniversaries of the tragedy.

Forgetting, obviously enough, plays a rather different role in relation to the tragic event as opposed to the joyous event. It would seem strange to suggest that England's World Cup victory has in any way been forgotten within public discourse. Yet, as far back as 2002, the author Hunter Davies mused, 'perhaps it's about time we started to forget it … it's all ancient history now … part of the dark ages when football and life were so different'.[3] The remark concludes 'England's 1966 World Cup victory', a brief essay by Davies among forty-nine others, written by prominent journalists and sportspeople (including an essay by Bobby Charlton on Stanley Matthews), in a book – *British Sporting Greats* – seeking nomination of the 'all-time greats' (happenings, sport stars, or sporting arenas) of British sport.[4] In his essay, Davies provides not merely a detached journalistic account of the World Cup Final, including his opinion that 'England was the better team', but his autobiographical memory of being in attendance at Wembley for the match. His essay commences:

> I was there in 1966. And I still have my ticket to prove it – Seat 37, Row 9, Entrance 36, Turnstile K. It was not to be forgotten, which about half a million English persons have regularly not forgotten, their first-hand memories crystal clear, even though there were only 93,000 present in the flesh.[5]

Thus, for Davies, the personal experience of being there at the Final is unforgettable, the forgetting he calls for in the conclusion of his essay applies to a general public remembering of the World Cup Final, a memory he suggests to be apocryphal because it is built largely on the embellishments and imaginings of those who were not actually there at Wembley on 30 July 1966. It is now fourteen years on since his essay was published and Davies may be either more or less concerned than he was in 2002. With the passing of years, both the numbers of people who were actually at Wembley on 30 July 1966, and those who merely claim to have been there, are steadily diminishing. As those with an autobiographical memory of the World Cup Final (wherever they may have been at the time) die off, the remembering of the occasion becomes totally reliant on the historical memory of those who are either too young to remember the Final or were not yet born at the end of July 1966. The 'autobiographical memory' thus refers to personal, firsthand memory experience while the 'historical memory' refers to memory that comes to us only through the historical record. The two are related and together form what the French sociologist Maurice Halbwachs referred to as 'collective memory'. Importantly for Halbwachs, even autobiographical memory is not an entirely personal or individual matter, as 'all individual remembering takes place with social material, within social contexts and in response to social cues'.[6]

The social bearing on autobiographical memory formation is apparent enough in Davies's account of his firsthand attendance at Wembley for the World Cup Final. The ticket he keeps as material evidence for his claim to have been there also locates him within a context alongside others, the ticket holder of Seat 38 etcetera, those whom Davies would regard as members of a privileged memory community. Davies's opening claim, 'I was there in 1966' is made as a result of him recognising a social cue; that having actually been at Wembley for the Final carries a special significance to an audience wanting to hear about the occasion. But, despite the presumed authority of this claim, Davies's recollection of 'England's 1966 World Cup victory' is based as much on a secondhand historical memory as it is on his firsthand autobiographical memory. This is apparent in his description of the match and such details as Alf Ramsey's extra-time pep talk. An awareness of the words Ramsey supposedly said to his players is obviously based on subsequent reports, rather than on Davies's firsthand memory. The autobiographical memory presented by Davies offers little more than a lead into the story before the historical memory takes over. To be fair, Davies's essay is fit for purpose in the illustrated coffee-table book for which it was written. Its brevity doesn't really do justice to either Davies's autobiographical memory of the 1966 World Cup Final or to a fuller case he might care to make for the sporting historical importance of that occasion. But it does offer a glimpse into relevant uses of autobiographical memory and historical memory respectively.

The final part of this book takes the discussion of these forms of memory further. The present chapter focuses on the theme of autobiographical memory, via a consideration of particular textual representations of remembrance and recollection of the 1966 World Cup Final. The justification for focussing on memory of the Final, rather than the World Cup competition in England overall, was set out in the introductory chapter.[7] The next, and concluding, chapter incorporates a consideration of historical memory of the World Cup Final, particularly in regard to the theme of 'public memory' and commemoration of the Final and England's victory. The relationship between public memory and collective memory will be discussed at that point. In the present chapter, although the focus is on autobiographical memory and individual accounts thereof, collective memory is used as a term to explain the ways in which such memories come together to form a common story of the World Cup Final, and also to retain an understanding that the recollection and retelling of autobiographical memory of the occasion is impacted upon by a store of accepted knowledge that constitutes a commonly shared or collective memory.

As noted above, the term collective memory has been derived from the work of Halbwachs, the principle book being *La Mémoire Collective*, originally published in French in 1950. Translation of this book into English in 1980 – *The Collective Memory*[8] – has led to the growth in academic memory studies since that time. These studies have largely followed Halbwachs's lead as a left-thinking sociologist by interpreting collective memory critically in regard to the ideological function it serves for the maintenance of the social status quo. Collective memory, thus regarded, becomes 'a mere tool in the arsenal of power', used to deceive and manipulate the general population into accepting a view of the world that benefits dominant interest groups.[9] To a considerable extent, the academic accounts, discussed in Chapter 7, reflect a critical engagement with what they perceive as a collective memory construction of England's World Cup victory by the mass media into a conservative discourse that can be referred to as the 'myth of 1966'. The necessity of such critical engagement is not in dispute, but a focus on collective memory in this way is not particularly insightful to understanding the possible significances of individual or autobiographical memory accounts.[10]

Following the advice of Jeffrey Olick, the use of collective memory in this chapter is considered against the related term 'collected memory'.[11] Collected memory may be used to refer to the aggregation of individual memories within remembrance projects, should this be a book, a television show or a museum exhibition. This understanding becomes particularly relevant to the next chapter. The term may also refer to the collecting and juxtaposition of individual memories within research, and it is this understanding and related process that is relevant to the present chapter. An intention is to discuss individual memories in some detail and to avoid them being subsumed within a collective memory. A resolution of the inevitable antagonism between individual and collective memory positions is not proposed; more important here is the consideration of their engagement in a dynamic process of memory articulation.

Again, this is not to disconnect memory from social context. Indeed, listening to individual memory accounts can offer a different perspective on social issues to that found within sociological and related academic writing. Individual accounts presented in this chapter bring out matters of gender, religion and family relations in association with memories of the 1966 World Cup Final in a way that has yet to be addressed within the academic literature. Individual memory accounts considered within the academic work discussed in the previous chapter tend to be from a limited range of texts, mainly autobiographical and biographical works by England players and those positioned closely to football, such as journalists and broadcasters. Celebratory discussions of England's World Cup Final victory by players or others uninterested in the politics of sport are easily slotted into a critical academic stance on collective memory. What has been missed is a large-scale oral history project concentrated on the recording of autobiographical memories of the 1966 World Cup and the significance of England's victory. While such a survey would be open to differing interpretation by scholars, there can be little doubt that few would question the value of such a project in principle.[12]

This chapter draws upon a small range of textual materials that offer an autobiographical memory of the 1966 World Cup Final. The intention is to move away from 'official' voices associated with football, so player autobiographies and, for example, autobiographies such as Kenneth Wolstenholme's predictably titled *They Think It's All Over...* have been avoided. Fictional, as well as non-fictional representations of memory are discussed in the chapter. This is in the belief that imaginative works, blending fictionalised accounts of being at the Final with 'real' memory experience, offer interesting insights into the cultural significance of the occasion.[13] Fictionalised accounts can also be seen to disrupt the 'I was there' privilege assumed in Davies's essay. The chapter is not interested in acknowledging this privileged position, but in making sense

of how memories of the 1966 World Cup Final have been expressed and interpreted within written – and in one case visual – accounts.

Presumably, in all cases discussed in the chapter, the Final was watched at
the time, either in person at Wembley or on television. Unfortunately there is
little on record from those individuals who did not see the match, but who may
have had relevant memory accounts to share, for example people who missed
watching the Final because they had to work that afternoon. Other people
missed watching the Final because they were abroad on summer holidays at
the time. There are those who deliberately avoided seeing the game because
of a dislike for football and there will have been those who watched it on television, largely against their will, to please other family members. Little has
been recorded of these memories, and facile gender-based assumptions about
non-watching have resulted in lieu of evidence. Assumptions too have been
made about the comprehensiveness of support for the England team within
Britain. If the prevailing (mis)assumption in 1966 was that all British football
fans were behind England in the Final, this now seems to have been displaced
by the contrary assumption, certainly in regard to the Scots. However, there is
little on record to make the view that the majority of Scots wanted England to
lose anything more than a sweeping claim. And without such evidence, Denis
Law's anti-England attitude and avoidance of the television broadcast of the
Final is taken as the typical mindset of his countrymen.

The first item pertaining to memories of the 1966 World Cup Final to be
addressed in this chapter comes from the book *Voices of '66* by Norman Shiel.[14]
This is a non-academic work of oral history presentation, originally published
in 2000, with a further edition (or reprint) following in 2006. The second
round of publication was presumably targeted to coincide with the fortieth
anniversary year of the World Cup. No explanation is provided in the book
of the methodology used to obtain or present the memory pieces (most pieces
are between a quarter and half a page in length). Each piece may be described
as offering an autobiographical memory, in terms of the definition discussed
above. These memory pieces are set out in four sections, sequentially titled,
'The Preparations', 'Games Before the Final', 'The Final' and 'Aftermath'.
Given the focus of this chapter on the 1966 World Cup Final, the third section of the book is concentrated upon here. Particular attention is given to the
memory pieces provided by women in Shiel's chapter. Such a focus is well
justified given the paucity of recorded material on women's thoughts about the
1966 World Cup.

Shiel's chapter gathers fifty-nine written statements, or fragments of statements, relevant to the 1966 World Cup Final. As indicated above, no explanation is given on the methodology used in the book, and, thus, no information

is given on how memory statements were attained, recorded, edited and con-solidated into the overall text. No explanatory information is given on any of the individuals quoted. Any biographical details to be learnt about them come out of their brief statements. The surnames of individuals are given after each memory statement, sometimes with their first name and/or title, sometimes with just the initial of their first name. In the majority of cases where the first name or title is not indicated, the gender of the person can be ascertained from their statement. Most of the statements appear to be from members of the general public, a few are from football-related figures, Kenneth Wolstenholme and the trainer Wilf McGuiness being the best known of these. Roger Hunt is the only player from the World Cup Final to have a statement included in the chapter. Perhaps Shiel has selectively included Hunt because of his low-key profile relative to other players. Seven statements are provided from individu-als clearly identified as female. Forty-two of the statements are from individuals who were in attendance at the Final (including Roger Hunt), eleven statements are from individuals that saw the Final on television, three statements are from individuals that do not indicate how or whether or not they actually watched the match, and three statements are from individuals that, for one reason or another, did not see the game on the afternoon of 30 July 1966.

The seven individuals identified as female are split between three who watched the match on television, two who were in attendance at Wembley, one who gives no indication of whether or not she saw the match and one who gives indication she did not watch the match. The other forty individ-uals who attended the match appear to be male, as do the remaining seven individuals who watched the match on television. Given the small sample of female memory providers (and the selective, if somewhat larger, sample of male memory providers), it is not scientifically feasible to draw general con-clusions from information in the statements regarding gender patterns for the watching/non-watching of the World Cup Final. On the whole, and reasonably enough for his particular book project, Shiel has sought memory statements from people interested in football and in watching the World Cup Final. How he acquired statements from the women included in the book again is not revealed and, thus, the deliberateness with which he sought out female voices is unknown. The lack of information on process also denies explanation as to why certain themes arise within the memory statements of women, i.e. of marriage, family and domesticity. How much this reflects questioning and editing as opposed to open-ended commentary would be interesting to know.

Mrs P. Higgins tells of the 3 p.m. kick off at Wembley coinciding with her wedding. The ceremony was rushed by the vicar and some male guests did not show up at the reception until the Final had finished. A number of those who did attend kept ducking out to listen to the match on the wireless.[15] Mrs M. Greenwood and husband Eric were unable to afford their own television set, so they watched the Final at her parents' home in Fulham.[16] A statement from Mrs M. Ridge refers not to her own interest (or lack of interest) in the match, but how her son's confirmation at Exeter Cathedral was delayed because an 'eccentric' bishop had forgotten all about his ceremonial duties on the afternoon in preference to watching the World Cup Final on television.[17] Mrs S. Jones of Liverpool is the only statement provider in the chapter to confess a hatred for football. But, despite her antipathy to the sport and seemingly in the spirit of family togetherness, she sat with others 'round the television to watch the final'. But her abiding memory of the occasion was of her brother being seriously injured by a hit-and-run driver while out that night to celebrate England's victory.[18] Mrs L. Dane attended the match with her husband and her teenage nephew. Although they were saving most of their money to buy a bungalow, Mr Dane decided that seeing a World Cup in England was likely to be a once in a lifetime opportunity, so they saw a number of games including the Final. Mrs Dane holds a bittersweet memory of the occasion as her husband passed away in 1972, never to see another World Cup match in person.[19]

Mrs Dane is one of three declared female football fans among Shiel's commentators. A Queens Park Rangers season ticket holder, Mrs Dane kept her World Cup Final programme as a 'treasured' memento of the occasion. She 'will never forget the patriotism at Wembley and the sheer joy on the faces of the players'.[20] Her positive memory of attending the Final is shared by Mrs P. Chaston, who, as a 20-year-old at the time, is presumably some years younger than Mrs Dane. Mrs Chaston recalls the Final as a 'wonderful but totally exhausting and draining experience': she jumped up and down as the England team ran past on their victory lap and her hands were stinging for some time afterwards due to the exuberance of her clapping.[21] Like Mrs Dane and Mrs Chaston, Gill Haynes is a self-declared football fan but, unlike them, she saw the World Cup Final on television rather than in person at Wembley. She is the only statement provider of this type in Shiel's chapter. Ms Haynes, like her mother, is a 'fanatical' Tottenham Hotspur supporter and recalls one of her earliest childhood memories as seeing the Spurs 'double' winning team displaying both trophies from an open-topped bus in 1961. Five years later she watched the World Cup Final at home with her mother and father. Ms Haynes and her mother 'found the tension of extra time so unbearable' that they left the room and sat on the stairs with hands over their ears.[22] Her father was instructed to let them know if England scored. Difficulty in coping with the tension of the Final was also noted in the statement of Mrs Chaston. When the equalising goal was scored by West Germany, just ahead of regular full time, it was 'too much' for her and she 'burst into tears'.[23]

Again, without knowledge of the editing process used in Shiel's book, the reader is left to ponder the rationale for the highlighting of certain themes. Reference to the expression of personal emotions comes through in each of the statements provided by women who enthusiastically watched the World Cup Final. In one case, that of Mrs Dane, the joyous emotion she experienced at Wembley in 1966 is recalled against a feeling of sadness over the subsequent loss of her husband.

An alternative representation of a statement from a female football fan who attended the 1966 World Cup Final is featured in *Backpass*, a 'retro' magazine dedicated to stories, mainly British focussed, on football in the 1960s, 1970s and 1980s. A fan of Wolverhampton Wanderers, Ros Pedley tells of winning a standing ticket for the Final via success in a ballot for people who had attended the group stage games held at Villa Park.[24] Ms Pedley recounts the detail of her journey to the Final, made with her friend Liz: car from Wolverhampton to Stanmore tube station and from there by tube train to Wembley Park station. Upon reaching the ground around 1 p.m. Ms Pedley and Liz took up standing positions behind the goal at which Geoff Hurst would secure England's victory in the final seconds of extra time. So many years on, she confesses that memories of the game itself 'are somewhat hazy', but she recalls the 'non-stop running of Alan Ball, the constant nuisance of Roger Hunt and the unselfish off-the-ball running of Martin Peters' as key signs that England 'was a team determined to win'. Ms Pedley notes the 'indescribable elation when the final goal was thumped into the net at the end' at which she was standing and the respective emotional responses of the Charlton brothers, Jack 'sinking to his knees' and Bobby shedding tears.

Ms Pedley's recounting of her journey to and from Wembley to see the World Cup Final is similar to accounts in the statements in Shiel's chapter by male supporters who travelled to London from provincial locations to see the game. The effort entailed in getting to and from the match is suggested as an indicator of dedicated support for the England team. Ms Pedley's brief comment on the performance of England players displays her knowledge of football play, an opportunity afforded to only some of the male statement providers in Shiel's chapter. Her highlighting of Hunt's 'nuisance' to the West German defence is particularly telling, as such an observation is unlikely to have been made by a person inexperienced in watching football. Her comment on the emotional response of the Charlton brothers also positions her differently to women discussed above. Rather than her emotions being put in the foreground, Ms Pedley is able to comment on those of players, and in this way she becomes an 'objective' observer on the aftermath of the game in the manner of other male commentators. The conclusion of her narrative points back to the importance of personal experience; 'it was a never-to-be-forgotten day and I will always be proud to say "I was there!"' Having been at Wembley to see the Final in person is offered in good faith and with conviction as a privileged memory status. A similar conclusion is detectable in a number of the statements gathered in Shiel's chapter. For example:

I still feel tremendously privileged to have been present at England's greatest football success – D. Roberts[25]

It was an unforgettable introduction to Wembley and the feeling of 'being there' will always be with me – P. di Giuseppe[26]

The date 30 July was an unforgettable day for me. It is not often you can really say of something important, 'I was there' – K. Porter[27]

The reminiscence of attending the World Cup Final in these examples is, like that of Hunter Davies, commonly positive and happily 'unforgettable'.[28] This representation of collected memory, which gives voice to a collective memory, is steeped in commemorative significance, according to which each of the articulators desired an England victory. The collective memory also exhibits a reflexive awareness that the World Cup has not been won subsequently and, possibly, an assumption that it is unlikely to be won again by England any time soon. The collected memory to be constructed from these examples, as well as others in Shiel's chapter does not involve a renunciation of the event that was the 1966 World Cup Final; however, the odd critical observation is recorded in some memory statements, including reference to an expression of nationalistic inspired resentment by some people in the crowd when England conceded the late second goal, thus renewing a chance for West Germany to win in extra time.[29] A number of statements refer to the overall memory of the match being a blur, although certain highlights, especially the controversial third England goal by Hurst, are recalled vividly, if not with certainty of interpretation at the time. Mr K. Metcalfe recalls people turning to each other to ask, 'Did it go in?', but, the query was lost in the 'ecstatic' celebration once the goal was awarded. Doubts about the correctness of the referee's decision came some time 'afterwards', according to Mr Metcalfe.[30]

Of course, Mr Metcalfe's account is from the perspective of an England supporter, as are most others presented in Shiel's chapter. A memory account from a supporter of West Germany present at Wembley for the World Cup Final would probably reverse the emphasis of interpretation. Although uncertainty as to whether or not Hurst's shot went in might have been shared with England supporters, the resultant awarding of the goal was no doubt commonly experienced by West German supporters with a feeling of dismay rather than joy. In similar contrast, we may assume a West German supporter's memory of the equalising goal, scored just ahead of regular full time, which so galled England fans, to be one of relief at the very least. This rather states the obvious, but in doing so it highlights how different collective memories may be formed in regard to one episode, one incident, or one historical moment. A commitment to the importance of the memory may be determined by the intensity with which the incident or happening was felt at the time, such as the feeling prompted by the awarding of Hurst's goal, or the blowing of the referee's whistle to sound England's winning of the World Cup Final and West Germany's loss. In regard to an event such as a World Cup Final the expression of feeling is underpinned by attitudes towards patriotism and nationalism. Shiel's chapter assembles memories of people seemingly unanimous in their wont for England to win the Final in 1966. By seeking out a majority of English informants in attendance of the Final at Wembley the intensity in positive expression of the memory of England's win is not surprising.

Book-length fan and supporter reflections upon the 1966 World Cup are few. That autobiographical memory accounts from those who attended the Final tend to be the preserve of football journalists and commentators is understandable, given the way that book contracts are awarded by publishing houses. For someone not professionally associated with football to publish such a book would require them to be a known author or to turn to 'vanity publishing'. Such seems to be the case with *I was There in '66* by Steve Batchelor, published by Athena Press in 2006.[31] Seventeen years old at the time, Batchelor purchased tickets for the games at Wembley and was then successful in a ballot, much in the way of Ros Pedley, which allowed him to purchase two tickets for the Final. By writing a book-length account Batchelor is able to embed his memories of the World Cup into a story of his life at the time. Via the provision of this fuller context his reflections upon key moments during the episode gain poignancy less likely to come through in the fragments of a brief edited statement. For example, in isolation, Batchelor's remark that he was 'quivering with excitement', upon receiving the letter from the FA about his success in the draw for tickets to the Final[32] may sound like mere boyish exaggeration, but, read within the context of the lead-up to his receipt of the letter on 20 July 1966, his peaked emotional state seems justifiably described.

Fuller discussion also provides reflection upon potentially controversial themes that tend to be left out of briefer, purely celebratory memory accounts. Such is the case with Batchelor's recalling of chants directed by England supporters, within his standing position vicinity at the Final, towards supporters of West Germany. This occurred, according to Batchelor, following West Germany's scoring of the equalising goal that denied England victory in regular time.

> from nowhere a shout developed that was taken over by hundreds of people around me. It seemed like an almost childlike reaction against the beastly Germans as if this would somehow avenge the injustice of their last goal: 'We won the war – we won the war!'[33]

Despite recognising (perhaps subsequently) that a 'retaliatory chant resonated throughout the area where I was standing and brought a sinister chill to the day'[34] Batchelor admits he joined in to what he mistakenly believed to be a continuation of the 'We won the war!' chant when Hurst scored in the first half of extra time. However, with the score now at England 3–West Germany 2 the collective chant had actually changed to the similar-sounding 'We want four!' This chant soon gave way to another 'war cry', 'Attack, attack – attack, attack, attack!'[35]

Batchelor's honest admission to having joined in momentarily with the morally unacceptable collective voicing is admirable. He could have easily recounted the belligerent chant coming from other England fans while 'forgetting' his own attempt to join the chorus. Admitting his own complicity also lends a certain power to his admonition of the England supporters' chant in regard to the discomfiture it brought to the supporters of West Germany within earshot.

> The Germans, who had been celebrating wildly, were bemused that the cheers of their supporters were completely drowned with this incessant, almost ethnic chant and their supporters, who undoubtedly understood English better than the average Englishman understands German, were incensed and the mood grimly changed from friendly rivalry to outright hostility within a minute as the ghost of World War II loomed over the occasion. I sensed the German supporters, even though they had snatched victory from within our grasp in the dying seconds, were simply embarrassed by such a puerile chant and the hostile change of atmosphere and they became strangely quiet.[36]

Batchelor also reflects critically upon the failure of television replays, despite 'We won the war' being 'repeated in unison for several minutes' by England supporters, to give any indication of the chant having occurred. He wonders whether it might have 'been dubbed out' because it was deemed by broadcasters as 'politically offensive'.[37] It is a provocative suggestion, one in keeping with the view of critical academics regarding the possibility of a sanitised collective memory having been constructed by powerful interests, such as the mass media, to present a positive impression of the 1966 World Cup.

A more subtle flagging of lingering post-war antipathy towards German people existing just below the surface of respectable English society is provided in the novel *Sean's World Cup Final Day Out: Wembley 1966* by John Riding.[38] Primarily for a young readership, this book tells the story of ten-year-old Sean, who, while out for a walk on farmland with his dog Rocket, is caught in a downpour and takes shelter in a barn. Rocket's entry into the barn agitates the resident horse, which kicks Sean in the head, rendering him unconscious. The story resumes with Sean waking up in his room at home in a suburb near

Newcastle-upon-Tyne. To his surprise and consternation, his surroundings are not as they should be. The year is 2006, but the posters on Sean's bedroom wall are of footballers from a bygone era and the clothes in his wardrobe are of a style worn by boys before his father was a lad. Stepping out on to the street, Sean sees that the few cars about are makes from decades well before he was born. These startling discoveries are compounded when Sean is congratulated by his father for having found the missing Jules Rimet trophy while out for his walk with Rocket. As a reward, Sean and his family are given tickets to attend the World Cup Final at Wembley. At this point Sean realises he has somehow slipped into a time-warp, from the summer of 2006 to that of 1966. As much as Sean wants to return to his own time, and the comforts and gadgets with which he is familiar, he cautiously embraces the opportunity to relive England's great moment in international football, so he keeps his awareness of the bizarre occurrence to himself and just hopes that his 'real' life will return at some point after the World Cup Final (as happens in the story).

A particular difficulty faced by Sean is to avoid revealing his knowledge of the result in advance of his family's trip to the Final. He succeeds against the temptation to blurt out the score, his only falter coming at Wembley when upon seeing the England manager walk by he yells, 'Good luck Sir Alf!', to the bemusement of those around him.[39] *Sean's World Cup Final Day Out* is a charming and fun story, which prompts enquiry from young readers into historical aspects of its narrative, including the tacit reference to Pickles finding the stolen and abandoned Jules Rimet trophy when out for a walk with his owner. The back-to-the-future type scenario also provides Sean with a glimpse of how individual personalities are shaped by the circumstances of the time in which people live. The man before him is certainly his father, but this man exhibits attitudes which Sean does not recognise in his father of 2006. His comment on the beyond sport significance of the outcome of the World Cup Final is a case in point.

> It's going to be a great day Sean. England versus West Germany in the World Cup final at Wembley. Who'd have thought it eh? The war just twenty years over and here we are playing the old enemy at football. We don't want to lose this one.

Sean's mother challenges her husband's representation of what she regards as past enmity:

> Now, now Alexander. We don't want any talk of the war, not now or tomorrow. That's behind us thank goodness, and we all need to move on.[40]

His mother's attitude is more recognisable to Sean. He refers to her being 'sensible as ever'. Nevertheless, Sean admits he understands his father's position, acknowledging 'it must have been very strange back in 1966 to be playing such an important football match against a country that England had so recently been at war with'.[41] From a biographical note on the cover of the book we learn that, like Sean, John Riding was ten years old at the time of the 1966 World Cup. Sean's story seemingly carries his own autobiographical memory of the World Cup Final, but in this fictionalised form affords him the opportunity to have been at Wembley on the day. In reality, Riding watched the match on television rather than in person. It also allows him to convey to a young, contemporary reader the perspective of a ten-year-old boy at the time. Riding perhaps heard, in his own home, the type of exchange that Sean witnesses between his mother and father about football and wartime enmity. By presenting the episode through the eyes and voice of Sean, directly from the time, rather than from his own memory in documentary form by a 50-year-old man in 2006, Riding sits the reader down in that Newcastle kitchen in 1966 to hear the dad's comment about the war via Sean's sympathetic ear. A mere retelling in the present day of such an episode from the past would more likely involve not a sympathetic hearing, but a purely judgemental response.

Sean's return to the present comes after he falls from his father's shoulders during the celebrations at Wembley and is knocked unconscious. He awakens in a hospital bed being told by his parents that he has just emerged from a coma after having been kicked in the head by a horse. Mentioning the return to 1966 seems too preposterous, so Sean settles on asking his father if he thinks England will ever win the World Cup again. He is heartened by an affirmative response and his father's assurance that they 'will be there' when it happens.[42]

The father-and-son relationship theme finds its way into other stories recalling the 1966 World Cup Final. *The Timeless Zone – A Return to '66*, by Bob Cox, is another novel favouring a back-to-the-future type narrative.[43] However, this story goes into the realm of science fiction when its protagonist, 12-year-old Matthew Sharp, after finding an old football during a garage clean-up, becomes trapped in an air bubble hovering above his real life surroundings. Although offered the opportunity of eternal existence within this ethereal state and the chance to determine what goes on in the world below him, Matthew wants a return to normal mortality and, with the help of his grandfather (who is in similar air-bubbled condition), works out that the key to his return is the decrepit football entrapped in the air bubble with him. The ball carries twelve fading signatures and Grandad is able to recognise eleven of them being the names of the England players from the World Cup winning team.

Grandad took Matthew's father to see the Final at Wembley and was able to have a ball signed by the England team, the very ball now in Matthew's possession. However, Grandad is puzzled by the twelfth signature and Matthew becomes certain that a trip back to Wembley on 30 July 1966 is needed to reveal the signatory and thus enable him to be released from his suspended state. In a fanciful twist (within a narrative already stretched to the limits of science-fiction credulity) the mysterious twelfth signature is revealed to be that of 'Russian' linesman Tofiq Bahramov, who becomes implicated in the creation of the 'Timeless Zone' state in which Matthew and his grandfather find themselves. By pressing hard on the signature, and through his growing power to determine events, Matthew is able to will himself back into the present and the garage at home, which he has still to clean up. The story started with Matthew cleaning the garage as a punishment imposed by his father for a failed attempt to run away from home. The trip back to the 1966 World Cup Final, and seeing his father as a boy in the company of his own father at Wembley, has given Matthew a new appreciation for the mutual love between father and son, and his desire to return home is driven largely by his intention to rehabilitate this relationship. *The Timeless Zone* does not reflect an authorial autobiographical memory as clearly as *Sean's World Cup Final Day Out* seems to do. Whether or not based on Cox's own memory, and father–son relationship, *The Timeless Zone* is written from an unstated autobiographical perspective, from which this theme is developed. Both books are derived from their respective author's obvious belief that the 1966 World Cup Final provides an ideal occasion through which a father-and-son unification narrative can be told. Accordingly, the narrative in both is interwoven into the now familiar commemorative collective memory of 'England's greatest day'.[44]

A similar usage of collective memory of the World Cup is made in the film *Sixty Six* (2006).[45] The film is based on what is conceded to be an embellished personal account of the events surrounding the bar mitzvah of the film's writer and director Paul Weiland. The lead character in the film, Bernie Rubens, is 13 years old in 1966 (Weiland was born in July 1953) and his bar mitzvah is scheduled for the afternoon of 30 July. The son of a timid, sickly and pessimistic greengrocer, Bernie is subject to bullying by boys at school, and the same at home from his tyrannical older brother. Feeling generally overlooked in life, Bernie sees the bar mitzvah as the one occasion when he can be the centre of attention, if just for a few hours. However, two unrelated problems arise to thwart Bernie's plan for the bar mitzvah to be a grand affair. Firstly, upon learning that the World Cup Final will be played at Wembley on 30 July Bernie fears that if England make the Final, guests will choose to watch the match on television rather than attend his bar mitzvah. Bernie is spurred into action, taking an interest in football, a sport that he has previously avoided to the best of his ability. However, this is only so as to get to know more about England's prospects of making the Final. Despite the consensus of opinion around him that England have no chance of playing at Wembley on 30 July, Bernie is not convinced and he conspires to jinx the England team via the enactment of various rituals, including sticking pins in a cuddly World Cup Willie and incinerating the photographs of England players.

As England advance through the competition to reach the Final, Bernie's worst fears are confirmed. To compound his woes, financial problems brought about by his father's business incompetence mean that the celebration following his bar mitzvah in the synagogue is switched from a function centre to a back garden turnout at home. But even the numbers for this reduced gathering dwindle, as Bernie had anticipated. Once England's place in the Final is confirmed, following the semi-final defeat of Portugal on 26 July, invited guests start phoning with false excuses as to why they will not be able to make his occasion. By the afternoon of the bar mitzvah, Bernie's emotions are at rock bottom. He becomes so fed up that he actually deserts the party to roller-skate down the street alone, still wearing his yarmulke and tallit. Upon becoming aware of Bernie's absconding, his parent's finally realise the extent of their son's upset, and his father Manny heads off in the car to look for him. Manny's finding of Bernie results in a late turning point in the film, a lifting of their respective spirits and their joining together in a most unexpected mutual cause. In an apparent reassessment of the impact of his own pessimism on his son, Manny philosophises:

> I suppose there's another way of looking at it. How many boys can say that on the day of their bar mitzvah, England played in a World Cup final? It may never happen again. And besides, this team, this England team, no-one believed in them, people were ridiculing them, calling them this, calling them that. But they never gave up, did they? They never gave in. It seems to me that this is a team we should be supporting [pause] especially on the day of your bar mitzvah. Now, be honest with me Bernie, when all is said and done, who do you want to win?

Bernie considers the question for about five seconds before unequivocally answering, 'England'. Manny then turns on the car radio and they listen to the last minutes of the match as they head home. When West Germany equalises in the final seconds both express disappointment before Manny, ignorant in the rules of football, turns to Bernie to ask if the game now goes into extra time. He greets Bernie's affirmation with an enthusiastic 'good!' and, in totally uncharacteristic fashion, puts his foot on the accelerator and speeds off with the intention of getting to Wembley for the conclusion of the match. They enter the stadium in time to see the final goal and together wave Bernie's tallit in celebration, as though it were a football scarf. The final sequence of the film features a family back garden football kick about at home that evening. In voice-over, Bernie declares his coming-of-age insight as the need to stop expecting his father to be perfect and to 'love him for the man he is'. 'On my bar mitzvah', Bernie declares, 'my dad became my friend for one day, and I loved it, and I always will.'

The opening credits for the film describe *Sixty Six* as a 'true-ish story'. A more formal disclaimer is included at the end of the film's closing credits:

While this film is based on a true story, in dramatising the story for the screen some characters have been composited or invented and certain events, dialogue and chronology have been fictionalised.[46]

Where Weiland's autobiographical memory gives way to historical memory is uncertain, but if it is the case that his bar mitzvah was held on 30 July 1966, it is entirely feasible that the attendance numbers were adversely affected by the clash of date with the World Cup Final. So perhaps Weiland did live through the dread of England making the Final and undertake the jinxing rituals we see perpetrated by Bernie in the film. Perhaps he did have a last-minute change of heart and rush to Wembley with his father to see England win. But, irrespective of where the 'truth' lies, most interesting is Weiland's use of this deliberately mixed memory to connect the World Cup Final to the father-and-son bonding tale. The account he gives of the World Cup Final – including his father receiving a speeding ticket from an unsympathetic Scottish policeman – is in keeping with the commemorative stereotype, effectively done with emotional music accompanying excellent quality footage of the England team players rejoicing on the pitch after the game. The most original dimension to the story is the linking of the World Cup to Bernie's cultural identity and his related shift in attitude, stirred by his father's speech towards the end of the film. Manny's reference to the England team being ridiculed and derided, but not giving up, can be read as a likening to the Jewish people, and thus his claim that this is a team that he and Bernie should be following, especially on the day of Bernie's bar mitzvah. The prevailing of this England team allows Manny and Bernie – as perhaps was the case for Weiland and his father – to accept and celebrate their own Englishness and, as evidenced by the subsequent kick around in the back garden, to adopt football as a game of their own.[47]

A much less romantic father-and-son story is threaded through David Thomson's detailed account of the 1966 World Cup Final in his part memoir, part popular history *4–2*.[48] Thomson provides an almost kick-by-kick account of the Final interspersed with reflections on football, life and 1960s' culture. Thomson's profession as film critic is in evidence with his sometimes stretched comparisons of football figures to film stars and luminaries, including Alf Ramsey to Alfred Hitchcock. His constant asides to tales from other sports, including cricket, American football and baseball, are explained in his afterword by the intention of a 'narrow book in one way' to be at once 'expansive, about all sport'.[49] The book was published in 1996 by which time Thomson had moved from his native England to live and work in the US. An Anglo-American identity is in evidence in the trans-Atlantic hopping of the storytelling between the passages of commentary on the 1966 Final. Thomson watched the match on television as a 25-year-old man in his then London home in the company of his near two-year-old son. He obviously draws on the autobiographical memory of that experience to relay his thoughts as he recalls them from the time. However, for the detail of the match description the observation was fresh, reliant on Thomson 'studying the none-too-fine tape of the match'.[50] His stated intention in this aspect of the book was to be accurate in describing the particulars of the game.

However, he admits, even in this endeavour, 'feelings were creeping in' regarding a tendency to express admiration for some players, notably Moore and Beckenbauer, and disfavour for others, notably Hunt and Peters.[51] A related consideration, not addressed by Thomson, is whether or not the objective reading of the match, involving opinion on the individual performances of players, remained affected by his more subjective watching of the match live on television back in 1966 as an England fan. If he came to watch the tape in 1996 without the autobiographical memory of the game from 1966, would he, for argument's sake, have been as prone as he was to highlight Martin Peters' presumed shortcomings? Thus, a perfectly accurate pass back to Moore is interpreted as characteristic of Peters' timidity, his unwillingness to act on adventurous impulse in the manner of the 'really great players'.[52] Yet there is enough within the detailed description of the match in *4–2* to overcome the intrusion of Thomson's preformed opinion into the commentary. In sheer number, and contrary to the author's intention, the unavoidable mentions of Peters' contributions to England's play effectively overcome Thomson's perfunctory tone and free the player from a possible damning with faint praise.[53]

The information about Thomson having watched the World Cup Final live on television and then thirty years later on video tape in preparation for the writing of *4–2* is provided, respectively, at the commencement and end of the book. Drawing upon the real viewing experiences of the match, the commentary on the Final within the central text imagines Thomson being at Wembley on 30 July 1966. He is there, standing in the crowd watching the game and describing the play out loud when a 'stranger' beside him asks, 'Blimey mate … you going to go through every single move?'[54] Related conversations periodically interrupting Thomson's commentary on the match, voicing Cockney truisms about football and life, soon reveal the stranger's articulations as an expression of the author's alter-ego. Via these conversations, Thomson discusses his father's estrangement from the family home throughout the week and his 'heroic returns' at the weekend to take his son to watch football (Chelsea as well as non-League club Tooting and Mitcham) and cricket in their respective seasons. In the final conversation, the stranger's identity seems to merge with that of Thomson's father when he refers to his two-year-old grandson: 'I'll tell him I was here … got a programme for him … he'll love it, however, I won't tell him about you.'[55] *4–2* closes with Thomson critically reflecting upon being abandoned by his father, apart from weekend sport, and the difficulty of his relationship with his own children, caused by his marital desertion and move to the US. However, the fantasy return to Wembley for the World Cup Final allows for a reconciliation of sorts across generations. When Thomson cradled his son while cheering England on to televised victory in 1966, he could only suppose his father to be watching the game on television elsewhere, at his home near St Albans. They were not in touch at the time.[56] Regret is evident enough in his words to indicate Thomson's belief that the World Cup Final was an occasion he would have best shared with his father as well as his son. Writing *4–2* gave him the chance to imaginatively redress the missed opportunity.

The recollections, retellings and reconstructions of the 1966 World Cup Final addressed in this chapter reflect what Carolyn Steedman has recognised as a tension between the ways in which stories are told and the 'compulsions of historical explanation'. But this is a symbiotic or synergistic tension, not in need of resolution because stories of this kind 'aren't stories in their own right: they exist with other more central ones'.[57] This is not to suggest the existence of *a* central story to which individual stories are orientated. Indeed, this chapter has warned against the use of the term collective memory for the marshalling of individual memories. The fictional texts discussed in the latter half of the chapter show the 1966 World Cup Final as a 'central' story in some lives, a story which is used to make sense of other stories, particularly those concerning familial relationships. The focus here, given the texts that are available, has been on father/son relationships, with mothers given a secondary role within those stories. The brief statements from women taken from the book by Shiel and the account given by Ros Pedley, shown in the earlier part of the chapter, indicate the importance of the 1966 World Cup Final as an occasion within the lives of some English women. Some of these accounts give glimpse to familial relationships but nothing more. Unfortunately, there is no fan-based text by a woman of the 1966 World Cup in the manner of Julie Welch's fictionalised autobiographical reflection upon her life as a North London schoolgirl during the 1960/61 double winning season of Tottenham Hotspur, provided in the screenplay for the 1983 film *Those Glory Days*.[58]

Perhaps the fiftieth anniversary of the 1966 World Cup will provide an opportunity for the publication of a further, probably final, round of 'autobiographical memory' production, in the manner of both non-fiction and fictionalised accounts, including film. That this should happen before the chance to get such memories into public access is lost is important. Access to more autobiographical memories of the 1966 World Cup and England's victory will be helpful to establishing a greater sense of balance against the ongoing 'historical memory', and, for this sense of balance, that vague notion academics continue to refer to as the 'collective memory' will be maintained as a richer repository.

Notes

1 'Sniper in Texas U. tower kills 12, hits 33', *New York Times*, 2 August 1966, pp. 1 & 14.
2 Eberly, 'University of Texas Tower Shootings'.
3 Davies, 'England's 1966 World Cup Victory', p. 185.
4 Davies also contributed to this volume an essay titled, 'The Twin Towers of Wembley', pp. 168–9.
5 Davies, 'England's 1966 World Cup Victory', p. 184.
6 Olick, 'Collective Memory', p. 337.
7 See, pp. 4–5.
8 Halbwachs, *The Collective Memory*.
9 Olick, 'From Collective Memory', p. 159.
10 Memory studies within Britain have been significantly influenced by the Gramscian strain of cultural studies to emerge from the Centre for Contemporary Cultural Studies (CCCS) at the University of Birmingham, with a related focus on memory as ideology (see Erll, *Memory in Culture*, p. 11). This influence is noticeable in academic work discussed in Chapter 7, especially the essays by Chas Critcher and John Clarke, both formerly associated with the CCCS.
11 Olick, 'Collective Memory', p. 337.
12 Relatedly, the Heritage Lottery Fund has awarded £302,500 to a consortium bid by the National Football Museum (NFM), the Sporting Memories Foundation and the FA to include a memories component within the 1966 World Cup 50th anniversary exhibition at the NFM in the summer of 2016.
13 See Erll, *Memory in Culture*, pp. 144–71, for a detailed account in favour of fiction as a means of representing 'cultural memory'.
14 Shiel, *Voices of '66*.
15 *Ibid.*, p. 143.
16 *Ibid.*, p. 133.
17 *Ibid.*, p. 138.
18 *Ibid.*, pp. 138–9.
19 *Ibid.*, p. 156.
20 *Ibid.*
21 *Ibid.*, p. 121.
22 *Ibid.*, p. 146.
23 *Ibid.*, p. 121.
24 'I Was There', *Backpass*, Issue 37, 2014, pp. 18–19.
25 Shiel, *Voices of '66*, p. 118.
26 *Ibid.*, p. 123.
27 *Ibid.*, p. 134.
28 Davies, 'England's 1966 World Cup Victory'.

29 See comment by journalist Clive Toye in Shiel, *Voices of '66*, p. 130.

30 Shiel, *Voices of '66*, p. 124.

31 Batchelor, *I Was There in '66*. Athena Press of Twickenham, London appears to have been an author 'pay to publish' press that is now defunct.

32 *Ibid.*, p. 89.

33 *Ibid.*, p. 140.

34 *Ibid.*, p. 140.

35 *Ibid.*, p. 144.

36 *Ibid.*, p. 141.

37 *Ibid.*, p. 140.

38 Riding, *Sean's World Cup Final Day Out*. This book was published in 2006 by Exposure Publishing, an imprint of Diggory Press. The latter is known as a 'vanity publisher' (the term 'independent publisher' is sometimes used) and would suggest Riding paid to have the book published on a small print run. This is mentioned not in criticism, but to indicate, again, the difficulty faced by unknown authors in getting books published. To reinforce the point of relevance to this chapter – the limitation of such authorial opportunity has restricted the public articulation of memories of the 1966 World Cup to certain privileged speakers and writers.

39 *Ibid.*, p. 72. Alf Ramsey was knighted in 1967, thus, in the year after the World Cup win. On the front page of the *Daily Mail*, 1 August 1966, following the World Cup Final victory, Roy Peskett reported that England players, jokingly but respectfully, referred to Ramsey as 'Sir Alf'. Knowledge of this nickname may have influenced Riding's related use in his narrative.

40 Riding, *Sean's World Cup Final Day Out*, pp. 58–9.

41 *Ibid.*, p. 59. This is similar to a thought had by Jack Charlton as he lined up to take the field at Wembley for the Final, *For Leeds and England*, p. 126: 'Ranged alongside us as we waited in the tunnel were the West German players – our opponents. The thought flashed through my mind. For six years we had waged war against Germany; now we were preparing to do battle on the football field.'

42 Riding, *Sean's World Cup Final Day Out*, p. 97.

43 Cox, *The Timeless Zone*. This book was also published by an 'independent publisher'.

44 *Ibid.*, p. 59.

45 *Sixty Six*, produced by T. Bevan, E. Felner and E. Karlsen, distributed by Universal Pictures, 2006. DVD released 2010.

46 For a discussion of the representation of sport within film, see Hughson, *The Making of Sporting Cultures*, pp. 118–33.

47 For a discussion on the theme of male Jewish identity and enculturation in England via football, see Clavane, *Does Your Rabbi Know You're Here?*, pp. xxi–xxxix, and Dee, 'Football, Integration and Jewish "Anglicisation"'.

48 Thomson, *4–2*.

49 *Ibid.*, p. 229.

50 *Ibid.*, p. 225.

51 *Ibid.*

52 *Ibid.*, p. 29.

53 In a recent book Geoff Hurst regards Martin Peters to be one of the most underrated players in the history of football. See Hurst, *50 Greatest Footballers*, p. 44.

54 Thomson, *4–2*, p. 19.

55 *Ibid.*, pp. 194–5.

56 *Ibid.*, p. 12.

57 Steedman, *Landscape for a Good Woman*, pp. 21–2.

58 *Those Glory Days*, produced by C. Griffin, distributed by Film 4, 1983. DVD released 2008.

9

That was the World Cup that was

... he had no desire to defy Germany and to exalt England. The distinction between German and English was not for him the distinction between good and bad. It was the distinction between blue water-flowers and red or white bush-blossoms: just difference. The difference between the wild boar and the wild bear. And a man was good or bad according to his nature, not according to his nationality. (D.H. Lawrence)

Rather than appreciating England's victory at the 1966 World Cup on its own terms, many commentators have been preoccupied with the win as a historical marker of a rightful state of football affairs. However, as the years roll by, the success of Ramsey's team tends to be adjudged more as an aberration of past achievement than as an index of future possibility. The suggestion throughout this book has been that recalling the 1966 World Cup only in regard to England's chances at forthcoming World Cups muddies the process of commemoration. This chapter addresses the theme of commemoration in relation to public engagement projects, such as museum exhibitions. It considers the challenge faced in planning an exhibition to have popular appeal while not being celebratory in a facile way.[1] The term 'public history' is favoured in this regard and it is used in the discussion of not only exhibition contexts, but also permanent commemorative sites, sculptures in particular. It is used here in accordance with the understanding provided by the US based National Council on Public History[2] whereby public history involves an engagement with and presentation of historical themes and subject matter, occurring within public sphere locations.

The creation and display of public history in museum exhibitions involves constructing and presenting a 'public memory'. The term is preferred here to 'collective memory' because the latter can connote an already established group or societal memory, a memory constantly rehearsed within mass media at anniversary and other convenient moments. While the influence of this collective memory is unavoidable, the professionals working with a public memory, in the creation of a public history display, will be mindful to avoid the stereotypes and lazy mythologies that are incorporated into a collective memory. This is not an easy undertaking. The title of historian John Bodnar's book *Remaking America* was meant as a cautious reminder of what is involved in commemorative projects.[3] From exhibitions regarding westward-bound pioneers to memorial events for Vietnam War veterans, a public memory undergoes 'remaking' and, in doing so, can disrupt a historical consciousness already steeped in certain beliefs, including patriotism. A brave exhibition will risk upsetting established views and, without necessarily being intended to adopt a political stance of its own, will lend to an open interpretation of events in a way to challenge politically based, taken-for-granted assumptions. In a democratic society, the representation of public memory can reasonably be expected to reflect a diversity in belief and values and, therefore, to be pluralistic in orientation to allow for the possibility of differing political interpretations by the observer.

A public-history, museum-based exhibition on the 1966 World Cup will necessarily involve imagery of and some text about Queen Elizabeth in attendance at the Final and the opening ceremony. However, this can be achieved in a historically representative way without presenting an either pro- or anti-monarchy viewpoint. In keeping with what was said above in regard to US examples, this may still be unsettling as it can involve taking issue with some popular articulations that are drawn into the presentation of public memory. Statements from the day claiming England's winning of the World Cup as a triumph in keeping with past imperial glory may well be displayed as part of a public memory record, but in a critical way to indicate that such a viewpoint is, at best, rather outdated. The expression of such criticism in an exhibition may be disagreeable to some viewers but, then, they will be free to reinterpret England's victory – visually displayed in the exhibition – as they please. Patriotic overkill may also be defused by way of humour. For example, something might be made of the type of statement put forward by the journalist Peter Allen:

> The image of them [Ramsey and team] on the most glorious day of so many lives is a stirring example of England's true heritage. It should be displayed every morning at school assemblies before our subdued nation becomes any more like Sweden.[4]

Rather than seriously suggesting the formalising of such ceremony, Allen mocks the exaggeration of England's World Cup victory as a signifier of national character. But using light-heartedness to expose the silliness, or worse, chauvinism need not detract from the seriousness of claims made for the importance of the World Cup and England's victory as a cultural event and even as a milestone. A key claim of this book has been for Ramsey's team playing strategy to be reconsidered within discussions about the history of football coaching and tactics.

Without rehearsing the case set out in Chapter 5, the claim is that, contrary to most interpretations, Ramsey's team playing pattern involved a certain type of modernist aesthetic, an aesthetic bearing parallel to other cultural happenings in Britain at the time. The edited volume *Moments of Modernity* includes chapters covering the period from the end of the Second World War in 1945 up to the election of the Wilson Government in 1964.[5] Had the editors stretched the period until, say, 1967's 'summer of love', then other inclusions would be pertinent, certainly the Beatles, popular music and the recording of *Sgt. Pepper's Lonely Hearts Club Band*, and also from the case made here, football, modernity and England's World Cup win. In a more recent publication, titled *1965*, Christopher Bray heralds that mid-1960s' mark as 'the year Modern Britain was born'.[6] Central to the claim is recognition of a change in the cultural landscape against Labour's first full year in office. 1965 was the year in which popular culture became serious as, *inter alia*, the Beatles were awarded MBEs and Stanley Matthews retired as a player and became the first footballer to be knighted. In 1967 Matthews was joined by Alf Ramsey as football's second knight, the latter on the basis of his achievement as a modern football manager, not as a player from the same romantic generation as Matthews. The respective claims of Matthews and Ramsey to their honouring, two years apart, are symbolically significant to the cultural history of English football.

As noted by Bray, 1965 was the year in which a black footballer first played in an FA Cup Final. This was South African Albert Johanneson for Leeds United in the 1–2 loss to Liverpool.[7] A teammate of Johanneson's in that match was Paul Reaney, who played at right back for Leeds. Fulham-born, Yorkshire-raised, Reaney was of mixed-race background, but did not identify publicly as such. Reaney was selected by Ramsey as a member of the 40-player preliminary World Cup squad, but was not included at the penultimate stage for the training camp at Lilleshall. Reaney first played for England when brought on by Ramsey as a substitute against Bulgaria in December 1968. He might well be remembered as the first black footballer to have played for England, his reluctance to so identify notwithstanding.[8] Race is a theme that raises difficulty for a public history project on the 1966 World Cup. This is largely due to the perceived non-engagement of non-white Britons with the tournament. The recorded autobiographical memories, such as those discussed in the previous chapter, say little on race, and photographic and filmic imagery of matches – there being more of the Final than other games – give little more than a glimpse of non-white people in attendance. However, this does not confirm that people from non-white and immigrant backgrounds were not interested in the World Cup or football in England more generally in the mid-1960s. To assume this, especially in regard to young people would be very inaccurate.

The example of author Caryl Phillips is worth considering in counterpoint. Phillips came to England from St Kitts with his parents as a baby in the year of his birth, 1958.[9] This was at the end of the first wave of post-war migration from the Caribbean between 1948 and 1958.[10] The Phillips family settled in Leeds and by 1963 the five-year-old Caryl had become a fan of Leeds United and was taken to his first home game by his baby-sitter in that year. Phillips believes he was 'probably the youngest fan in the stadium and undoubtedly the only black one'. His passion for football was not shared by his parents. Phillips's father was a fanatical cricket enthusiast and his son's obsession with football and lack of interest in cricket not only bemused him, but also opened a 'cultural gap' between child and parents.[11] By the time of the 1966 World Cup finals, Caryl Phillips was eight years old. Given the involvement of Leeds players – Norman Hunter as well as Jack Charlton being in the squad, and Paul Reaney in the preliminary squad – Phillips is likely to have taken some interest in the tournament. Thirty-two years on, Phillips was in attendance at England's 1998 World Cup group match against Columbia in Lens. He recalls an 'impassioned' atmosphere inside the stadium and being shocked by the 'vigour' with which he 'belted out' *God Save the Queen*, along 'with the thirty thousand other English fans', when the anthem was played.[12] At that moment Phillips felt a sense of 'belonging' to an identity he otherwise regarded with ambivalence and treated with vigilance. His years as a Leeds supporter had made him customarily wary of football fraternity. A public history of the 1966 World Cup will not be unrelated to the experience described by Phillips. The non-visibility of non-white fandom at the time does not make the themes of race and ethnicity irrelevant to the public memory. Indeed, the challenge is to show how England's victory in 1966 held out humanistic and inclusive possibilities of the kind carried over by Phillips into his support for England in subsequent international football tournaments during his adulthood.[13]

As indicated in the previous chapter the term 'collected memory' is significant to exhibition projects related to the 1966 World Cup. Collected memory, in a material sense, refers to the existence of items in which memory 'lives'. These items might be pictures, statues, or other such items familiarly seen in museum exhibitions and collections. Together, these items contribute to the public memory encapsulated within the museum setting. The items of collected memory gathered in specialist museums will reflect the particular specialism. Accordingly, the National Football Museum (NFM) possesses many items of football apparel, equipment and trophies, as well as less expected items, such as artworks pertaining to football. Museum studies scholar and Director of the NFM, Kevin Moore, has undertaken a detailed 'material culture' analysis of one item within the NFM collection – the football used in the 1966 World

Cup Final – to demonstrate that items of popular culture are as viably examined by curatorial method as traditional kinds of museum objects.[14] As well as detailing more routine aspects of an item's material nature and provenance, the examination seeks to explain the item's symbolic significance in regard to the social and cultural meanings that it carries. The significance of the 1966 World Cup football is heightened by the story of its journey from the conclusion of the Final to the time of its 'repatriation' to England in coincidence with the hosting of the European Football Championship in 1996. The Slazenger-made amber-coloured football was, during those thirty intervening years, in the possession of West German player Helmut Haller. Haller snatched up the ball at the conclusion of the match, allegedly in good faith of rightful claim based on a German tradition that 'if the winners get the Cup, the losers keep the ball'.[15]

An English tradition – that the scorer of a hat-trick in a football match keeps the ball – sat at odds with Haller's claim and laid the grounds for disputation over the cultural legitimacy of the ball's ownership. In this case, according to the English tradition, ownership honours rest with three-goal scorer Geoff Hurst, a privilege Hurst attempted to exert when he met up with Haller at a dinner in 1988. Haller declined a request to relinquish the ball. Countering with another German tradition he presumed to doubly indemnify his right of possession over that of Hurst: 'The first man to score in the final always gets to keep the ball'.[16] The matter quietened until 1996 when Hurst took his appeal to the British press. Given the newsworthiness at the time of Euro 96 coming to England, a tabloid duel commenced between *The Sun* and the *Daily Mirror* in pursuit of the ball's return 'home'. The *Mirror* won out, reportedly reaching an agreement with Haller to return the football in exchange for a sizeable donation to an unnamed charity. The *Daily Mirror* and its partners in the arrangement, Eurostar and the Virgin Group, remain the owners of the football, which, as indicated above, is now kept at the NFM. Given the controversy of Hurst's second goal in the Final, the ball is assured a strong public memory resonance in this particular exhibition context. The story of the protracted haggling over its ownership merely adds to its evocativeness.

The ball's reputation precedes its appearance in public display. Exhibition visitors will draw on their own memories in what will be for some a ready interpretation of its significance. As Kevin Moore points out, the ball will carry a different meaning to different people. In the public memory and public history context it is a 'polysemantic' object, 'capable of being viewed in a multiplicity of ways'.[17] This applies by degree of subtlety and nuance to all display items; especially so sporting items, given the rivalrous nature of sport. An extremity in differing interpretation of the 1966 World Cup ball is made likely by the contested nature of the circumstances in which it has been embroiled.[18] Visitors to the NFM from Germany are likely to regard the ball differently to most English people. Yet the division between West and East Germany, as existed in

1966, will have a bearing on present-day interpretations.[19] Unanimity cannot be assumed for how English visitors will respond to the ball's exhibition presence. For those who believe the second Hurst goal was wrongly awarded and that this sours a commemoration of England's victory, the ball may signify unworthiness. Others will distance themselves from thoughts of controversy and social circumstance and regard the ball purely in association with the football played in the Final. This is to bring more of an aesthetic interpretation to the object having an intrinsic cultural meaning and value. Seeing the ball can evoke a different response for people of this mindset. They might be immediately taken into thoughts of the athletic grace summoned by Geoff Hurst to alter his run, retrieve a cross from Alan Ball, and, in a fluid swivelling movement, pull the ball with his right foot from behind to in front of his body and then drive it towards the goal, above the reach of West Germany's goalkeeper, Tilkowsksi.[20]

Public memory of the 1966 World Cup and England's victory is also prompted by existing commemorative markers such as statues. Prominent in this regard is *The World Cup Sculpture* (or *The Champions*), located near West Ham United's Boleyn Ground at Upton Park in the East End. The statue, designed by Philip Jackson, in situ since April 2003, is based on photographs of a familiar scene from World Cup Final day, Bobby Moore raising the Jules Rimet trophy in his right hand whilst perched on the shoulders of Geoff Hurst and Ray Wilson, with Martin Peters positioned immediately to Hurst's right. The statue was funded by a mixed contribution, the largest portions coming from a Government grant and an allocation from West Ham United football club. It was unveiled in April 2003, two months after the tenth anniversary of Bobby Moore's death, and acknowledged then by a local councillor instrumental to its commissioning as a tribute to Moore.[21] As of the commencing 2016/17 Premier League season, West Ham United will relocate from the Boleyn Ground to the nearby Olympic Stadium. This has created speculation that the statue could be moved to the new vicinity within the Queen Elizabeth Olympic Park.[22] This suggestion may be regarded with irony. *The World Cup Sculpture*, tucked away in an area of the East End generally visited by outsiders only for away football games, is understandably reclaimed by locals as their own, providing a material reminder of the old adage that 'West Ham won the World Cup'. However, should the statue be moved near to the Olympic Stadium, in proximity to West Ham's new 'home', it would receive a much greater public viewing from tourists visiting the area around the London 2012 Olympic site. A somewhat unintended legacy of the Olympic Games perhaps, but one in which *The Champions* would be given to the people of England as well as to those of the East End.

   Whether or not relocated, *The Champions* statue bears its own evidence that England's World Cup win was more than a West Ham affair. Taking most of the load of Bobby Moore's bodyweight at the celebratory moment depicted in the statue is Everton player Ray Wilson. The photographs of those few seconds show Wilson grimacing under the strain. After all, this was a man who had just played two hours of gruelling football. As willing as he no doubt was to provide a human chair for his triumphant captain, the look on his face during this last call of duty on that hectic afternoon indicates the point of total physical exhaustion from which he was only a breath or two away. However, this is not so in *The World Cup Sculpture* (*The Champions*) statue. In preparing the sculpture, Jackson deemed it reasonable that Wilson should be seen to enjoy the celebration as much as his England teammates from West Ham, so he assumed 'artistic license' to replace the player's pained countenance with an expression approximating a grin. 'I don't think he would mind', claimed Jackson in presuming Wilson's agreement to the change.[23] And thus, Jackson makes a significant alteration to the materialised public memory of that celebratory moment. The non-London player alongside Moore, Hurst and Peters now appears happy, symbolising perhaps that a World Cup win can overcome the grim fate of being from up North.[24]

A subsequent commission awarded to Philip Jackson was for *The Bobby Moore Sculpture* at the end of Wembley Way outside the north entrance to the new

11 The West Ham three. Martin Peters, Bobby Moore and Geoff Hurst, with the Jules Rimet trophy.

12 Bobby Moore raises the Jules Rimet trophy as Ray Wilson struggles to raise him.

Wembley Stadium. The bronze statue was unveiled on 11 May 2007, a week ahead of the official opening and playing of the first FA Cup Final at the new stadium. A dignified looking Moore stands, arms folded, with a ball trapped beneath the foot of his bent left leg. The statue, at a height of approximately twenty feet, is twice that of most other football player statues in Britain. Jackson had agreement from the stadium's designing architect Sir Norman Foster that the statue needed to attain relative dimension to the new Wembley structure, otherwise it would be dwarfed in the shadow of the building.[25]

Relative to the size of the stadium behind him though he may be, this Bobby Moore seems chunkier than the player who captained England in 1966. The hair also looks different: longer, wavier, more like that of the England captain at the 1970 World Cup. The brim of a bronze cap attached to the left hand side of the plinth on which the Moore statue stands is marked 'World Championship, Jules Rimet Cup 1970'. Perhaps this confirms the suspicion, yet the solidness of physique looks like a Moore from even later than this time. The team assembled in the plaque on the plinth directly below Moore's statue creates further uncertainty. We might suspect this to be the 1966 winning team, but to this viewer's eye, only Moore in the centre and Peters on the far left in the line of players can be readily identified. An oversupply of hirsute figures seems to negate the possibility of Bobby Charlton, George Cohen, Ray Wilson and Nobby Stiles all being present in this grouping. We seemingly have to accept that this is a composite gathering of players and that the captain standing above is a composite Bobby Moore, the Bobby Moore of 1966, but also the Bobby Moore in other stages of his football career. Perhaps this is, after all, a Bobby Moore for a new Wembley, not the Wembley at which he took England to World Cup victory? Perhaps this new Wembley signifies a shift to postmodernity and a need to realise that a 'public memory' of the 1966 World Cup cannot be pinned down in the way Bobby Moore captures the football beneath his giant bronze boot.[26]

However, there is another statuary presence at the new Wembley that may give us pause to think again. Looking rather like Mino da Fiesole's bust of the Florentine statesman Diotisalvi Neroni, Philip Jackson's sculptural portrait of Alf Ramsey's head looks on pensively from its position in the player's tunnel.[27] Mino's portrait has been described as showing Neroni's 'profound public awareness … far from losing himself in selfish thoughts, he has nothing but the good of his city in mind'.[28] The 'public man' Ramsey was of the same outlook, albeit with a much more limited scope. The stoic concern, apparent in the portraits of both men, evinces a dubious regard for the political overlords who ultimately controlled their fates. Neroni initially held favour with the Medici under Cosimo, but was banished from Florence upon son Piero's succession to rule over the 'divided city'.[29] At no point during his time as England Football manager could it be said that Alf Ramsey enjoyed the support of the FA, yet throughout his tenure he remained a faithful servant to football. Much has been written in criticism of the FA's discarding of Ramsey as manager when the chance arose in 1974.[30] Perhaps in some attempt to make good, the FA touted the idea of a joint statue of Ramsey and Bobby Moore at the planned new Wembley Stadium in May 1999. This was shortly after Ramsey's death, and the consideration seems to have been prompted by members of the 1966 England team.[31] The joint statue did not materialise. The plan for a solo Moore statue was already on the drawing board and, as discussed above, went ahead for the opening of the new Wembley in May 2007. The bust of Ramsey was subsequently commissioned and unveiled by the England manager at the time, Fabio Capello, in November 2009.[32]

Given the way Ramsey left the limelight to his players following the World Cup Final victory in 1966, it is unlikely he would have wanted to reclaim its glare alongside Moore in statuary over forty years later. We can imagine him quite happy with his place in the tunnel, overseeing England teams before they take the field. What he would make of the new Wembley is another matter. In *Talking Football* Ramsey declared his love for Wembley, the 'finest playing pitch' he ever appeared on.[33] However, that was in 1952, stated towards the end of Ramsey's playing career. Ramsey the football modernist would not be one to stand in the way of well-considered progress and he might have been open to the idea of Wembley undergoing some transformation ahead of the new millennium. But Ramsey's modernism did not extend beyond his own cultural domain. In regard to architecture he appeared more a traditionalist, as reflected in his choice of the Georgian Hendon Hall as residence for the England squad during the World Cup tournament.[34] The initial discussion for a new Wembley involved the understanding that tradition would be preserved by the retention of the iconic twin towers.[35] This position received support from the 1966 players via Geoff Hurst as spokesman.[36] By this time Ramsey's health was in decline and he would not have been in a condition to give any consideration to the matter. Had he been able to, it is hard to imagine him abiding the destruction of the twin towers and buying into corporate propaganda about the arch over the north stand being a more than worthy replacement to signify the new national stadium's prominence.[37]

The officially sponsored book on the new Wembley includes a colour photograph of one of the twin towers under demolition and, on the opposite page, a large caption making light of the tower's destruction with reference to 'a German excavator known as "Goliath" being charged with the task'. Such a flippant remark lends confirmation to the suspicion that those concerned with a postmodern future have little respect for the dignity of the past. And, with such spirit prevailing, the twin towers of Wembley did not survive for the fiftieth anniversary of the 1966 World Cup. Like the matches of the tournament itself they are now only viewable in photos and on film. Some grounds involved in the World Cup competition have disappeared altogether, the sites of Ayresome Park and Roker Park now occupied by housing estates, and White City Stadium also demolished. The other grounds featured in the tournament have all undergone significant alterations in appearance since 1966. Changes of this kind around the grounds of the country were inevitable, known about and foreseen. This adds weight to a case for at least one landmark of the 1966 World Cup having been kept and there was none more appropriate for that purpose than the twin towers of the competition's main venue, Wembley Stadium.[38]

There has been much discussion in the last few chapters of this book about the 1966 World Cup and memory, discussed under various terms. Without re-entering that discussion it seems pertinent to close by emphasising the importance of debating memory in regard to how an event such as the World Cup and England's victory might be remembered. At certain points along the way in a book-length discussion, the author's opinions will show through, and such has been the case here. However, it is hoped that the critical engagement with views that may be at odds with those opinions has been fair. This is the intention, and it is one aimed, as much as anything else, at opposing the trivialisation of this important cultural event to the glossy nonsense of coffee-table books and brochures of corporate interest. Such uses will no doubt occur, but memory of the event warrants a much fuller consideration than much of what is said, written and broadcast in populist representations. Hopefully *England and the 1966 World Cup* offers an original and worthwhile contribution to existing scholarship and will attract debate and criticism from other scholars within the cultural history of sport and related fields, while encouraging yet further scholarship into this significant moment of modernity.

Notes

1 At the time of writing (July 2015) the author is a member of the National Football Museum's planning committee for a commemorative exhibition of the 1966 World Cup, to open during the fiftieth anniversary year, 2016. The National Football Museum relocated from its original location at Deepdale Stadium, Preston, to the Urbis Building in Manchester in July 2012. Sir Bobby Charlton is President of the Museum and Sir Geoff Hurst one of its Vice-Presidents.

2 http://ncph.org/cms/what-is-public-history/. Accessed 3 July 2015.

3 Bodnar, *Remaking America*.

4 Allen, *An Amber Glow*, p. 6.

5 Conekin et al., *Moments of Modernity*.

6 Bray, *1965*.

7 *Ibid.*, pp. 275–6.

8 'Black Footballers', p. 36. Viv Anderson became the first black footballer on record to play for England, in a match against Czechoslovakia on 29 November, 1978.

9 Phillips, 'Leeds United', p. 298.
10 Phillips, 'The Pioneers', p. 268.
11 Phillips, 'Leeds United', p. 298.
12 Phillips, 'High Anxiety', p. 308.
13 Humanism is meant here not in the manner of a traditional, exclusivist 'liberal humanism', but as an open, non-racial understanding of humanism; what Gilroy refers to in his book *Between Camps* as 'planetary humanism'.
14 Moore, *Museums and Popular Culture*, p. 106.
15 *Ibid.*, p. 108.
16 *Ibid.* The German writer Hesse-Lichtenberger (*Tor!*, p. 184) defends Haller's right to ownership on the even simpler basis that he was the first player alert enough to gather the ball as a 'souvenir' after the game.
17 Moore, *Museums and Popular Culture*, p. 133.
18 Hughson and Moore, 'Hand of God', pp. 219–22.
19 There was some television broadcasting of the 1966 World Cup in East Germany. The main concern of the communist authorities in sanctioning this was to counter any western cultural influence of broadcasting, whether coming from either Western Germany or England. It remains uncertain as to which team in the 1966 Final received most allegiance in East Germany, although supposition might be drawn from evidence pertaining to the 1954 World Cup, which indicates widespread support for West Germany against Hungary in the Final of that tournament. This compares to popular support being afforded to Hungary (i.e. a team from another communist country) during the matches against England in November 1953 and May 1954. See McDougall, *The People's Game*, pp. 169–70, 83–4 and 80–1.
20 Thompson, *4–2*, p. 180, offers a rare aesthetic appreciation of Hurst's shot on goal.
21 http://news.bbc.co.uk/1/hi/england/london/2982419.stm. Accessed 3 June 2015.
22 www.dailymail.co.uk/sport/football/article-2834007/West-Ham-s-Champions-Sculpture-near-club-s-new-Olympic-Park-home.html. Accessed 3 June 2015.
23 http://news.bbc.co.uk/1/hi/england/london/2982419.stm. Accessed 3 June 2015.
24 A number of statues of football players and managers appear at different locations, mainly football grounds, around the country. A statue of Gordon Banks (raising the Jules Rimet trophy) is in place at Stoke City's Britannia Stadium. Banks transferred to Stoke City from Leicester City the year following the World Cup victory. A triple statue of Jimmy Armfield, Geoff Hurst and Simone Perrotta is located at the Roy Oldham Sports Village in Ashton-under-Lyne, in honour of the three World Cup winning players born in the Tameside borough of Greater Manchester. Perrotta, born in 1977, migrated with his parents back to their home country as a four-year-old and then went on to become an international player for Italy. He was a member of the 2006 World Cup winning team. The inclusion of Hurst in this statue is especially interesting as it relocates him from a fixed and better-known East End identity to his place of origin in the North of England. A statue of a besuited Sir Alf Ramsey stands astride Sir Alf Ramsey Way across from Ipswich Town's Portman Road

Stadium. It is a statue primarily in honour of Ramsey's achievement as manager of Ipswich. However, the inscription on the plinth also notes his taking England to World Cup success in 1966. Information about these statues and others is recorded comprehensively in *From Pitch to Plinth: The Sporting Statues Project* www.offbeat. group.shef.ac.uk/statues/biogs.htm. Accessed 3 June 2015.

25 The author is grateful to Dr Chris Stride for providing this insight via his research interview with Philip Jackson. Correspondence with Stride, 28 May 2015.

26 For an image of *The Bobby Moore Sculpture* see *From Pitch to Plinth: The Sporting Statues Project* www.offbeat.group.shef.ac.uk/statues/STUK_Moore_Bobby_1. htm. Accessed 28 May 2015.

27 The statue of Diotisalvi Neroni by Mino da Fiesole, dated 1464, is located in the lower ground floor of the Denon wing in the Louvre.

28 Jonathan Jones www.theguardian.com/culture/200/aug/30/art. Accessed 6 June 2015.

29 *Ibid.*

30 Leo McKinstry, 'Hero cast aside: Sir Alf Ramsey', www.theguardian.com/ football/2009/may/21/seven-deadly-sins-football-alf-ramsey-england. Accessed 6 June 2015.

31 Thomas Russell and Peter White 'Wembley statue for Ramsey and Moore', www. theguardian.com/football/1999/may/07/newsstory.sport6. Accessed 6 June 2015.

32 'Fabio Capello admits World Cup dreams at unveiling of Alf Ramsey bust', www. theguardian.com/football/2009/nov/06/fabio-capello-world-cup-dreams-alf- ramsey. Accessed June 6 2015.

33 Ramsey, *Talking Football*, p. 90.

34 The Hendon Hall Hotel has been in operation since 1912. At the centre of its premises is Hendon Hall which dates from the mid-1750s.

35 Inglis, *Football Grounds of Britain*, p. 397.

36 'Wembley towers demolition begins', www.theguardian.com/uk/2002/dec/06/ wembleystadium.football. Accessed 7 June 2015.

37 In the latter regard see the volume *Wembley Stadium*, published under the imprimatur of Wembley Stadium Limited.

38 An argument against the retention of Wembley's twin towers was that the rebuilding of the new stadium involved a repositioning of the playing pitch on to the space occupied by the towers. *Ipso facto*, they needed to be removed. This point was made public by a spokesperson from the FA in late 1998. See www.independent.co.uk/ news/wembley-may-lose-the-twin-towers-1183755.html. Accessed 7 June 2015. Presented as an imperative this does not entirely reconcile with earlier expert reference to a proposed new Wembley, which categorically assumed the towers would remain within a rebuilding project. See Inglis, *Football Grounds of Britain*, p. 390.

Bibliography

A Rational Aesthetic: The Systems Group and Associated Artists, exhibition catalogue Southampton City Art Gallery, 11 January–31 March 2008.

Allen, P., *An Amber Glow: The Story of England's World Cup-Winning Football* (Edinburgh: Mainstream Publishing, 2000).

Armfield, J., *Right Back to the Beginning: The Autobiography*, with A. Collomosse (London: Headline, 2004).

Arnold, M., *Culture and Anarchy*, J. Dover Wilson edition (Cambridge: Cambridge University Press, 1944).

Atherton, M., *The Theft of the Jules Rimet Trophy: The Hidden History of the 1966 World Cup* (Aachen, Germany: Meyer & Meyer, 2007).

Ball, A., *It's All About a Ball: An Autobiography* (London: W.H. Allen, 1978).

Ball, A., *Playing Extra Time*, with James Mossop (London: Pan Books, 2005).

Banks, G., *Banks of England* (London: MacDonald Futura, 1981).

Banks, G., *Banksy: My Autobiography* (London: Michael Joseph, 2002).

Batchelor, S., *I Was There in '66* (London: Athena Press, 2006).

Bates, S., '1966 World Cup Football Competition', *Special Stamp History*, no. 43 (Royal Mail unpublished document).

Baudelaire, C., 'The Painter of Modern Life' [1863], *Selected Writings on Art and Literature*, trans. P.E. Charvet (London: Penguin, 1992), pp. 390–435.

'Black Footballers', unnamed author entry in *When Saturday Comes: The Half Decent Football Book* (London: Penguin, 2005), pp. 34–7.

Bockris, V., 'Fifteen Minutes of Fame', introduction to F. Dennis and D. Atyeo, *Muhammad Ali: The Glory Years* (London: Ebury Press, 2002), pp. 17–27.

Bodnar, J., *Remaking America: Public Memory, Commemoration and Patriotism in the Twentieth Century* (Princeton: Princeton University Press, 1992).

Booker, C., *Neophiliacs: Revolution in English Life in the Fifties and Sixties*, new edition (London: Pimlico, 1992).

Bose, M., *The Sporting Alien: English Sport's Lost Camelot* (Edinburgh: Mainstream Publishing, 1996).

Bowden, M., 'Soccer', in K.B. Raitz, *The Theatre of Sport* (Baltimore: Johns Hopkins University Press, 1995), pp. 97–140.

Bowler, D., *Winning Isn't Everything: A Biography of Sir Alf Ramsey* (London: Victor Gollancz, 1998).

Bray, C., *1965: The Year Modern Britain Was Born* (London: Simon & Schuster, 2014).

Burns, J., *The Hand of God: The Life of Diego Maradona* (London: Bloomsbury, 1997).

Busignani, A., *Mondrian* (London: Thames and Hudson, 1968).

Butler, B., *The Official History of the Football Association* (London: Queen Anne Press, 1991).

Butler, B., *The Football League: The Official Illustrated History*, revised edition (Enderby, Leicester: Blitz Editions, 1993).

Butler, B. and R. Greenwood, *Soccer Choice* (London: Pelham Books, 1979).

Charlton, B., *My Soccer Life* (London: Pelham Books, 1964).

Charlton, B., *Forward for England* (London: Pelham Books, 1967).

Charlton, B., *This Game of Soccer* (London: Cassell, 1967).

Charlton, B., *My Manchester United Years: The Autobiography*, with James Lawton (London: Headline, 2007).

Charlton, B., *My England Years: The Autobiography*, with J. Lawton (London: Headline, 2008).

Charlton, C., *Cissie: Football's Most Famous Mother Tells Her Story*, with V. Gledhill (Morpeth, Northumberland: Bridge Studios, 1988).

Charlton, J., *For Leeds and England* (London: Stanley Paul, 1967).

Charlton, J., *Jack Charlton: The Autobiography*, with P. Byrne (London: Partridge Press, 1996).

Chinitz, D.E., *T.S. Eliot and the Cultural Divide* (Chicago: University of Chicago Press, 2003).

Chisari, F., '"Shouting Housewives!" The 1966 World Cup and British Television', *Sport in History*, 24:1 (2004), pp. 94–108.

Chisari, F., 'When Football Went Global: Televising the 1966 World Cup', *Historical Social Research*, 31:1 (2006), pp. 45–54.

Clarke, J. and C. Critcher, '1966 and All That: England's World Cup Victory', in A. Tomlinson and G. Whannel (eds), *Off the Ball: The Football World Cup* (London: Pluto, 1986), pp. 112–26.

Clavane, A., *Does Your Rabbi Know You're Here? The Story of English Football's Forgotten Tribe*, updated paperback edition (London: Quercus, 2013).

Clayton, J., 'It's Only a Game: 150 Years of Association Football', *Soccer & Society*, 16:2/3 (2014), pp. 153–5.

Clough, B., *The Autobiography*, with J. Sadler (London: Partridge Press, 1994).

Cohen, G., *My Autobiography*, with J. Lawton (Pinhoe, Exeter: Greenwater Publishing, 2003).

Colman, J., *A 'Special Relationship'? Harold Wilson, Lyndon B. Johnson and Anglo-American Relations 'at the Summit', 1964–68* (Manchester: Manchester University Press, 2004).

Conekin, B., '"Here is the Modern World Itself": The Festival of Britain's Representation of the Future', in B. Conekin, F. Mort and C. Waters (eds), *Moments of Modernity: Reconstructing Britain, 1945–1964* (London: Rivers Oram, 1999), pp. 228–46.

Conekin, B., *'The Autobiography of a Nation': The 1951 Festival of Britain* (Manchester: Manchester University Press, 2003).

Conekin, B., F. Mort and C. Waters, 'Introduction' to B. Conekin, F. Mort and

C. Waters (eds), *Moments of Modernity: Reconstructing Britain, 1945–1964* (London: Rivers Oram, 1999), pp. 1–20.

Cox, B., *The Timeless Zone: A Return to '66* (Brighton: Pen Press Publishers, 2006 [2000]).

Critcher, C., 'Football since the War', in J. Clarke, C. Critcher and Richard Johnson (eds), *Working Class Culture: Studies in History and Theory* (London: Hutchinson, 1979), pp. 161–84.

Critcher, C., 'England and the World Cup: World Cup Willies, English Football and the Myth of 1966', in J. Sugden and A. Tomlinson (eds), *Hosts and Champions: Soccer Cultures, National Identities, and the USA World Cup* (Aldershot: Arena, 1994), pp. 77–92.

Crolley, L. and D. Hand, *Football, Europe and the Press* (London: Frank Cass, 2002).

Crosland, S., *Tony Crosland* (London: Jonathan Cape, 1982).

Crossman, R., *The Diaries of a Cabinet Minister, volume one, Minister of Housing, 1964–66* (London: Hamish Hamilton and Jonathan Cape, 1975).

Davies, H., 'England's 1966 World Cup Victory', in A. Merullo and N. Wenborn (eds), *British Sporting Greats* (London: Cassell Illustrated, 2002), pp. 184–5.

Davies, H., 'The Twin Towers of Wembley', in A. Merullo and N. Wenborn (eds), *British Sporting Greats* (London: Cassell Illustrated, 2002), pp. 168–9.

Davies, H., *The Beatles: The Authorised Biography* (London: Ebury Press, 2009).

Davies, H., *Postcards From the Edge of Football: A Social History of the British Game* (Edinburgh: Mainstream Publishing, 2010).

Dawson, J., *Back Home: England and the 1970 World Cup* (London: Orion, 2001).

Dee, D., 'Ironing Out the Ghetto Bend: Football, Integration and Jewish "Anglicisation"', in *Four Four Jew: Football, Fans and Faith* (London: Jewish Museum / Oxford: Shire Publications, 2013), pp. 30–5.

Dickinson, W., 'World Cup Football on … Merseyside', *FA News*, XV: 6 (1966), pp. 213–15.

Dougan, D. and P.M. Young, *On the Spot: Football as a Profession* (Newton Abbot: Readers Union, 1975).

Downing, D. *The Best of Enemies: England v Germany* (London: Bloomsbury, 2001).

Eberly, R.A., '"Everywhere You Go, It's There": Forgetting and Remembering the University of Texas Tower Shootings', in K.R. Phillips, S. Browne and B. Biesecker (eds), *Rhetoric, Culture and Social Critique: Framing Public Memory* (Tuscaloosa: University of Alabama Press, 2004), pp. 65–88.

Edgerton, D., 'The "White Heat" Revisited: The British Government and Technology in the 1960s', *Twentieth Century British History*, 7:1 (1996), pp. 53–82.

Eliot, T.S., *Notes Towards the Definition of Culture*, 2nd edition (London: Faber and Faber, 1962 [1948]).

Erll, A., *Memory in Culture*, trans. S.B. Young (Basingstoke: Palgrave Macmillan, 2011).

Featherstone, S., *Englishness: Twentieth Century Popular Culture and the Forming of English Identity* (Edinburgh: Edinburgh University Press, 2008).

Finn, R.L., *England World Champions 1966* (London: Robert Hale, 1966).

Fiske, J., *Power Plays, Power Works* (London: Verso, 1993).

Fowler, A. 'The Systems Group and Its Constructivist Context', in *A Rational Aesthetic:*

The Systems Group and Associated Artists, exhibition catalogue Southampton City Art Gallery, 11 January–31 March 2008, pp. 12–21.

Games, N., C. Moriarty and J. Rose, *Abram Games, Graphic Designer: Maximum Meaning, Minimum Means* (Aldershot: Lund Humphries, 2003).

Gee, H., *Wembley: Fifty Great Years* (London: Pelham, 1972).

Gilroy, P., *Between Camps: Nations, Culture and the Allure of Race* (London: Penguin, 2000).

Gilroy, P., *After Empire* (London: Routledge, 2004).

Giraudoux, J., 'King of Sports, King of Games', in B. Glanville (ed.), *The Footballer's Companion* (London: Eyre & Spottiswoode, 1962 [1933]), pp. 537–9.

Glanville, B., *The Sunday Times History of the World Cup* (London: Times Newspapers Limited, 1973).

Glanville, B., 'The FA Cup Final', in A. Merullo and N. Wenborn (eds), *British Sporting Greats* (London: Cassell Illustrated, 2002), pp. 51–5.

Goldblatt, D., *The Ball is Round: A Global History of Football* (London: Penguin, 2007).

Goldblatt, D. and J. Williams, *A History of the World Cup in 24 Objects* (Leicester: De Montfort University, 2014).

Grayson, E., 'England's Duty to the Past', *FA News*, XV: 12 (1966), pp. 486–7, continued p. 495.

Greaves, J., *This One's on Me* (London: Arthur Baker, 1979).

Greaves, J., *Greavsie: The Autobiography* (London: Time Warner, 2003).

Greaves, J., *The Heart of the Game* (London: Time Warner Books, 2005).

Green, G., 'A Glorious Occasion for British Sport', *FA News*, XV: 12 (1966), pp. 468–70.

Greenwood, R., *Yours Sincerely*, with B. Butler (London: Willow Books / Collins, 1984).

Gregory, C., *Who Could Ask For More? Reclaiming The Beatles* (London: Plotted Plain Press, 2008).

Grieve, A., *Constructed Abstract Art in England: A Neglected Avant-garde* (New Haven: Yale University Press, 2005).

Halbwachs, M., *The Collective Memory*, trans. F.J. Ditter, Jr and V. Yazdi (New York: Harper and Row, 1980).

Hall, S. and P. Whannel, *The Popular Arts* (London: Hutchinson, 1964).

Hampton, J., *The Austerity Olympics: When the Games Came to London in 1948* (London: Aurum, 2008).

Harris, A., *Romantic Moderns: English Writers, Artists and the Imagination from Virginia Woolf to John Piper* (London: Thames & Hudson, 2010).

Harris, J., S. Hyde and G. Smith, *1966 and All That: Design and the Consumer in Britain 1960–1969* (London: Trefoil Books, 1986).

Harrison, C., *English Art and Modernism 1900–1939* (New Haven: Yale University Press, 2nd edition, 1994).

Haynes, R., 'The BBC, Austerity and Broadcasting the 1948 Olympic Games', *The International Journal of the History of Sport*, 27:6 (2010), pp. 1029–46.

Hesse-Lichtenberger, U., *Tor! The Story of German Football* (London: When Saturday Comes Books, 2003).

Hewison, R., *Culture and Consensus: England, Art and Politics Since 1940* (London: Methuen, 1995).

Hill, J. *Sport, Leisure and Culture in Twentieth-Century Britain* (Basingstoke: Palgrave, 2002).

Hoggart, R., 'Culture: Dead and Alive', in *Speaking To Each Other – Volume One: About Society* (London: Chatto & Windus, 1970), pp. 131–4.

Holt, R., *Sport and the British: A Modern History* (Oxford: Clarendon Press, 1992 [1989]).

Holt, R. and T. Mason, *Sport in Britain: 1945–2000* (Oxford: Blackwell, 2000).

Hopcraft, A., *The Football Man: People and Passions in Soccer* (London: Aurum, 2006 [1968]).

Horne, J., A. Tomlinson, G. Whannel and K. Woodward, *Understanding Sport: A Socio-cultural Analysis* (London: Routledge, 2012).

Horne, J., 'Managing World Cup Legacy', in S. Frawley and D. Adair (eds), *Managing the Football World Cup* (Basingstoke: Palgrave Macmillan, 2014), pp. 7–24.

Howell, D., *Soccer Refereeing* (London: Pelham, 1968).

Howell, D., *Made in Birmingham: Memoirs* (London: Macdonald / Queen Anne Press, 1990).

Hudson, A., *The Working Man's Ballet* (London: Robson, 1998).

Huggins, M. and J. Williams, *Sport and the English: 1918–1939* (London: Routledge, 2006).

Hughson, J., 'Why He Must Run: Class, Anger, and Resistance in *The Loneliness of the Long Distance Runner*', in R. Briley, M.K. Schoenecke and D.A. Carmichael (eds), *All-Stars & Movie Stars: Sports in Film and History* (Lexington: University of Kentucky Press, 2008) 261–78.

Hughson, J., *The Making of Sporting Cultures* (London: Routledge, 2009).

Hughson, J., 'The Cultural Legacy of Olympic Posters', *Sport in Society*, 13:5 (2010), pp. 749–59.

Hughson, J., 'The Friendly Games: The "Official" IOC Film of the 1956 Melbourne Olympics as Historical Record', *Historical Journal of Film, Radio and Television*, 30:4 (2010), pp. 529–42.

Hughson, J., 'Not Just Any Wintry Afternoon in England: The Curious Contribution of C.R.W. Nevinson to "Football Art"', *International Journal of the History of Sport*, 28:18 (2011), pp. 2670–87.

Hughson, J. 'An Invitation to "Modern" Melbourne: The Historical Significance of Richard Beck's Olympic Poster Design', *Journal of Design History*, 25:3 (2012), pp. 268–84.

Hughson, J., 'Modern Design for Modern Events: Olympic Games Posters 1948 and 1956', paper presented to the North American Society for Sport History, Berkeley, California, 1–4 June 2012.

Hughson, J., 'Watching the Football with Raymond Williams: A Reconsideration of the Global Game as a Wonderful Game', in J. Scherer and D. Rowe (eds), *Sport, Broadcasting and Cultural Citizenship: Signal Lost?* (New York: Routledge, 2013), pp. 283–99.

Hughson, J., '"Ten Years Ahead of His Time": The East End Elegance of Martin Peters', *Sport in History*, 35:1 (2015), pp. 108–26.

Hughson, J., D. Inglis and M. Free, *The Uses of Sport: A Critical Study* (London: Routledge, 2005).

Hughson, J. and K. Moore, '"Hand of God", Shirt of the Man: The Materiality of Diego Maradona', *Costume*, 46:2 (2012), pp. 212–25.

Huizinga, J., *Homo Ludens: A Study of the Play Element in Culture* (Boston: Beacon Press, 1955).

Hurst, G., *1966 And All That: My Autobiography*, with M. Hart (London: Headline, 2001).

Hurst, G., *Geoff Hurst's 50 Greatest Footballers of All Time* (London: Icon Books, 2014).

Hutchinson, R., '... It Is Now': The Real Story of England's 1966 World Cup Triumph* (Edinburgh: Mainstream, 1995).

Inglis, D. and J. Hughson, *Confronting Culture: Sociological Vistas* (Cambridge: Polity, 2003).

Inglis, S., *Football Grounds of Britain*, 3rd paperback edition (London: Collins Willow, 1996).

Inglis, S., *Engineering Archie: Archibald Leitch – Football Ground Designer* (Swindon: English Heritage, 2005).

Irving, D., *The West Ham United Football Book* (London: Stanley Paul, 1968).

Jefferys, K., *Sport and Politics in Modern Britain: The Road to 2012* (Basingstoke: Palgrave Macmillan, 2012).

Jenkins, R., *A Life at the Centre* (London: Macmillan, 1991).

Johnes, M. and G. Mellor, '"The 1953 FA Cup Final": Modernity and Tradition in British Culture', *Contemporary British History*, 20:2 (2006), pp. 263–80.

Jones, T., *Remaking the Labour Party: From Gaitskell to Blair* (London: Routledge, 1996).

Keller, H., *Music, Closed Societies and Football* (London: Toccata Press, 1986).

Kidd, P. and M. Scanlan, 'The Beautiful Game', *Freemasonry Today*, 53 (Summer 2010).

Laselles, G., *The Tongs and the Bones: The Memoirs of Lord Harewood* (London: Weidenfeld and Nicolson, 1981).

Law, D., *The King*, with B. Harris (London: Ted Smart / Transworld Publishers, 2003).

Lawrence, D.H., 'England my England', in *England my England* (Harmondsworth: Penguin, 1960 [1922]).

Leatherdale, C., *England's Quest for the World Cup: A Complete Record* (London: Methuen, 1984).

Leaver, J., 'Fútbol and Modernist Aesthetics', *X-TRA Contemporary Art Quarterly*, 17:2 (2015), pp. 1–19.

Lee, J., 'A Policy for the Arts: The First Steps', extract in M. Wallinger and M. Warnock (eds), *Art For All? Their Policies and Our Culture* (London: Peer, 2000 [1965]), p. 146.

Levin, B., *The Pendulum Years: Britain and the Sixties* (London: Jonathan Cape, 1970).

Levin, B. 'At the Cup Final', in B. Levin, *Taking Sides* (London: Pan Books, 1979), pp. 197–201. Originally published in the *New Statesman*, 20 May 1966.

Lichfield, J., 'Jules Rimet: the man who kicked off the World Cup', *The Independent*, 5 June 2006.

Lipsyte, R., 'Winner by a Decision', *Smithsonian Magazine* (February, 2004), www.smithsonianmag.com/arts-culture/winner-by-a-decision-106452969/?no-ist. Accessed 4 March 2015.

Lodziak, C. *Understanding Soccer Tactics* (London: Faber & Faber, 1966).

Lopez, S., *Women on the Ball: A Guide to Women's Football* (London: Scarlet Press, 1997).

MacDonald, I., *Revolution in the Head: The Beatles Records and the Sixties*, 3rd revised edition (London: Vintage, 2008).

Magdalinski, T., 'Cute, Loveable Creatures: The Place and Significance of Mascots in the Olympic Movement', *OLYMPIKA: The International Journal of Olympic Studies*, XIII (2004), pp. 75–92.

Mason, T., 'England 1966: Traditional and Modern?', in A. Tomlinson and C. Young (eds), *National Identity and Global Sports Events: Culture, Politics and Spectacle in the Olympics and the Football World Cup* (Albany: State University of New York Press, 2006), pp. 83–98.

Mayes, H., *World Cup Report 1966* (London: William Heinemann (for The Football Association), 1967).

McColl, G., *England: The Alf Ramsey Years* (London: Chameleon Books, 1998).

McDonald, I., 'Situating the Sport Documentary', *Journal of Sport and Social Issues*, 31:3 (2007), pp. 208–25.

McDonald, I., 'Critiquing the Olympic Documentary: Kon Ichikawa's *Tokyo Olympiad*', *Sport in Society*, 11:2/3 (2008), pp. 298–310.

McDougall, A., *The People's Game: Football, State and Society in East Germany* (Cambridge: Cambridge University Press, 2014).

McFarland, R., *Roy Mac: Clough's Champion*, with W. Price (Liverpool: Sport Media, 2014).

McGhee, F., 'The Ramsey Era', in *World Cup Winners 1966* (London: A Soccer-Print Publication, 1966), pp. 11–13.

McGuinness, M., 'Some Reflections on Representations of the England Football Team Through Ephemera from the 1966 World Cup to the Present', unpublished paper, available online http://idrottsforum.org/articles/mcguinness/mcguinness110330.html. Accessed 10 March 2015.

McIlvanney, H. (ed.), *World Cup '66* (London: Eyre & Spottiswoode, 1966).

McIlvanney, H., 'England v. Argentina', in H. McIlvanney (ed.), *World Cup '66* (London: Eyre & Spottiswoode, 1966), pp. 111–18.

McIlvanney, H., 'England v. West Gemany', in H. McIlvanney (ed.), *World Cup '66* (London: Eyre & Spottiswoode, 1966), pp. 149–64.

McIlvanney, H., 'Portugal v. Brazil', in H. McIlvanney (ed.), *World Cup '66* (London: Eyre & Spottiswoode, 1966), pp. 83–7.

McIlvanney, H., 'Summary: Looking Forward', in H. McIlvanney (ed.), *World Cup '66* (London: Eyre & Spottiswoode, 1966), pp. 165–73.

McKibbon, R., *Classes and Cultures: England 1918–1951* (Oxford: Oxford University Press, 2000).

McKinstry, L., *Sir Alf: A Major Reappraisal of the Life and Times of England's Greatest Football Manager* (London: HarperSport, 2006).

Mellor, P. and C. Shilling, *Re-forming the Body: Religion, Community and Modernity* (London: Sage, 1997).

Meyer, J.C., '"Erecting a European Lieu de *Mémoire*": Media Coverage of the 1966 World Cup and French Discussions About the "Wembley Goal"', in W. Pyta and N. Havemann (eds), *European Football and Collective Memory* (Basingstoke: Palgrave Macmillan, 2015), pp. 119–38.

Moore, K., *Museums and Popular Culture* (London: Cassell, 1997).

Moore, R., *England!, England!* (London: Stanley Paul, 1970).

Moore, T., *Bobby Moore: By the Person Who Knew Him Best* (Leicester: W.F. Howes, 2007 [2005]).

Moorhouse, G., *The Other England* (Harmondsworth: Penguin, 1964).

Moorhouse, P., *POPARTPORTRAITS* (London: Portrait Gallery, 2007).

Moran, J., *Armchair Nation: An Intimate History of Britain in Front of the TV* (London: Profile, 2013).

Morris, D., *The Soccer Tribe* (London: Jonathan Cape, 1981).

Morse, G., *Sir Walter Winterbottom: The Father of Modern English Football* (London: John Blake Publishing, 2013).

Moynihan, J., *Soccer Syndrome: From the Primeval Forties* (London: Simon & Schuster, 1987 [1966]).

Naughton, B., *Alfie* (London: Panther, 1966).

Norman, P., *John Lennon: The Life* (London: Harper, 2009).

Olick, J.K. 'Collective Memory: The Two Cultures', *Sociological Theory*, 17:3 (1999), pp. 333–48.

Olick, J.K. 'From Collective Memory to the Sociology of Mnemonic Practices and Products', in A. Erll and A. Nünning (eds), *Media and Cultural Memory Studies: An International and Interdisciplinary Handbook* (Berlin / New York: Walter de Gruyter, 2008), pp. 151–61.

O'Mahony, M., *Olympic Visions: Images of the Games Through History* (London: Reaktion, 2012).

Orwell, G., 'The Sporting Spirit', in S. Orwell and I. Angus (eds), *The Collected Essays, Journalism and Letters of George Orwell*, vol. IV: *In Front of Your Nose, 1945–50* (London: Secker and Warburg, 1968 [1945]), pp. 40–4.

Orwell, G., 'England Your England', in S. Orwell and I. Angus (eds), *The Collected Essays, Journalism and Letters of George Orwell*, vol. II: *My Country Right or Left, 1940–43* (Harmondsworth: Penguin, 1970 [1941]), pp. 74–133.

Orwell, G., 'Notes on Nationalism', in S. Orwell and I. Angus (eds), *The Collected Essays, Journalism and Letters of George Orwell*, vol. III: *As I Please, 1943–45* (Harmondsworth: Penguin, 1970 [1945]), pp. 410–31.

Osmond, G. and M. Phillips, 'Enveloping the Past: Sport Stamps, Visuality and Museums', *The International Journal of the History of Sport*, 28:8–9 (2011), pp. 1138–55.

Parkinson, M., *Michael Parkinson on Football* (London: Hodder and Stoughton, 2001).

Pawson, T., *100 Years of the FA Cup: The Official Centenary History* (London: Heinemann, 1972).

Pawson, T., *The Football Managers* (London: Eyre Methuen, 1973).

Peters, M., *Goals From Nowhere*, as told to Peter Corrigan (London: Stanley Paul, 1969).

Peters, M., *The Ghost of '66: Martin Peters, the Autobiography*, with M. Hart (London: Orion, 2006).

Phillips, C., 'The High Anxiety of Belonging', in C. Phillips, *A New World Order* (London: Secker & Warburg, 2001), pp. 303–9.

Phillips, C., 'Leeds United, Life and Me', in C. Phillips, *A New World Order* (London: Secker & Warburg, 2001), pp. 298–301.

Phillips, C., 'The Pioneers: Fifty Years of Caribbean Migration to Britain', in C. Phillips, *A New World Order* (London: Secker & Warburg, 2001), pp. 264–82.

Physick, R., 'Football and the Fine Arts: The Football Association Art Competition and Exhibition, 1953', in J. Hill, K. Moore and J. Wood (eds), *Sport, History, and Heritage: Studies in Public Representation* (Woodbridge, Suffolk: Boydell Press, 2012), pp. 45–57.

Pimlott, B., *Harold Wilson* (London: Harper Collins, 1992).

Polley, M., 'The Diplomatic Background to the 1966 Football World Cup', *The Sports Historian*, 18:2 (1998), pp. 1–18.

Polley, M., *The British Olympics: Britain's Olympic Heritage 1612–2012* (Swindon: English Heritage, 2011).

Pope, S., 'Female Fan Experiences and Interpretations of the 1958 Munich Air Disaster, the 1966 World Cup Finals and the Rise of Footballers as Sexualised National Celebrities', *International Review for the Sociology of Sport*, 15 July 2015, DOI: 10.1177/1012690214558284.

Porter, D., 'Your Boys Took One Hell of a Beating! English Football and British Decline, *c.*1950–80', in A. Smith and D. Porter (eds), *Sport and National Identity in the Post-War World* (London: Routledge, 2004), pp. 31–48.

Porter, D., 'Eggs and Chips with the Connellys: Remembering 1966', *Sport in History*, 29:3 (2009), pp. 519–39.

Poulton, E., 'English Media Representation of Football-related Disorder: "Brutal, Shorthand and Simplifying"', *Sport in Society*, 8:1 (2005), pp. 25–47.

Powell, J., *Bobby Moore: The Life and Times of a Sporting Hero* (London: Robson Books, 2002).

Priestley, J.B., *The Good Companions* (London: Heinemann, 1980 [1929]).

Priestley, J.B., *English Journey* (London: William Heinemann / Victor Gollancz, 1934).

Ramsey, A., *Talking Football* (London: Stanley Paul, 1952).

Reid I. and A. Zisserman, 'Goal-directed Video Metrology', *Lecture Notes in Computer Science*, 1065 (1996), pp. 647–58.

Rees, N., *Brewer's Famous Quotations* (London: Weidenfeld and Nicolson, 2006).

Riding, J., *Sean's World Cup Final Day Out: Wembley 1966* (Liskeard, Cornwall: Exposure Publishing, 2006).

Robinson, P., '1966 Photography: The How and Who of Covering the World Cup', in P. Robinson, D. Cheesman, and (text by) H. Pearson, *1966 Uncovered: The Unseen Story of the World Cup in England* (London: Mitchell Beazley, 2006), pp. 250–3.

Robinson, P., D. Cheesman, and (text by) H. Pearson, *1966 Uncovered: The Unseen Story of the World Cup in England* (London: Mitchell Beazley, 2006).

Rogan, J., *The Football Managers* (London: Macdonald / Queen Anne Press, 1989).

Rollin, J., *England's World Cup Triumph* (London: Davies Books, 1966).

Ross, A., 'World Cup', in *Poems: 1942–1967* (London: Eyre and Spottiswoode, 1967), p. 204.

Rous, S., *Football Worlds: A Lifetime in Sport* (Newton Abbot: Readers Union, 1979 [1978]).

Russell, D., *Football and the English: A Social History of Association Football in England, 1863–1995* (Preston: Carnegie Publishing, 1997).

Russell, J., *The Meanings of Modern Art* (London: Thames and Hudson, 1981).

Rutherford, J., *Forever England: Reflections on Masculinity and Empire* (London: Lawrence & Wishart, 1997).

Sandbrook, D. 'The Age of Boom: Britain and the United States in the 1950s–1960s', in P. Moorhouse, *POPARTPORTRAITS* (London: National Portrait Gallery, 2007), pp. 15–30.

Sandbrook, D., *White Heat: A History of Britain in the Swinging Sixties* (London: Abacus, 2007).

Sargeant, A., *British Cinema: A Critical History* (London: British Film Institute, 2005).

Scannell, P., 'Public Service Broadcasting: The History of a Concept', in A. Goodwin and G. Whannel (eds), *Understanding Television* (London and New York: Routledge, 1990), pp. 11–29.

Sennett, R., *The Fall of Public Man* (London: Penguin, 2002 [1977]).

Shanes, E., *Pop Art* (New York: Parkstone Press, 2009).

Shaoul, M. and T. Williamson, *Forever England: A History of the National Side* (Stroud, Gloucestershire: Tempus, 2000).

Shepherdson, H., *The Magic Sponge*, with R. Peskett (London: Pelham, 1968).

Shiel, N., *Voices of '66: Memories of England's World Cup*, 2nd edition (Stroud, Gloucestershire: Tempus, 2006).

Shils, E. and M. Young, 'The Meaning of the Coronation', *The Sociological Review* (new series), 1:2 (1953), pp. 63–81.

Schulze, F. and E. Windhorst, *Mies van der Rohe: A Critical Biography*, new and revised edition (Chicago: University of Chicago Press, 2012).

Silk, M. and J. Francombe, 'All these Years of Hurt', in S. Wagg (ed.), *Myths and Milestones in the History of Sport* (Basingstoke: Palgrave Macmillan, 2011), pp. 262–86.

Silk, M., J. Francombe-Webb and D.L. Andrews, 'The Corporate Constitution of National Culture: The Mythopoeia of 1966', *Continuum: Journal of Media and Cultural Studies*, 28:5 (2014), pp. 720–36.

Simmel, G., 'The Sociology of Sociability', *American Journal of Sociology*, 55:3 (1949), pp. 254–61.

Smith, B., 'The Death of the Artist as Hero', in B. Smith, *The Death of the Artist as Hero: Essays in History and Culture* (Melbourne: Oxford University Press, 1988), pp. 8–29.

Smith, C., *Creative Britain* (London: Faber & Faber, 1998).

Smith D., 'England's Victory in the World Cup', in D. Smith (ed.), *The Boys' Book of Soccer 1966* (London: Evan Brothers, 1966), pp. 7–16.

Snow, C.P., *The Two Cultures: And a Second Look* (Cambridge: Cambridge University Press, 1964).

Speight, J., *It Stands to Reason: A Kind of Autobiography* (London: Michael Joseph, 1973).

Steedman, C., *Landscape for a Good Woman* (London: Virago, 1986).

Steen, R., *The Mavericks: English Football When Flair Wore Flares* (Edinburgh: Mainstream Publishing, 1994).

Stiles, N., *Soccer My Battlefield*, ed. P. Keeling (London: Stanley Paul, 1968).

Stiles, N., *After the Ball: My Autobiography*, with J. Lawton (London: Hodder and Stoughton, 2003).

Taylor, D.J., *On the Corinthian Spirit: The Decline of Amateurism in Sport* (London: Yellow Jersey Press, 2006).

Taylor, M., *The Association Game: A History of British Football* (London: Pearson / Longman, 2008).

Taylor, M., 'From Source to Subject: Sport, History, and the Autobiography', *Journal of Sport History*, 35:3 (2008), pp. 469–91.

Thomson, D., *4–2* (London: Bloomsbury, 1996).

Todd, C., 'Cover Driving Gracefully: On the Aesthetic Appreciation of Cricket', *Sport in Society*, 10:5 (2007), pp. 856–77.

Tomlinson, A., *FIFA: The Men, the Myths and the Money* (London: Routledge, 2014).

Triesman, D., 'Introduction' to G. Vinnai, *Football Mania: The Players and the Fans; the Mass Psychology of Football* (London: Orbach and Chambers, 1973), pp. 11–28.

Turner, B., *Beacon for Change: How the 1951 Festival of Britain Helped to Shape a New Age* (London: Aurum, 2011).

Tyler, M., *Boys of '66: The England Team that Won the 1966 World Cup – Then and Now* (London: Hamlyn, 1981).

Vaizey, M., *Peter Blake* (London: Weidenfeld and Nicolson, 1986).

Walvin, J., *The People's Game: The Social History of British Football* (London: Allen Lane, 1975).

Ward, A. and J. Williams, *Football Nation: Sixty Years of the Beautiful Game* (London: Bloomsbury, 2010).

Watson, J., 'World Cup Football Competition, 1966', *Philatelic Bulletin*, 15:11 (1978), p. 4.

Weight, R., *Patriots: National Identity in Britain 1940–2000* (London: Macmillan, 2002).

Wembley Stadium: Venue of Legends (Munich, London and New York: Prestel, 2007).

West, C., *First Class: A History of Britain in 36 Postage Stamps* (London: Square Peg, 2012).

Whitley, E., 'The Postmodern White Album', in I. Inglis (ed.), *The Beatles: Popular Music and Society* (Basingstoke: Palgrave, 2000), pp. 105–25.

Wilk, C., 'The Healthy Body Culture', in C. Wilk (ed.), *Modernism 1914–1939: Designing a New World* (London: V&A Publications, 2006), pp. 249–95.

Williams, J., *Entertaining the Nation: A Social History of British Television* (Stroud, Gloucestershire: Sutton, 2004).

Williams, R., *Culture and Society 1780–1950* (London: Chatto & Windus, 1958).

Williams, R., *Keywords*, revised edition (London: Fontana, 1988).

Williams, R., *The Long Revolution* (London: Chatto & Windus, 1961).

Williams, R., *Raymond Williams on Television: Selected Writings*, ed. A. O'Connor (London: Routledge, 1989).

Williams, R., *Television: Technology and Cultural Form* (Glasgow: Fontana, 1974).

Wilson, H., *The Labour Government 1964–1970: A Personal Record* (London: Weidenfeld and Nicolson / Michael Joseph, 1971).

Wilson, H., *Memoirs: The Making of a Prime Minister, 1916–64* (London: Weidenfeld and Nicolson / Michael Joseph, 1986).

Wilson, J., *Inverting the Pyramid: The History of Football Tactics* (London: Orion, 2008).

Wilson, J., *The Anatomy of England: A History in Ten Matches* (London: Orion, 2010).

Wilson, J., *Brian Clough: Nobody Ever Says Thank You: The Biography* (London: Orion, 2012).

Wilson, R. *My Life in Soccer* (London: Pelham, 1969).

Winner, D., *Brilliant Orange: The Neurotic Genius of Dutch Football* (London: Bloomsbury, 2001).

Winner, D., *Those Feet: A Sensual History of English Football* (London: Bloomsbury, 2005).

Wolstenholme, K., *They Think It's All Over…: Memories of the Greatest Day in English Football* (London: Robson Books, 1996).

World Championship Jules Rimet Cup 1966 Official Handbook (no publication details given).

World Cup Winners 1966 (London: A Soccer-Print Publication, 1966).

Young, C., 'Two World Wars and One World Cup: Humour, Trauma and the Asymmetric Relationship in Anglo-German Football', *Sport in History*, 27:1 (2007), pp. 1–23.

Young, P.M., *The Appreciation of Football* & *Football Facts and Fancies* (London: The Sportsman's Book Club, 1953).

Young, P.M., *A History of British Football* (London: Stanley Paul, 1968).

Index